T0243574

THE MEN OF 1924

Ramsay MacDonald and his cabinet of 1924

Back: Sidney Webb, John Wheatley, F. W. Jowett
Middle: Charles Philips Trevelyan, Stephen Walsh, Christopher Thomson (Lord Thomson), Frederic Thesiger (Viscount Chelmsford), Sydney Olivier (Lord Olivier), Noel Buxton, Josiah Wedgwood, Vernon Hartshorn, Thomas Shaw
Front: William Adamson, Charles Cripps (Lord Parmoor), Philip Snowden, Richard Haldane (Viscount Haldane), Ramsay MacDonald, John Clynes, James Thomas, Arthur Henderson

The Men of 1924

Britain's First Labour Government

PETER CLARK

First published in 2023 by
Haus Publishing Ltd
4 Cinnamon Row
London SW11 3TW

A CIP catalogue for this book is available from the British Library

ISBN 978-1-913368-81-4
eISBN 978-1-913368-81-1

Typeset in Garamond by MacGuru Ltd
Printed in the UK by Clays Ltd, Elcograf S.p.A.

www.hauspublishing.com
@HausPublishing

In memory of
PETER MACKENZIE SMITH
(1946–2020)

and

BYRON CRIDDLE
(1942–2021)

Contents

Introduction

In January 1924 a British government was formed with a Cabinet consisting of twenty white men in dark suits of Christian background, with an average age of fifty-seven. They succeeded a Cabinet consisting of nineteen white men in dark suits of Christian background, with an average age of fifty-six. In November 1924, they were replaced by a Cabinet of twenty-one white men in dark suits of Christian background, with an average age of fifty-three.

And that is where the resemblances end, for Ramsay MacDonald's Labour government of 1924 was the most diverse there had been in British history. Stanley Baldwin's Conservative government of 1923 contained six men who had been to one school, Eton College, and five who had been to another, Harrow; his second government, following MacDonald's first, had seven Old Etonians and five Old Harrovians. In each of Baldwin's Cabinets, all but four had studied at the universities of either Oxford or Cambridge.

This privileged class and educational background was typical for Cabinets of the previous 200 years. By contrast, the majority of MacDonald's Cabinet had completed their full-time education by the time they were fifteen. Five of them had started work by the time they were twelve years old. The deputy prime minister ceased full-time education when he was ten. There were no Old Etonians in the Cabinet – was this for the first time ever?

The core of this book is about the twenty men who made up that first Labour Cabinet. It included former Conservatives, former Liberals, socialist intellectuals, and trade unionists. There was a great diversity of expertise and experience around the Cabinet table: men who were familiar with the way modern industrial Britain functioned, sometimes literally at the level of the coalface (three were working down the mines before they entered their teens); men versed in local government administration and finance, including a former mayor of Darlington; three former colonial administrators, including an ex-viceroy of India; one man who had played cricket for Middlesex; a translator of German philosophy; and a successful capitalist – regarded as the Cabinet's most left-wing member. There were men who had served in war-time governments, two of whom had forged distinguished careers in active service during the Great War, one ending up with the rank of brigadier general; others had opposed British participation in that war. Two were illegitimate, one was a foundling, three were of working-class Irish immigrant descent. Five were born in Scotland. They were also a well-travelled lot. At least three had journeyed to Australia and New Zealand, and several of them had been to the United States. One had had personal dealings with both Lenin and Mussolini; another had survived an assassination attempt in the Balkans. One was a Methodist lay preacher, another a Primitive Methodist Sunday school teacher, and a third had been a senior Church of England lawyer. Altogether it was a Cabinet that was representative of the multifaceted nature of early-twentieth-century Britain.

Or at least half of it. Novelty and diversity did not stretch to the inclusion of women in the Cabinet. That had to wait for Labour's second government in 1929, when Margaret Bondfield was appointed minister of labour, becoming the first female privy councillor. In 1924 she had to be content with being a junior minister outside of the Cabinet.

The first four chapters of this book look at the political, social, and cultural contexts of the late nineteenth and early twentieth centuries that led to the forming of a Labour government in 1924, which would have been regarded as beyond the realm of fantasy just ten years before.

The following four chapters focus on the men of 1924. The first of these central chapters is about the man who brought them all together, Ramsay MacDonald. History has not been kind to MacDonald. In 1931 he allied himself with the Conservatives and was reviled by the Left, without ever being embraced by the Right. I have been mindful of the dictum of the historian F. W. Maitland, who said: 'It is very hard to remember that events now long in the past were once in the future.'[1] Following this precept I have concentrated on the careers of MacDonald and his colleagues in the years leading up to and including 1924. One of MacDonald's achievements was to form a government that bridged two major political faultlines in the Labour movement of the time – between socialists and trade unionists, and between those who supported the Great War and those who opposed it.

The men who formed MacDonald's inner circle of the Labour Party in 1924 were J. R. Clynes, Arthur Henderson, Philip Snowden, and J. H. Thomas. Personal relationships between them were not without tensions and jealousies. These four men are the subject of one chapter.

The remaining fifteen members of the Cabinet fall into two categories. Some had spent years, decades even, in the service of either socialism or the Labour movement. It seems natural to call them Old Labour; they are the subject of one chapter. The others, by contrast, were recruits to Labour over the previous five years or so from the older parties. I have called them New Labour, and their profiles form a separate chapter.

The final chapter reviews the performance of the men of the 1924 government. What did they achieve?

PETER CLARK

Frome, Somerset, England

2023

1

Tuesday, 22 January 1924

The King and the Prime Minister

On the evening of Tuesday, 22 January 1924, King George V wrote in his diary: 'Today 23 years ago dear Grandmama [Queen Victoria] died. I wonder what she would have thought of a Labour Government!'[1]

That afternoon James Ramsay MacDonald, the illegitimate son of a Scottish maidservant, had kissed the hand of the monarch on appointment as prime minister, head of Britain's first Labour government. It was a turning point in British history. For nearly a century the country had adjusted to the language of democracy. Before 1924 the people who formed governments, all men, were mostly from either the landed aristocracy or prosperous professional families. A few outsiders, such as William Gladstone, Benjamin Disraeli, and David Lloyd George, had reached the top of politics, but they had all unquestioningly accepted the class bias of the distribution of political power. A Labour government challenged all this. The weasels were taking over Toad Hall.

The king was at the apex of a pyramid of aristocracy, wealth, and power. Officials in the royal household close to him were mostly from these privileged classes. That upper tier of the social system included the upper ranks of the professions – the civil service, the church, the army, the navy. Wealth and achievement were co-opted to reinforce the system. Newspapers and magazines, catering for a new mass readership, did not challenge the distribution of power, influence, and privilege; indeed, they took it as the manifestation of the laws of nature. There were some excellent Liberal journalists who wrote for the *Manchester Guardian*, *Daily News*, and the *Daily Chronicle*, but apart from the small-circulation newspaper *Daily Citizen* and the Labour Party's 'house' newspaper, the *Daily Herald*, the great majority of the London press were indifferent, ill-informed, or hostile to the Labour Party. Readers of these newspapers would not have had much of an idea of the world or backgrounds of the men who were forming the new government. The provincial press, especially the *Manchester Guardian*, were, however, sympathetic.

Many of the comfortable classes were incredulous at the challenge posed by a Labour Party, with its language of socialism. Labour governments had been in power in the British Empire – in New Zealand and in five of the six states of Australia. Socialism in Europe was geographically closer and seen as far more menacing. The Bolshevik Revolution in 1917, which resulted in the bloody overthrow of the tsar and the Russian upper classes – a revolution applauded by many in the Labour Party – was enough to make the flesh of the British bourgeoisie crawl. There had been socialist and Labour governments, in coalition or in control, in Sweden and Germany. In Germany and Hungary socialist revolutions had been violently reversed.

The king of Britain liked to think of himself as a man of the people. As a teenager and young man, he had had an older brother and was not expected to inherit the throne. He spent fourteen years in the Royal Navy where he met men from outside the ranks of privilege and entitlement. He would often draw attention to this.

The role of King George V in British public life was pivotal. According to Lloyd George, there was 'not much in his mind',[2] but he had a stiff sense of public service and decorum. He was two years older than his new prime minister and was probably bored by royal rituals, having lived in a cocoon of deference and flattery.

He was aware of the massive social changes that had transpired in the country over the previous half-century. It turned out that he hit it off personally with Ramsay MacDonald. There had been a few weeks to prepare for a Labour government, and MacDonald was very keen to reassure the Establishment and to comply with accepted procedures. The king's secretary, Lord Stamfordham, went to see MacDonald the previous year when he was leader of the Opposition and was gratified to find him amenable to compliance with social codes, such as the wearing of court dress in the presence of the king at Buckingham Palace. He was pleased to find the Labour leader 'quite a gentleman'.[3] When the king met MacDonald, he expressed his anxieties about the singing of the socialist anthem 'The Red Flag', at Labour Party events. MacDonald said he would try to end the practice.[4]

A few days earlier the secretary of the Cabinet, Sir Maurice Hankey, had called on MacDonald at his house at Belsize Park.[5] There were assurances about the armed forces. No, they would not be disbanded.

There was one immediate problem. The prime minister had to be a member of the Privy Council. Ramsay MacDonald was not a member of that body of men from whose ranks ministers were appointed. So at 11.30 a.m. two Labour politicians, Arthur Henderson and J. H. Thomas, both of whom were privy councillors, were summoned to Buckingham Palace with MacDonald, who was duly sworn in.[6] He was then able to return later to the palace to kiss hands and be appointed prime minister and first lord of the Treasury. The names of the new ministers were presented and then the new prime minister spoke with the king for an hour.

They got on well. Each was anxious to please the other. It was the beginning of a good relationship, the king demonstrating what his official biographer, Sir Harold Nicolson, described as 'forthright friendliness'.[7] MacDonald found the king 'most friendly'.[8] The king wrote in his diary that he was 'impressed' by Mr MacDonald, whom he thought wished 'to do the right thing'.[9] The new prime minister acknowledged that he and his colleagues were inexperienced in government. He was able to reassure the king that they were 'honest and sincere'. They may fail in their endeavours but it would not be for want of trying. The king said that he would help whenever he could and asked only for frankness. (During this period of office, MacDonald did refuse one personal request from the king, who wanted MacDonald to appoint his cousin, Prince Arthur of Connaught, as lord lieutenant of London. MacDonald knew this would not go down well with his left wing.[10] There was, in any case, no vacancy.)

The king expressed his concern about the 'extreme' language of some Labour MPs. For example, when in December there had been suggestions that the Liberals and Conservatives might unite to thwart the appointment of a Labour administration, George Lansbury made dark allusions to a previous king who had got in the way of the will of the people: namely Charles I, who lost his head. Fortunately MacDonald chose not to include Lansbury in his first government.

The king wondered whether it was wise for MacDonald to take on the burden of being foreign minister as well as prime minister. George V was particularly interested in foreign affairs. Anticipating the possibility of the Labour government recognising Bolshevik Russia, he was concerned that the head of the mission should not be someone who had been closely involved in the killing of the tsar and his family, the tsar having been his first cousin. The head of any Russian mission should not have the designation of an ambassador who was accredited to the Royal Court but that of minister, which implied only an accreditation to the government.

The king arranged to have conversations with (or grant audiences to) all the new ministers. 'I must say they all seem to be very intelligent,' he wrote on 17 February to Queen Alexandra, his mother, the widow of King Edward VII, 'and they take themselves very seriously. They have different views to ours, as they are all socialists.'[11]

Ramsay MacDonald had been preparing for this moment. On 6 December 1923 the Conservatives lost their majority in the general election. When they subsequently lost a vote of no confidence in January 1924, the king called on MacDonald to form a minority Labour government, with the tacit support of the Liberals. Some advised MacDonald against forming a minority administration that would be dependent for its survival on the support of political opponents. It would be impossible to carry out socialist reforms. MacDonald thought it was of paramount importance to have a Labour government in office and assure people that it would not 'cut the throats of every aristocrat and steal all their property', as one noble lady had feared.[12] Labour should not fudge the opportunity.

MacDonald was ready to take over the government and had proclaimed his belief in pragmatism and gradualism. He was also aware of the risks of a Labour government coming to power in unpropitious times. 'God knows full well', his colleague J. R. Clynes reported him as saying, 'that none of us wants office now. None of us wants to face this mess. But somebody has got to do it.'[13]

The new prime minister had spent some weeks getting his Cabinet together. They were formally announced on the evening of Tuesday, 22 January 1924, and they trooped off to Buckingham Palace the following morning. One major point of contention among MacDonald's ministers was the wearing of court dress. In his eagerness to reassure the public, outside the ranks of the Labour enthusiasts, MacDonald was keen to show that a Labour government was outwardly like any other government. Court dress should be worn by ministers on appropriate occasions. King George V had a record of being touchy about these matters. In the early years of his reign he had refused to allow working-class Cabinet minister John Burns to accompany him in his carriage because he chose to wear a bowler hat rather than the prescribed top hat.[14] In 1927 Viscount Byng of Vimy, a former governor-general of Canada and future field marshal, was refused admittance to a function at Buckingham Palace in honour of the visiting French president because he was wearing 'court dress' and not 'full dress'.[15]

MacDonald seemed to relish dressing up in full court gear – a blue frock coat with gold braid and white knee breeches, buckled shoes, cocked hat, and 'toy sword'. He was supported by Labour's leading intellectual backer, the playwright George Bernard Shaw. Shaw spoke at a Fabian Society party held for all newly elected Labour MPs at the home of the Countess of Warwick, arguing that people should not imagine that wearing evening dress or court dress was in any way snobbish or a betrayal of the movement. Some new MPs were taken aback by this, but most ministers, with varying degrees of enthusiasm, did comply, although some later took umbrage with wearing a sword at receptions hosted by the speaker.

For calling on the monarch, the requirement was a frock coat and a silk hat. The king's private secretary had helpfully written to Ben Spoor, the Labour chief whip, to say that the necessary dress could be bought for £30 at Moss Bros.[16] MacDonald and J. H. Thomas were more than happy to oblige, and men such as Noel Buxton and Charles Trevelyan were able to go along with the idea, but for others it presented a major problem – both of practicality and principle. Some of MacDonald's men did the best they could. Philip Snowden, for example, had given away his court suit to a jumble sale in previous years, but he managed to borrow a substitute.[17] Sidney Webb had a suit that he had last worn on a visit to Japan twelve years earlier. The new ministers were briefed and drilled by the Cabinet secretary about how to behave in the presence of the sovereign.

J. R. Clynes expressed feelings of awed incredulity:

> Amid the gold and crimson of the Palace, I could not help marvelling at the strange turn of fortune's wheel, which had brought MacDonald, the starveling clerk, Thomas, the engine driver, Henderson, the foundry labourer, and Clynes, the mill hand to this pinnacle.[18]

The tension was relieved later when many of the new ministers met up for a meal. One who was present described the hilarity of the occasion. 'Altogether we were a jolly party – all laughing at the joke of Labour in office.'[19]

The new ministers carried out their rituals with good humour. There was laughter at the sight of John Wheatley, the fiery Glasgow revolutionary, 'going down on both knees and actually kissing the king's hand.'[20] The king, it was noted, seemed tongue-tied. 'He went through the ceremony', Charles Trevelyan observed, 'like an automaton.' A photograph was taken of two Cabinet ministers, the very tall Noel Buxton and the very short Sidney Webb, in their top hats. This was published in a Glasgow socialist journal with the caption 'Is this what you voted for?'[21]

The pageantry at Buckingham Palace disturbed much of the government's core support among Labour partisans. Some in the party expressed fierce ideological objections to Labour ministers wearing court dress, not to mention their inflated salaries. Some Labour MPs proposed that ministers should take a salary of only £1,000 a year rather than £5,000.[22]

In going through these rituals, MacDonald wanted to emphasise continuity with previous governments that had been in power, in order to legitimise Labour and its socialist agenda. They were new men, but they retained the services of the principal civil servants, including the Cabinet secretary, Sir Maurice Hankey, who had served Lloyd George, Bonar Law, and Stanley Baldwin.

Cabinet Making

How did MacDonald pick his team?

Shortly after the general election, MacDonald had dinner with Sidney and Beatrice Webb. The other guests were J. R. Clynes, Arthur Henderson, Philip Snowden, and J. H. Thomas. They agreed that they should accept office, despite what they saw as a situation that was not favourable to Labour. Snowden had reservations, arguing that Labour should stand aside and force a Conservative–Liberal coalition. But the lure of imminent office and the prospect of being able to institute free trade policies – a key part of their programme – helped them to overcome their scruples. At the dinner it was agreed not to push for more controversial parts of the Labour programme, such as the capital levy or nationalisation.[23]

A few days later the National Executive Committee (NEC) of the Labour Party formally agreed that Labour should accept the invitation to form a government, and also that MacDonald should be free to nominate ministers.

A few days before Christmas, MacDonald had retreated to his home at Lossiemouth in the north of Scotland to ponder his options. There was a core of Labour men whom he had no choice but to appoint to senior posts. However, there were some people, he thought, whose appointments would puzzle the Labour base but might reassure others whose fears of a socialist government had to be overcome if the steady increase in the Labour vote over the previous six years was to be maintained.

One man whom he consulted was Lord Haldane, who had been lord chancellor in Herbert Henry Asquith's Liberal government. He had drifted away from his Liberal roots and MacDonald wanted to appoint him to a senior post. Haldane invited him to stop off at Cloan, Haldane's country house in Perthshire, as he travelled south to London. After some discussion Haldane was offered the post of lord chancellor and chairman of the Imperial Defence Committee. He was also consulted about other possible office holders, and the leadership of the party in the House of Lords.[24]

J. H. Thomas recalled that some of the Cabinet-making was worked out at his house in Dulwich. So unschooled were they that they did not know what all the posts to be filled were. Thomas sent his son – who a generation later was elected Conservative MP for Canterbury – to look up *Whittaker's Almanac* and check all the government offices.[25]

In general MacDonald kept his counsel to himself, although he was subject to much lobbying. People had a clearer idea of what was in MacDonald's mind when seventeen men were invited to dinner at Haldane's mansion in Queen Anne's Gate, a short walk from both Downing Street and the Houses of Parliament, on Monday, 14 January. As well as the core of the Labour leadership – Arthur Henderson, J. R. Clynes, J. H. Thomas, Philip Snowden, William Adamson, Stephen Walsh, Arthur Greenwood, and Sidney Webb – guests included the former Conservative Lord Parmoor, the former Liberal MPs Charles Trevelyan and Noel Buxton, the lawyer Patrick Hastings, the left-wing General Thomson, and the Labour chief whip Ben Spoor. It was a good-humoured gathering. Jobs were discussed, but MacDonald gave nothing away.

'I have not the remotest notion what I am going to be,' Snowden said. 'Thomson is going to be Colonies,' Henderson told Webb.[26] To the rest of the party, however, it was no surprise when Snowden was appointed chancellor of the exchequer, having been Labour's economic and financial expert for nearly twenty years previous.

MacDonald had a wariness about trade unionists, even though he relied on them heavily. Beatrice Webb, despite being a historian of British trade unionism, was similarly patronising about them. She suggested that the appointment of trade union bosses in a Labour government was equivalent to the need of eighteenth-century prime ministers to appoint a duke or two to an administration.[27]

Negotiations took place over the weekend of 19 January. On the Monday, MacDonald summoned a meeting of his proposed ministers. They were to meet in the House of Commons room he occupied as leader of the Opposition. As they waited for the meeting to start they chatted to each other. The complete outsider was Frederic Thesiger, 1st Viscount Chelmsford, considered a Conservative, who had worked with Sidney Webb on the London County Council twenty years earlier.

Arthur Henderson had lost his seat at the general election. At first MacDonald had wanted him to concentrate on work at the Labour Party headquarters: everybody thought another general election was likely within months. MacDonald then had an idea: if

Henderson was able to return to Parliament through a by-election, he could have him made chairman of ways and means, a parliamentary rather than a government appointment. Henderson insisted on being home secretary. 'If I had not been a good Wesleyan, I should have sworn at him,' he told Snowden.[28] George Lansbury was offered an under-secretaryship but felt it was beneath his dignity, and so he was not included in the government. Sidney Webb was first intended to be minister of labour, but he thought that was too low status for him, although he agreed to be president of the board of trade, a post coveted by Josiah Wedgwood.[29]

MacDonald's deputy and immediate predecessor as party leader, J. R. Clynes, was appointed to post with the bewildering title of lord privy seal; he was expected to deputise for MacDonald in the House of Commons in the prime minister's absence. But what were the duties of lord privy seal? Clynes consulted his Conservative predecessor, Lord Robert Cecil. 'Can you tell me ... exactly what my official duties will be as lord privy seal?' 'None whatsoever,' Cecil replied with a smile, 'except the pleasant one of signing a receipt once a month for your salary.'[30]

One serious challenge to MacDonald's premiership was the House of Lords. Apart from new allies such as Haldane, Parmoor, and Chelmsford, there were only two hereditary members of the Upper House who were members of the Labour Party. One was the twenty-three-year-old ninth Earl De La Warr, who was made a lord-in-waiting. The other was the second Earl Russell, grandson of the Victorian prime minister Lord John Russell and older brother of the philosopher Bertrand Russell. He was not interested in taking office.

Some appointments were to ministerial posts outside the Cabinet. Emanuel Shinwell – a Clydesider (one of the group of militant MPs from Glasgow), although born in London – became minister for mines. Harry Gosling, a former Liberal who had been a London trade unionist, and a founder member of the Amalgamated Society of Watermen, Lightermen, and Bargemen, was made minister of transport.

The principal legal officers, apart from Haldane, were Sir Patrick Hastings, who became attorney general, and Henry Slesser, an old Fabian Anglo-Catholic who was made solicitor-general.

Among the junior appointments were men (and one woman) who were later to play a prominent part in Labour politics. *Major* Clement Attlee may have been a reassuring counterweight to the military establishment at the War Office. The civil lord of the Admiralty, representing the first lord, Lord Chelmsford, in the Commons, was Frank Hodges, a South Wales miners' trade union official. Lord Thomson and the Air Ministry were represented in the Commons by William Leach, a Yorkshire businessman and stalwart of the Bradford Independent Labour Party. John Wheatley's deputy at the Ministry of Health was Arthur Greenwood, who, fifteen years later, was to be deputy leader of the party. And Margaret Bondfield, the leading woman trade unionist, was parliamentary secretary at the Ministry of Labour, supporting Thomas Shaw.

Contrasting Experiences

After the swearing in ceremony, the new Cabinet moved on to Downing Street for the first Cabinet meeting.

Ramsay MacDonald was the first prime minister to take office without any previous government experience. Only Lord Haldane and Arthur Henderson had been in previous Cabinets – Haldane in the Liberal Cabinets of Henry Campbell-Bannerman and Asquith, and Henderson in the war-time coalition Cabinets of Asquith and Lloyd George. Clynes, Trevelyan, and Parmoor had held previous government offices. The Cabinet included four former Liberal MPs – Buxton, Haldane, Trevelyan, and Wedgwood

Just over five years had passed since the end of the Great War. The Cabinet included men who had opposed the war, such as MacDonald himself, the chancellor of the exchequer, Philip Snowden, and the former Conservative Lord Parmoor; others, such as Josiah

Wedgwood and Lord Thomson, had had successful military careers in the Great War. Thirteen of the Cabinet had been trade union officials.

The Junta

According to Beatrice Webb, there was an inner core, which she described as a 'junta'.[31] They were all long-established Labour loyalists – MacDonald, Snowden, Thomas, Clynes, and her husband, Sidney Webb. That was Beatrice Webb's perception. More generally, Labour's collective leadership was seen as being made up of five men, 'the big five', with Henderson in the place of Webb, who had been committed to the Labour Party only for the previous decade. The activism of the others went back to the previous century.

They were an interesting five, thrown together in this great venture, sometimes distrustful of each other. When MacDonald was elected chairman of the Parliamentary Labour Party (PLP), in effect party leader, none of the others had voted for him. Despite this, his leadership was accepted.

They were all committed to the idea of a Labour government run by Labour people. They themselves were all from working-class backgrounds. None of them had any formal full-time education after the age of fifteen. None had a London or home counties background. None spoke 'received pronunciation' English. MacDonald was emotionally tied to his birthplace, Lossiemouth, in the north of Scotland, to which he retreated more frequently than was appreciated by his colleagues; he was ultimately buried there. Clynes came from Oldham and was MP for a constituency within a morning's walking distance of his birthplace. Henderson, although born in Glasgow, had his political base in Tyneside. Snowden was a gritty Yorkshireman from the Pennines. Thomas was a Welshman with strong (railway) connections in Swindon and Derby. He was MP for Derby and was later buried in Swindon.

The five were from religiously diverse backgrounds. Only Thomas was a nominal Anglican. MacDonald was a Scottish Presbyterian. Clynes was an immigrant Irish Catholic. Snowden was brought up in a Methodist village. Henderson was the most committed in terms of religion. From his late teens he had been a Methodist lay preacher who reluctantly attended political meetings on a Sunday but otherwise tried to keep the Sabbath. All were inspired by a sense of public duty and the need to work hard. None of them had any sense of entitlement. Thomas later had what might have been called a 'drink problem', but otherwise they all led sober and upright lives.

Their political journeys had differed. Between them they straddled the uneasy alliance of trade unionism and socialism. MacDonald talked most about socialism. Snowden and Henderson were from strong Liberal backgrounds. Snowden adhered to Gladstonian principles in his financial policies and his budget. Henderson had been a Liberal Party agent when he was adopted as a Labour parliamentary candidate. Thomas denied that he was a socialist. Clynes combined absorption in trade union affairs and a socialist philosophy.

MacDonald and Snowden were intellectuals, propagandists, and prolific writers of books and pamphlets. The other three were rooted in trade unionism. For the latter, their principal goal was the emancipation of the working class, with socialism as the vehicle to that end.

Henderson, born in 1861, was the oldest of the five; Thomas, born in 1874, was the youngest. All but Thomas had been among the twenty-nine Labour MPs elected in 1906. Henderson, who was first elected in 1903, had the most parliamentary experience. Thomas became an MP in 1910. The war experience of the five also varied. MacDonald and Snowden had opposed Britain's involvement in the war. Clynes, Henderson, and Thomas accepted it. Clynes and Henderson became government ministers and Henderson entered Lloyd George's five-man War Cabinet. Thomas was supportive of the war-time coalition and performed useful tasks. The three of them were made privy councillors during the war. In 1924 all of them recognised and acknowledged MacDonald's leadership skills and oratory, although there were underlying tensions. Henderson, as secretary of the Labour Party, was personally popular, universally known as 'Uncle Arthur'. Thomas was popular, and totally without personal malice. Clynes was perhaps the man most rooted in the Labour movement. MacDonald was idolised and Snowden respected.

MacDonald, in 1924, was a widower, while the others had supportive wives. MacDonald and Thomas fell for the 'aristocratic embrace'. Snowden did too but more reluctantly, despite the social ambitions of his wife, Ethel. Three of the five had hopes of founding political dynasties. In the same year MacDonald (unsuccessfully) pressed his son, Malcolm, to be an MP. That son later became a National Labour MP and Cabinet minister in the government of Neville Chamberlain. Henderson had two sons who became MPs in 1924. Thomas had a son who became a National Labour candidate in the 1930s and a Conservative MP after the Second World War. The Snowdens had no children. Clynes's children did not enter politics, although one nephew became editor of the *Radio Times*.

Pride and Prejudice

'It had come at last! Few of us who had toiled through the years to achieve this object had expected to see it realised in our lifetime.'[32] So wrote Philip Snowden, who had spent the previous thirty years as a socialist propagandist.

The new Labour government faced the House of Commons. Just as there was elation on the Labour government benches, so too was there fury, disdain, and fear, mixed with curiosity, on the part of the opposition. One new office holder, the attorney general, Patrick Hastings, was from an upper-middle-class background – he had studied at Charterhouse School as a boy – and had been elected

MP for Wallsend in 1922. He was not a politician for long, and being in the government was not a joyous experience for him. In his memoirs he recalled that the opposition displayed an intolerance for the working men of the Labour Party that they would never have shown to MPs from the professional class. The expression 'class hatred', which was at that time frequently used, 'seemed to me much more fairly attributed to our opponents than to ourselves; and with so little excuse'.[33]

2

The Arrival of Labour

Labour's Impact on the House of Commons in 1906

In 1914, ten years before Labour formed its first government, there were forty-five Labour MPs. Twenty-five years before that there had been none.

The breakthrough in numbers had been in the general election of 1906, when the Labour Representation Committee (founded in 1900) gained twenty-nine seats in parliament and decided to rename themselves the Labour Party. This breakthrough had only been possible because of a secret electoral pact made between Ramsay MacDonald, then the secretary of the Labour Representation Committee, and Herbert Gladstone, liberal chief whip and son of the Grand Old Man, William Ewart Gladstone. The Liberals would not put up candidates in seats where Labour had a chance of winning. Labour would do the same in constituencies where they might otherwise split the anti-Conservative vote.

There had been working-class MPs before, going back to the 1880s – men like Henry Broadhurst, Thomas Burt, and Alexander MacDonald. They had been backed by trade unions in their districts and supported, or at least tolerated, by the Liberal Party. But as individuals they were absorbed into the culture and etiquette of the House of Commons, dressing formally and showing due deference to the parliamentary codes of behaviour. It had always been an all-male venue. Men sometimes wore top hats, often 'worn with a parliamentary tilt backwards',[1] within the chamber. James Keir Hardie, first elected in 1892, had struck a defiant line, in dress and commitment. He appeared at the House of Commons in a cloth cap. Later this was modified to a deerstalker, and then – he had a showman's touch – a broad sombrero.[2] But he was regarded as a court jester, in no way a challenge to the culture of the institution or the sense of entitlement enjoyed by his social superiors. From 1906 a critical mass of new Labour MPs entered parliament. A few Labour MPs wore top hats.[3] One Labour MP, John Hodge, wore a top hat that had been manufactured in his Manchester Gorton constituency, a centre for hat-making; his candidature had been supported by the Denton Hatters' Union.[4] Philip Snowden, on one occasion, sported a straw boater.[5] But most Labour MPs wore soft felt hats outside and short coats and square-toed boots inside the House of Commons. Their most marked innovation to the House was their rich north-country dialects.[6]

The new Labour MPs brought in an alternative way of life. Pipe smoking was a working-class habit, so now pipes were widely seen in the Smoking Room of the House of Commons for the first time. The habit steadily spread beyond working men. A generation later, Stanley Baldwin was rarely seen without his pipe.

Pipe smoking was cheaper than cigars, and the 1906 Labour MPs were frequently strapped for cash. They did not have the assured financial security of rents or income from investments, or the rewards from directorships, the legal profession, or other sources of easy money enjoyed by other MPs. They often stayed in cheap lodgings, and late-night sittings meant (for them) expensive taxi fares or a long nocturnal walk. The food available at the House of Commons was expensive. The Commons restaurant catered for the tastes and pockets of most MPs. It was possible to get a snack in the tea room for one shilling (5p, equivalent to £5 in 2023). Most of the Labour MPs were teetotallers, so there were few alcoholic extras or bar bills. The catering services responded to the demands of the new members and in time provided a meal for two shillings and sixpence, equivalent to £12.50 today.[41] Such economies mattered for MPs who relied on trade unions for financial support. Some MPs supplemented this support by writing for their constituency newspapers or for the national press.

Non-Labour MPs, particularly the Conservatives, often had a sense of entitlement. Their training grounds had been debating societies at school or university. The debating experience of Labour MPs, by contrast, had been forged in very practical circumstances – in trade union negotiations or the management of municipal public services. The subjects of their issues had been pay scales, working timetables, health and safety at work, or the Poor Law – matters of life and death. Detail was important. Detached rhetoric studded with classical quotations was not their thing.

Most Labour MPs were or had been trade union officials. They had moved on from the coal face, the mill, or the factory. They now wore suits and were familiar with administrative processes, working out deals and making compromises. They were a sober lot. Literally so, for Keir Hardie, tapping into a nonconformist conscience, laid down the rule that they refrain from consuming alcohol when they were on parliamentary duty.[8] They were not all insular minded, however; some had international interests. Hardie and Ramsay MacDonald had travelled widely. Others like J. R. Clynes, Fred Jowett, and Arthur Henderson had travelled in Europe to international socialist or trade union conferences.

Labour MPs, before and after 1906, had generally given their support to the Liberal Party. But this was not always so. In 1899, when Winston Churchill first stood (unsuccessfully) for the Conservatives in Oldham, his fellow candidate in the two-member constituency was the Conservative cotton workers' trade unionist James Mawdsley.[9]

Overall the Labour MPs of the 1906 Parliament did not make a huge impact on politics. Some were unwell, and others gave priority to their 'heavy responsibilities' as trade union officials.[10] They welcomed, but did not initiate, legislation that benefited their supporters in the first years of the new Parliament – the Workmen's Compensation Act of 1906, the Old Age Pensions Act of 1908, and the Trade Boards Act and the Minimum Working Law of 1909.

The Emergence of a Working-Class Identity

Why did representatives of Labour arrive on the parliamentary scene when they did? For centuries the world of national politics and decision-making was the task of wealthy, male landed aristocrats who had monopolised the major roles in politics since the Middle Ages. That same aristocracy had been flexible in absorbing new blood and new wealth, successful soldiers, royal favourites, and royal bastards. Even the Glorious Revolution of 1688 was the replacement of one such elite with another. Things started to change from the end of the eighteenth century. People from outside the upper classes were becoming interested in how the country's affairs were being managed. The Industrial Revolution brought the working classes together in a way that had not been experienced before. As a result, many realised they had common interests that were not politically represented by those with power over their lives. Ideas of representative accountability and talk of human rights drifted into Britain after the American colonies revolted and created the United States, and also from France after their revolution in 1789. These ideas were anathema to the powerful elites, and for a generation after the end of the Napoleonic Wars there were regular riots and confrontations between people representing fundamentally divergent ways of looking at the distribution of political power. The most iconic was the clash of gentlemen soldiers and demonstrators in Manchester that became mythologised as the Peterloo Massacre in 1819.

This popular discontent and extra-parliamentary activity was not ineffective. The political elite made the concession of a reform of Parliament in the Reform Act of 1832. It was not extensive, but it was a precedent that was noted and repeated over the next century, until universal franchise was achieved in 1929.

In the first half of the nineteenth century a working class emerged. The Industrial Revolution created new systems of economic and social organisation. In the pre-industrial world, society was hierarchical in a vertical way. People were scattered, communications across the country were limited, and society was made up of hundreds of small units. Those at the top of the social pyramid had some kind of class solidarity in their education, way of speaking, and shared habits. This did not extend to the lower orders of society. The widespread introduction of mills, factories, and mines operated with a large proletarian workforce brought in from rural areas to the towns and cities, where they lived in close proximity to each other. They clearly had common interests that did not coincide with those who were richer or more privileged. A working-class culture appeared with its own narratives, songs, and poetry, its own leaders and even its own forms of Christian worship. This emergence of a working-class consciousness peaked with the Chartist movement of the 1830s and 1840s. Parliament was petitioned. There were huge mass demonstrations. However, the movement was crushed by the authorities, and things went quiet for forty years.

Quiet, that is, on the surface. There were plenty of radical ideas being exchanged, as well as social developments that consolidated class identity and solidarity. Radical ideas circulated and a radical wing of the Liberal Party crystallised, based in urban centres outside of London. Energies that had previously been spent on Chartism were channelled elsewhere. The cooperative movement started in Rochdale in 1844 and was a collectivist venture, whereby customers owned the profits of commercial activity. However, it was slow, even reluctant, to engage in political activity. The major working-class activities were trade unionism and religion.

The Trades Union Congress was a federation that first met in Manchester in 1868. Membership was mainly drawn from skilled craftsmen, who were primarily concerned with protecting their privileges and interests. They were barely touched by the masses of abject poor in the industrial counties of the north of England and the East End of London. At the beginning they were unaffected by ideas of socialism.

Socialist ideas began appearing in Britain in the middle of the century. They took many forms, but what these forms had in common was the idea that the state should be involved in the economy for the sake of the people as a whole. Socialism during this period sometimes manifested itself in a class consciousness, 'us against them', or a belief in human equality. It received a more precise and prescriptive definition in the work of Karl Marx and Friedrich Engels. Their *Manifesto of the Communist Party*, issued in 1848, ended with the resonating words, 'Workers of the World Unite! You have nothing to lose but your Chains.' Marx's revolutionary ideas of socialism with theories of history and economics were expounded in three volumes, *Capital*, better known in its original German form, *Das Kapital*. The first volume was published in 1867, the second and last volumes after Marx's death. Marx, who lived and died in London, had an influence in Britain, but it was not as great as in continental Europe.

The established national Church of England had no appeal to the emerging industrial working class. The church was knitted into the fabric of a hierarchical class system with the landed aristocracy in the most privileged position; its formulaic services had no emotional resonance for the underclasses. From the middle of the century a few Anglicans had a social message and were attracted to socialist ideas, but they were in a minority and were remote from trade unions and working-class lives. The class hierarchy was also replicated in the army. A former Conservative Cabinet minister, the son of a duke, writing his memoirs during the Great War, noted an alienation of nonconformity from what he saw as national institutions. 'The three great national interests', he observed, ' – Land, Army, Church – became the subject of obloquy and misrepresentation from an unceasing and ever-present agitation.'[11]

The various nonconformist churches began to hold greater popular appeal to the working classes than the Church of England. Every city and town and most villages throughout Britain bear witness to this through the huge number of nonconformist chapels that were constructed in the 1840s, 1850s, and 1860s. These new chapels were built in working-class districts, attracting the likes of miners, quarrymen, millworkers, and farm labourers. The older nonconformist denominations – such as Quakers, Congregationalists, and Unitarians – were led by well-established middle-class families. The newer denominations, and especially the Methodists, had a mass appeal to the working classes, among whom were developing a culture of nonconformity (or dissent). Characterised by hymn-singing, social work, self-help, mutual assistance, and a sense of being special that could come over as smug self-righteousness, nonconformists were outside the Establishment. There were no nonconformist dukes. There were no nonconformist generals.

Methodism had a direct influence on the growth and character of the Labour movement, their delegate conferences and meetings often reflecting religious services, complete with travelling 'preachers'. In 1898 it was reported that an Independent Labour Party (ILP) meeting 'was of a religious character, opened by a Hymn, Lesson and Prayer and Keir [Hardie] preached the sermon to a large and attentive audience'.[12] Future politicians were trained in public speaking at these early trade union meetings; it was the working-class equivalent to the Oxford and Cambridge Unions.

The Methodists were the strongest and wealthiest of the nonconformist denominations and had several branches. The first generation of Methodists were made up of leaders, middle-class men preaching to the working class. The Primitive Methodists, who sprouted up in the first decade of the nineteenth century, had working-class preachers preaching to the working class. Not only working-class men, but working-class women preachers too. The 'Prims' had a disproportionate influence on trade union politics.

The Political Classes and Reform

During the course of the nineteenth century the established political classes recognised the growing strength of these new vocal classes, and slowly extended membership of the political world, in terms of extending the right to vote. In 1867 the franchise was extended further to urban ratepaying men. The fear of intimidation by employers or landlords was averted by the Ballot Act of 1872, which ensured that the act of voting was secret. The franchise was further extended in 1884 to include rural ratepayers. Women, in spite of the advocacy of the philosopher John Stuart Mill, continued to be excluded. In legislation the Conservatives and Liberals competed with each other in wooing the new classes with ameliorative measures. The Conservative Earl of Shaftesbury sponsored Factory Acts that improved conditions and hours of work in industrial areas. The Conservatives had, in the 1870s and 1880s, made a bid for the emerging working-class vote. Their Conspiracy and Protection of Property and Employers and Workmen Acts of 1975 were bids for their support. They strengthened trade union rights and altered the Master and Servant Act, enabling both sides, theoretically, to be equal in law.

Liberal governments introduced laws regulating public health. A cautious extension of the franchise was part of the credo of advanced Liberals, but it was a Conservative government that extended the franchise in 1867, 'dishing the Whigs', as Disraeli put it. Disraeli had been a Radical in the 1830s, and insofar as he had any clear political principles, it was to see the landed aristocracy in partnership with a contented working class. Disraeli's government in the 1870s introduced a number of social reforms concerning public health and trade union rights.

Nonetheless, radical reformers and trade unionists were happiest allying themselves with the Liberals, especially under the leadership of W. E. Gladstone, 'the people's William', who dominated Liberal politics from the 1860s to the mid-1890s. With spellbinding oratory, he could transfix large audiences in Scotland and the north of England. His political opponents saw him as a scheming humbug, especially when it was his habit, after giving a speech to thousands of working men about being on the side of the masses and against the (upper) classes, to ride off to stay at a nearby aristocratic stately home. Nonetheless his communication of a sense of moral purpose in politics resonated with the nonconformist conscience. Other Liberals, such as John Stuart Mill, have been seen as preparing the way for a British brand of socialism.

Trade Unions Become Political

For two decades after its foundation the Trades Union Congress (TUC) had little direct interest in politics, and certainly none in the idea of a politics of class. Indeed one trade unionist who was elected to Parliament as a Liberal was actually a junior minister in a Liberal government. Henry Broadhurst, formerly a stonemason, was under-secretary at the Home Office in 1885. The TUC represented the aristocracy of Labour; they barely touched the masses of abject poor in the industrial and mining counties, who were either too exhausted, too cowed, or too apathetic to engage in collective action. It was reckoned that 90 per cent of the working classes at this time were not unionised.[13] Relative prosperity kept the TUC away from militancy.

Things changed in the 1870s and 1880s. A trade recession led to the vulnerable being laid off. The word 'unemployment' entered the English language. Trafalgar Square witnessed demonstrations of the unemployed, and the nature of trade unionism changed. Membership increased to include men who had hitherto been unionised. New unions were founded, others amalgamated, and others folded up, so while the number of unions declined, the number of trade unionists increased. The last decades of the century saw the growth of the joint-stock company. Instead of industrial concerns being owned by one man or family, they became corporations with an impersonal board and directors.

The 'new unionism', as it was called, mostly concerned men, but a pattern for public relations was set in 1888 with a publicised strike of badly paid matchgirls at the Bryant and May factory in the East End of London. This strike was inspired by the middle-class former wife of an Anglican Minister, Annie Besant. She helped to make the people of the luxurious West End aware of the conditions of life of people in the East End, four or five miles away.

The wider public also became aware of trade unionism with the dock strike of 1889. The new unionism brought an edge to industrial disputes, along with a new militancy and the whiff of class warfare. The dock strike was led by charismatic leaders who had an eye for public relations – Ben Tillett, Tom Mann, and John Burns. The strike helped to cultivate and mobilise a working-class consciousness.

There were setbacks to the advance of trade unionism. The militancy of the new unionism and the 1889 dock strike was met with a response from employers' organisations. Leaders of the latter set up the National Free Labour Association, with the objective of bypassing the unions.

The TUC had been reluctant to be too involved in politics. It had a parliamentary committee that approved of trade unionists becoming MPs with support from the Liberal Party. But with the binary class confrontations and the spread of socialist ideas, many thought that labour interests diverged from Liberal interests, and a more assertive and proactive representation of labour in Parliament was required. The TUC shifted its position when the employers' counter-offensive turned to legal action.

The railway management was traditionally hierarchical, even quasi-militaristic. Workers wore uniforms, and the senior management was paternalistic at best, authoritarian at worst. Railway workers were among the least unionised until the end of the nineteenth century, but the principal union was the Amalgamated Society of Railway Servants (ASRS). The Taff Vale Railway in South Wales was managed by an aggressive disciplinarian who refused to recognise or negotiate with the union. The company brought a case against the union, claiming that losses made by the company as a result of the strike action should be claimed from the union. Legal action went on for some years and was a sign to trade unionists that they needed legislation to guarantee their funds and freedom of action. This alarm spread to the whole trade union movement, stirring them to secure a policy of independent labour representation in Parliament, rather than relying on the benevolent paternalism of the other parties. At the same time, trade union leaders were becoming more interested in socialism, with an increase in membership of the ILP.[14]

The parliamentary committee of the TUC initiated a meeting of trade unions and socialist societies that was held at the Memorial Hall on Farringdon Street, London, at the end of February 1900. The meeting has been seen as the foundation of the Labour Party, and the beginning of the convergence of trade unionism with socialism.

The delegates in attendance were 129 in number, representing half a million workers and socialists. This was the first formal meeting of the two sides with a clear agenda.

The Independent Labour Party (ILP)

Working-class political activity had largely been manifest in the Liberal Party, although Disraeli's reforms and Lord Randolph Churchill's rhetoric about an alliance of upper and working classes was not enough to challenge the personality of William Gladstone, whose charisma had a huge prophet-like appeal to the Bible-reading working class. Pious trade unionists also responded to Gladstone's claim for an ethical foreign policy and his tirades against unethical imperialism. For many, he was a Moses or an Elijah, a liberator. For a generation from the 1870s, many two-member constituencies had a working-class member, a 'Lib–Lab', running alongside a more conventional Liberal.

The self-taught Scottish miner Keir Hardie, like many other pioneering Labour leaders, had first put his hopes in the Liberal Party, but he was spurned by the local party when he sought the parliamentary candidature at a by-election in Mid-Lanarkshire in 1888. Despite support from Liberal Party headquarters, the local party preferred a middle-class Londoner.[15] Hardie then set up a Scottish Labour Party. He surveyed the disparate Labour and socialist groups, and for the next twenty years dreamed of and worked for a 'Labour Alliance'. Four years after his snubbing in Lanarkshire he was returned as an MP for West Ham. Hardie was the most successful socialist individual during this time. Pragmatic and energetic, he was an accomplished orator whose socialism was motivated by Christianity and driven by memories of poverty and humiliation.

The Independent Labour Party (ILP) was founded in Bradford in 1893 and had a northern nonconformist ethos, to such an extent that Robert Blatchford claimed that it was controlled by 'lily-livered Methodists'.[16] Members included trade union activists as well as field professionals and even businessmen. Geographically its strength was in Yorkshire, Lancashire, and Scotland. Glasgow was a strong base. Its Methodism showed itself in its alliance with temperance. Many of its leading figures, such as Philip Snowden, were advocates of temperance. The brewing and liquor industries degraded the working classes, it was argued, distracting them from self-improvement. The ILP journal, *Forward*, would not take advertisements for alcohol; the editor's puritanism also extended to refusing to publish any news about gambling.[17]

ILP culture had a 'folksy' element. The members promoted cycling clubs – the bicycle was a great liberator of men and women. Ownership of a bicycle gave bargaining power to someone seeking work. He or (less frequently) she was no longer dependent on finding work within walking distance of home. Moreover marriage partners, and additional networks and information, could be found beyond the immediate neighbourhood. And it consolidated trade union support, for members who lived within a radius of ten or more miles could attend meetings.

There were ILP book clubs, rambling clubs, and cricket competitions. The ILP was allied to Labour Churches that held meetings and sang socialist songs and hymns, and organised Sunday schools for children. The idea of the Labour Church was the brainchild of a Unitarian minister, John Trevor. The church flourished brilliantly and briefly in the 1890s and then faded away. Its message was that life and work should be 'the basis of union rather than a profession of faith'.[18]

The party attracted enthusiasts for new progressive fads – vegetarianism, sexual freedom, and hostility to vaccination. Some members with an internationalist perspective encouraged the study of the invented language Esperanto, the very word for which derived from the Latin for 'hope': hope for a new world order when all men will be brothers – and sisters. The ILP was an early supporter of votes for women, and for the greater involvement of women in public life, including trade unions.

Reflecting a north-country choral tradition, the ILP members were great singers. Their preferred anthem was Edward Carpenter's 'England Arise' or the hymn 'When Wilt Thou Save Thy People?', rather than 'The Red Flag'.[19] The singing of socialist songs and hymns was an explicit borrowing from chapel services. A *Socialist Sunday School Tune Book* was available with hopes of redemption in this world rather than (or in addition to) the next:

> These things shall be! A loftier race
> Than e'er the world hath known shall rise
> With flame of freedom in their souls,
> And light of science in the eyes.[20]

Another was taken from a Baptist hymn book:

> Forward! The day is breaking,

Earth shall be dark no more;
Millions of men are waking
On every sea and shore.

One of the most popular songs was by Edward Carpenter. It became effectively the ILP anthem before 'The Red Flag' took precedence. It was similarly chiliastic:

England Arise, the long, long night is over,
Faint in the east behold the dawn appear,
Out of your evil dream of toil and sorrow
Arise, O England, for the day is here![21]

ILP conferences would end, after a day's earnest debate, with social gatherings around the tea urn – attendees were mostly teetotallers – when sentimental songs would be sung, the star turn being Keir Hardie crooning 'Annie Laurie'.[22]

The ILP was openly socialist and stated as its objective 'to secure the collective ownership of all means of production, distribution, and exchange.'[23] It was the spirit of revivalism channelled into politics. Its members' activities were described as a 'mission' or a 'crusade'. Philip Snowden recalled the advice of an old Bradford socialist to a young speaker: he had to 'keep it simple, and when th'art coming to t'finishing up tha' mun put a bit of "Come to Jesus" in.'[24] People were 'converted' to socialism. There were the 'socialist ten commandments'. In the 1970s one veteran socialist looked back wishing he could remember them all. He was able to recall some: 'Love learning which is the food of the mind. Be as grateful to your teachers as to you parents. Do not think that he who loves his own country should hate and despise other nations or wish for war which is a remnant of barbarism.'[25] There was a touch of self-righteousness, a feeling of being part of a virtuous elect that chooses to attend a political meeting rather than going to the pub.[26] The propagandists were earnest preachers of the good news of socialism, travelling around the country by railway and staying in the homes of fellow socialists. Politics was a moral evangelical endeavour. Some of the working-class leaders of the Labour movement in the early years of the twentieth century were also lay preachers who combined their religious and political professions. Branches of the ILP were not only interested in political work, they were also centres of culture and education.[27] People were addressed as 'Comrade' and letters opened with 'Dear Sir and Bro.'[28]

The early activists were great readers. The novels of Charles Dickens were devoured. Thomas Carlyle was a favourite, and so was John Stuart Mill. John Ruskin too, especially *Unto This Last*. There were more explicitly socialist writings, such as the works of William Morris, especially his novels *A Dream of John Ball* and *News from Nowhere*. Robert Blatchford's *Merrie England* sold over a million copies of a one penny edition.[29] Not all literary inspirations were British, however. Edward Bellamy and Henry George, both Americans, were of interest. The former's *Looking Backward* was, like *News from Nowhere*, a futuristic utopia. The latter's *Progress and Poverty* advocated a tax on land values and had an enormous influence on socialist ideas in the early part of the twentieth century. In 1882 George went on a speaking tour of Britain, and 400,000 copies of his book were sold.

The Fabian Society

The Fabian Society was intellectual, middle class, and London-based. It thus differed from the ILP, although some, such as Ramsay MacDonald, were members of both. It was named after a Roman general who introduced 'fabian' tactics, that is, a slow and patient strengthening of one's position. Many Fabians thought that with industrialism, social reforms – education, public health, and state monitoring of the private sector – were inevitable. Such developments should, to their mind, be encouraged in the public interest.

Cooperation and collectivism should temper the excesses of individualism and capitalism. Fabian thought also reflected the popular science of the age. Evolution was applied to society, and the body politic was seen as an organism with ills that could be scientifically diagnosed and remedied.

The society was founded in 1884 and its leading figures in the next two decades were George Bernard Shaw, Beatrice and Sidney Webb, and Graham Wallas. In London its middle-class membership was sometimes mocked as 'drawing room socialists'. In *Fabian Essays in Socialism*, published in 1889, they produced a collectivist programme. This publication had an impact on the society's character: it ceased to be overwhelmingly London-based society, and branches formed all over the country, especially in the north of England. Shaw and MacDonald both travelled around the country giving talks on the society's behalf. Members worked with all political parties. They had the idea of permeating other political parties with their ideas of gradualism and the inevitability of socialism. A methodical study of society would lead to greater efficiency. Poverty was not a phenomenon to be alleviated by charitable deeds but an evil to be eliminated. They aimed to make socialism acceptable, if not fashionable. To some extent they succeeded. The word 'socialist' was so accepted that when the Liberal chancellor of the exchequer, William Vernon Harcourt, introduced death duties in his budget in 1894, he could say, 'We are all socialists now.'

The society issued a stream of well-researched pamphlets, many written by Sidney Webb, on economics, finance, and social affairs. There was, however, a gulf between the world of the Fabians and the world of the classes who were to benefit from their efforts.

Although not revolutionary, some members did study the works of Karl Marx. In the late 1880s, Shaw, Webb, Wallas, Sydney Olivier, and others met to discuss *Das Kapital*.[30]

The society had received a good press, not least because at the time of its peak in the early 1890s up to 10 per cent of its male members were writers, journalists, or historians. About a quarter of its members were women.[31] Members were seen by staid outsiders as people wearing velvet jackets and Liberty gowns.[32]

The Social Democratic Federation (SDF)

The third socialist society around at this time was a little more in touch with the working classes and continental Marxism. The Social Democratic Federation (SDF) was the vehicle for the ideas and activism of the colourful H. M. Hyndman, Old Etonian, amateur county cricketer, and professional stockbroker. He read Marx's work in a French translation and was persuaded by its message. He was impatient with the gradualism of the Fabians, describing their politics as 'Mr Micawberism, waiting for something to turn up.'[33] He also thought the Fabian Society, probably correctly, lacked an international perspective.

Hyndman launched the Democratic Federation, soon to be renamed the Social Democratic Federation, in 1881. A number of branches were set up around the country – in 1884 Ramsay MacDonald was a member of the Bristol branch. Members took to wearing red ties and addressing each other as 'comrade'. The SDG survived rows, resignations, breakaways, and splits, and stood apart from the Labour Party after its foundation. It lasted for nearly forty years until it morphed in 1920 into the Communist Party of Great Britain. The SDF's doctrine was Marxism as interpreted by Hyndman, although Marx's daughter, Eleanor, who had been a founding member, fell out with Hyndman and, with William Morris, set up the Socialist League in 1885.

Unlike the Fabian Society, the SDF did have some working-class lieutenants, including for a while one of the leaders of the 1889 dock strike, Tom Mann. Like the Fabian Society, the SDF was very much London-based, but unlike the Fabian Society it participated in parliamentary elections.

In the 1885 general election an SDF candidate was accused of receiving support from the Conservatives, who saw the opportunity to split the anti-Conservative vote. The SDF was more successful thirteen years later when in 1898, in alliance with the local Irish community and radicals, they secured the first Labour/Socialist majority in a town council – West Ham, Keir Hardie's old constituency.

The Labour Representation Committee (LRC)

At a meeting convened by the TUC in February 1900, the differing strands of the trade union and socialist movements came together and resolved to secure independent Labour representation in Parliament. The chairman was a trade unionist, but an unusual one – a man who later disappeared from the Labour story. Frederick Rogers was a bookbinder and specialist in the production of books bound in vellum. An Anglo-Catholic, he was a national, if not international, authority on Elizabethan literature and early modern book production.

The conference established the Labour Representation Committee (LRC). A secretary was elected – James Ramsay MacDonald. Initially he had no salary, but his wife, a committed socialist, fortunately had a private income. Before the breakthrough in 1906, the path to secure MPs, independent of other parties, was not smooth. In September 1900 the prime minister called a general election. The Boer War was in progress and the election became known as the 'khaki' election because of its exploitation of military enthusiasm. The LRC had only £33 to spend on the fifteen candidates who stood. Two of them were successful, Keir Hardie in Merthyr Tydfil and Richard Bell in Derby.

The case for independent Labour representation was strengthened by the final judgment in 1901 on the Taff Vale case. The Amalgamated Society of Railway Servants (ASRS) was required to pay £23,000 in damages to the railway company to cover any losses incurred as a result of the strike. This challenged the integrity of trade union finances. As a result, more trade unions allied themselves to the LRC.

Success came at by-elections. In 1903 Labour took Barnard Castle in a three-cornered contest, followed by Woolwich. Labour, it was observed, was often competing for Liberal votes. Hitherto, in two-member constituencies that were solidly Liberal there had been agreement that one candidate might be a working man from Labour, the other a more mainstream Liberal. MacDonald, with Hardie's knowledge and support, entered into negotiations with the office of the Liberal chief whip, Herbert Gladstone, to formalise these arrangements in a secret pact. Although it went against the fundamental principle of the founding of the LRC and was concealed from the members, it was a shrewd strategic move, and transformed Labour's fortunes. One unforeseen consequence of the deal was that it curbed extremism. LRC candidates would have to be acceptable to Liberal voters; and, at the same time, in these constituencies the Liberal candidate would have to be sensitive to local Labour feeling. Winston Churchill shared a two-member constituency with a Labour MP in Dundee under this pact. In response to his constituents, he was at his most radical during these years.[34]

The Politics of 1906 and After

In the general election of 1906 the Liberals gained 216 seats, totalling 400 seats, facing 157 Conservatives. This more or less reversed the balance of the previous election – 184 Liberals and 402 Conservatives.

The twenty-nine successful Labour candidates had not owed much to local organisation, compared with those of the other parties. Canvassing was organised mostly by trades councils. MacDonald and Henderson did what they could to set up a skeleton of support through local committees.[35] Fifty-five LRC candidates stood, of whom thirty-two were allowed a straight fight with Conservatives. Their most successful region was Lancashire, where Liberals were weak. Of the total electorate, 5.9 per cent voted Labour.[36] Only two of those elected were in London and the South East, and none from the West Country. Seven owed their sponsorship to the ILP, and the rest were trade union nominees. Most were in their fifties and were placid, respectable trade union dignitaries. The majority of the trade unionists would not have described themselves as socialists. They left the political running to MacDonald and Snowden, both in their forties and ILP nominees. The most active trade unionist MPs were Arthur Henderson and David Shackleton. Henderson was chief whip of the group. Keir Hardie was initially the leader, or chairman, of the Parliamentary Labour Party (PLP), but he was prematurely ageing and not very good in this role. He was more a venerated leader than a respected party manager. He was replaced as leader two years later by the first of a succession of annually elected chairmen/leaders. Hardie became, in Beatrice Webb's words, 'little more than a figurehead'.[37]

The conservatism of the 1906 intake was illustrated in 1908 when Victor Grayson was returned at a by-election in Colne Valley. He was not endorsed by the LRC but stood as a socialist and won. He was in his twenties, and a dynamic and forceful orator who was scornful of the normal parliamentary conventions. He was shunned by Labour MPs, most of whom were a generation older. He lost his seat in the January 1910 general election, and gradually faded from public view.

At the first meeting of the new LRC-sponsored MPs, they decided to rebrand the Labour Representation Committee with the catchier name of Labour Party.

The new Liberal prime minister was a canny old Scottish radical, Sir Henry Campbell-Bannerman, and his appointment of John Burns to be president of the Local Government Board was seen as a significant gesture to any challenge from the Left. Burns had been a fiery young leader of the 1889 London dock strike. He had been elected to Parliament in 1892 but had not got on well with the other ILP member, Keir Hardie, and over the next decade drifted away from his roots, taking no part in the foundation of the LRC. Even so he had a popular base in London. On being told that he was to become a Cabinet minister, he grasped the prime minister's hand. 'I congratulate you, Sir Henry,' he said. 'It will be the most popular appointment you have made.'[38] Burns was a disappointment in office. He initiated nothing and was seen as totally deferential to his officials. He stayed in office until 1914 when, on the outbreak of the Great War, a flicker of his old radicalism flared up and he resigned in protest. According to his Cabinet colleague Lord Haldane, he was 'vain and ignorant'.[39] Burns disappeared from public life and lived on until 1943.

Over the next eight years Labour gave general support to the Liberal government. They succeeded in reversing the decision on the Taff Vale case, to the benefit of trade union funds, and the legislation dealing with social reforms that were close to Labour aspirations. Local authorities were encouraged to offer school meals. Old age pensions were introduced, albeit only for men over seventy years old, an age that most working-class men failed to reach. Unemployed insurance and employment exchanges were brought in. Labour MPs were also strongly concerned with legislation dealing with health and safety measures in the workplace, a minimum wage, and education.[40] The government's radical agenda was primarily driven by the chancellor of the exchequer, David Lloyd George, and the aristocratic president of the Board of Trade, Winston Churchill. In 1909 Lloyd George brought in his redistributive People's Budget, which imposed a tax on unearned income derived from an increase in land values. This roused fierce opposition from the landed interests, stoked further by inflammatory speeches from Lloyd George and Churchill. Labour, not surprisingly, backed the budget, especially as the increased revenue was being used to fund the social reforms (as well as increased armaments).

The year 1910 saw two general elections, in January and December. The two main parties obtained roughly the same number of seats each, and a Liberal majority was sustained with the support of Irish MPs and Labour. The number of Labour MPs was increased to forty in January and forty-two in December. The parliamentary progress of Labour was not smooth. Some seats were gained, others lost. Some seats won in 1906 were lost. It was clear that there was no irreversible Labour advance, and strategists like MacDonald might well have wondered whether Labour had already peaked. The sense of Labour irrelevance or marginality would have been accentuated when the new king, George V, summoned a constitutional conference at Buckingham Palace. Leaders of the government and of the Conservative opposition were invited, but not Labour.

In the years before 1914 Labour MPs were, in Beatrice Webb's caustic and not entirely fair words, 'a lot of ordinary workmen who neither know nor care about anything but the interests of their respective trade unions and a comfortable life for themselves', with three exceptions. The exceptions were MacDonald, the leader from 1911 to 1914, and Snowden, and they did not always work in harmony with each other.[41] The third was the figurehead, Keir Hardie.

Many of the more militant members of the working-class movement were disappointed with the performance of the Labour MPs. Initiative for activism switched to the trade unions. Sometimes external events stimulated militancy. Another legal case, the Osborne Judgment of 1909, curbed the practice of trade unions making payments to MPs. This caused panic among the MPs who temporarily resigned from the Labour Party, which then paid them what the unions had paid them. The issue was permanently resolved by a clause in the Parliament Act of 1911 that introduced payment for all MPs. During the hot summer of that year a number of strikes brought on a heavy police response, with the army standing by ready to intervene.

Trade union militancy was matched by the militancy of a number of movements at this time whose activities disregarded the accepted norms of peaceful protest. The years 1910 to 1914 saw an acceleration of bitterness and violence in the suffragette movement, but perhaps the most serious militancy was seen in resistance to the Home Rule Bill of 1912, which gave independence to Ireland. The resistance was led by senior army officers in collusion with leaders of the Conservative Party.

The notion of syndicalism derived from the ideas of the French political philosopher Georges Sorel. His theory was that trade unions should be aware of their power and determine the pace of social change. More could be achieved for the working classes through aggressive industrial action, or 'direct action' as it was called, than by the slow deliberations of Parliament. In the four years before 1914 prices rose but wages remained static,[42] and trade union membership grew. Unions continued to amalgamate, and the larger unions catered for general workers, not exclusively limited to one industry. Will Thorne, a gas worker, prepared the way for the creation of the General and Municipal Workers' Union. J. H. Thomas worked, not always successfully, to bring smaller unions into the National Union of Railwaymen. Ernest Bevin worked for the federation of dockers and transport workers, leading to the establishment of the Transport and General Workers' Union. Coal mining was scattered, and the regional mining unions joined up in the Miners' Federation, later the National Union of Miners. Until early in the century the political miners had been allied to the Liberal Party, but in 1908 they affiliated themselves to the Labour Party. In the next few years they acquired a reputation for militancy. This nonetheless coincided with the poor performance of the Labour Party in a series of by-election defeats.[43]

Beatrice Webb missed the point when deploring the lack of vigour in the Labour MPs at this time. They were not the harbingers of a new socialist commonwealth. They saw themselves specifically in Parliament to promote Labour interests. Just as there were Conservative trade unionists, so one of the 1906 new Labour MPs ended up as a Conservative member of Parliament. As George Shepherd, a long-term official in Labour Party headquarters, expressed it, 'A working man may be a Conservative, a Liberal or a Socialist, but he will always look upon these words as additional, as something that can be discarded at will. But to be a Labour man is another matter altogether.'[44] Their primary job was to represent Labour, and to lobby for legislation and reforms that directly affected the working conditions and family circumstances of their trade union members. Most of the new MPs had been, or still were, trade union officials. They were no longer at the coal face or the work bench. They wore suits and watch chains, had offices, and took home a regular and steady salary. They were familiar with administrative procedures, negotiating deals, and making compromises.

By 1914 the impact of Labour on the political scene had been superficial, indirect, and often overlooked. It had made stumbling, if not spectacular, progress over the previous decade, but nothing to suggest that it was anything more than an important pressure group, often reflecting progressive and collectivist ideas.

The Great War would change all that.

3

From Pressure Group to Government in Waiting

The Impact of the Great War

Britain declared war against Germany on Tuesday, 4 August 1914.

When, on 28 June that year, the heir to the Habsburg Empire was assassinated in Sarajevo in Austrian-occupied Bosnia by a young Serbian nationalist who claimed that Bosnia rightfully belonged to Serbia, few could have predicted that that event would trigger a European war. But the European nations were like a house of cards. Austria sent an ultimatum, making demands on Serbia. Russia backed their fellow Slav nation. Austria confronted Russia, and Germany came to the support of Austria. France saw a chance of regaining territory lost in the War of 1870 and challenged Germany. Britain had secret military agreements with both Russia and France. All the European nations were heavily armed for conflict. The balance of power lost its equilibrium and, to mix metaphors, the tower made from a pack of cards collapsed. Each country was fighting a defensive war. Every country had God on its side.

Alternatively, Germany, since Bismarck, had built up a navy that was challenging Britain's naval supremacy. There was an aggressive militaristic culture in Germany that was itching for a war with Britain. The chain of events gave Germany the opportunity to get even with France. To do this it had to overrun Belgium. Britain had undertaken to protect Belgium and so was, for reasons of honour, inevitably drawn into the European war.

The impact and consequences were colossal throughout Europe. The rest of the world was sucked in. After the war, the military correspondent for *The Times*, Colonel Repington, published his war-time diaries with the title *The First World War*. This was not an act of uncanny clairvoyance, prophesying a succession of world wars, but a recognition that this was the first war that involved not just the principal European belligerents but most of the rest of the world. Mary Agnes ('Molly') Hamilton, a Cambridge graduate and future Labour MP who was working as a journalist at *The Economist*, recalled that the war was 'a shock under which we reeled. Its impact destroyed our foundations; left us staring at a world alien, hostile, terrifying, in which we did not know our way about. We were involved, engulfed in nightmare; we had to accept nightmare, and not our previous waking thoughts, as reality.'[1] The conduct of foreign affairs was left to a Foreign Office and a diplomatic service that was composed of men from a narrow, exclusive, and moneyed class, not only in Britain but in all European countries. For most people in Britain, 'foreign affairs' suggested something alien, marginal to everyday life, something that could be ignored or left to others to worry about. Gradually the notion of 'foreign affairs' gave way to the less subjective 'international relations'.

British Labour and the World

The outbreak of the war split the ranks of Labour.

As in other political parties at the time, few in the Labour movement in 1914 took a close interest in foreign affairs. A spirit of theoretical internationalism pervaded the movement, and an ideological objection to 'colonialism', derived from Gladstonian liberalism, but it was not comprehensively articulated. In the previous fifty years foreign issues such as Italian unity or Bulgarian atrocities had stirred much popular enthusiasm, but interest was never sustained over decades.

There were no student exchanges or mass tourism that might have produced an awareness of people in other countries. Several trade unionist leaders and socialists had travelled to European conferences, but they were a minority. Many knew little and cared less about what happened beyond the English Channel. There were more pressing issues this side of the Channel. Five years after the war, David Kirkwood criticised Labour's concern for foreign affairs. 'I sincerely regret that many members of the Labour Party', he wrote in *New Leader*, 'should be eternally giving prominence to the Ruhr, or Montenegro, or Timbuctoo, when their prime duty is to emancipate the British working class.'[2]

When he was secretary of the Labour Party, Ramsay MacDonald was the British representative of the Socialist International (SI). The first SI had been set up by Karl Marx after the Revolutions of 1848. This met periodically in different European cities but broke down in the 1880s after doctrinal disputes, mostly between anarchists and socialists. After Marx's death a second SI was founded in 1889, and British socialists and trade unionists regularly attended their conferences. It was at these that MacDonald met, got to know, and found respect for such European socialist luminaries as August Bebel, Karl Liebknecht, and Jean Jaurès. Some socialist parties had shared power in both municipal and national governments. Socialist ideas had succeeded in the introduction of social welfare programmes in Germany, although socialist organisations were suppressed. In Vienna, the municipality had been under socialist control and had pioneered social housing.

Within days of the outbreak of the war the hopes of international socialists collapsed, as most people throughout Europe, as in Britain, were swept away by nationalism and chose to support their belligerent governments rather than fight for the rights of the working class. It was a bitter disappointment to idealists.

What did people in the Labour movement know about the rest of the world? Some had relations in the United States. The outside world also included the British Empire, where others had families who had migrated – to Australia, Canada, South Africa, and New Zealand. Not many – Keir Hardie and Ramsay MacDonald excepted – knew much about India. Some soldiers and sailors may have served in imperial bases such as Gibraltar, Malta, Cyprus, Aden, Singapore, and Hong Kong. As for the swathes of territory in South, East and West Africa, scattered smaller imperial possessions in Central America, Southeast Asia and the Caribbean, and islands in the Atlantic and Pacific Oceans, there was little Labour policy beyond 'be kind to the natives,' and perhaps a feeling of guilty pride, fed by the novels of John Buchan and Rudyard Kipling. Imperial possessions were just that. It was natural that European powers had possessions outside Europe. They were extensions of Europe.

A few saw lessons for Labour in the empire. In the lands of white settlement – the dominions – class divisions were significantly less rigid than they were in Britain. Those countries had strong trade unions. Both New Zealand and some of the Australian states had even had Labour governments before 1914. In the colonies and in India there had been no resistance to socialistic measures. Railways and banks were often state-owned.[3]

MacDonald and the Independent Labour Party (ILP)

On Saturday, 2 August 1914, there had been a great anti-war rally, organised by the British branch of the Socialist International in Trafalgar Square, addressed by Keir Hardie and Arthur Henderson. (Ramsay MacDonald was out of London that weekend.)

MacDonald had travelled extensively and made a study of international affairs. He was particularly close to German socialists. The British government, he argued, was at fault in assuming that the German government represented the whole of German public opinion. German socialists, he had pointed out in Parliament, had voted against the expansion of Germany's navy.

At first it seemed that the Labour Party as a whole would

not support the Liberal government in declaring war. But after Germany invaded Belgium a national wave of righteous pro-war feeling was reflected in the majority of the Parliamentary Labour Party. On Wednesday, 5 August, the party decided to support the vote for war credits in Parliament. MacDonald found himself at odds with the party and promptly resigned from his role as chairman and leader.

Philip Snowden was also opposed to the war. In August he was out of the country on a world tour to America and Australia. He cut short his world tour and returned to Britain.

MacDonald maintained a more or less consistent position throughout the war: entering the war was a mistake, and the way out was to negotiate a settlement with Germany. Together with other Radical Liberals, he had long been suspicious of the British government's closeness to France and the oppressive Russian government. He was not pro-German but wondered whether Britain would have declared war against France if France had invaded Germany. The war was a consequence of a belief in the policy of the balance of power, with two heavily armed camps glaring at each other, and with Britain bound to one of the camps. There was no justification for Britain getting involved. Britain was not, he argued, in any danger. He was not a pacifist; rather he thought this was the wrong war at the wrong time.

MacDonald was succeeded as leader by Arthur Henderson, for whom the invasion of Belgium, and thus the violation of a small nation, was justification for Britain declaring war against Germany.

Outside Parliament, the ILP was also divided. MacDonald, Snowden, and others in the leadership declared the war 'an appalling crime', while other members rallied to the flag to offer support to the government. In the first few months of the war about 10,000 members left the ILP, around a third of the total membership.[4]

The two most prominent Labour-supporting public intellectuals both wrote booklets backing the war. In October 1914 H. G. Wells published the tract *The War that Will End War*. He thought that an extension of liberal and peaceful values in Europe was irreversible, that the militarism of the German type was on the way out, and that the war against Germany would be its final blow. That autumn also saw the publication of a pamphlet by George Bernard Shaw, *Common Sense About the War*. In this Shaw argued that all the European powers were equally culpable for the war, but that as he was on one side, he would be supporting the British war effort. This somewhat cynical approach pleased nobody. At the same time he called for peace negotiations.

But the ILP became the main political opposition to the war. Keir Hardie was broken by it and died within a few months. MacDonald, paradoxically using a military metaphor, describing the ILP as 'the spear-head of the peace movement.'[5]

For many in the ILP the war was a vindication of their broader political and social outlook. The conduct of foreign affairs had been the business of an effete upper class, and they had failed. Indeed, the Conservative MP Lord Hugh Cecil said that the idea of the Labour Party running foreign affairs was like expecting a baby to be in charge of an aeroplane.[6] Conventional ideas such as the balance of power and the notion that security was guaranteed by an arms race were myths. One aristocratic radical, Bertrand Russell, the future third earl, related to ambassadors and diplomats as well as dukes, articulated what he saw as the inadequacy of his class's mismanagement of foreign affairs. International diplomacy 'has remained everywhere the exclusive domain of an aristocratic clique'. He argued that 'the world of finance, the world of learning, the world of socialism – to take only three examples – are international, each of great importance in its own way, each having interests that cut right across the divisions of States.'[7] Representatives of these interests should be associated with the formation and execution of foreign policy. Diplomacy should be 'in the hands of men'; not even Bertrand Russell in 1914 could contemplate women diplomats – 'less aloof and less aristocratic, more in touch with common life, and more emancipated from the prejudices of a bygone age.'[8] He expressed this opinion in various magazine articles within months of the outbreak of war. They were later reissued in a small book published by the National Labour Press.

New theories of international relations became attractive. One of the earliest theorists was an inspirational Cambridge don, G. Lowes Dickinson. In *The European Anarchy*, published in 1914, he argued that 'wars do not arise because one nation or group of nations is wicked, the others being good.'[9] He rejected the idea of exclusive war guilt. It may be, he conceded, that Germany's actions triggered the war (literally), but what was at fault was the 'international anarchy' with its build-up of mutual suspicion and fear, each country arming itself against the possibility of war. 'It is part of the irony that attaches to the whole system,' Dickinson wrote, 'that the preparations made against war are themselves the principal cause of war.'[10] No single power was ready to disarm unilaterally.

Russell exposed the rhetoric of the warmongers, both politicians and journalists. The paradox was, he argued, that every side was conducting a defensive war and that the other side was to blame.

> Serbia is defending itself against the brutal aggression of Austria-Hungary, Austria-Hungary is defending itself against the disruptive revolutionary agitation which Servia is believed to have fomented; Russia is defending Slavdom against the menace of Teutonic aggression; Germany is defending Teutonic civilisation against the encroachment of the Slav; France is defending itself against a repetition of 1870; and England, which sought only the preservation of the *status quo*, is defending its rights against a prospective menace to its maritime supremacy. The claims of each side to be fighting in self-defence appear to the other side as mere wanton hypocrisy.[11]

Cross-Party Cooperation Against the War

There were, in the first weeks of the war, developments that were to have a profound and lasting influence on the Labour Party over the next ten years. A number of Liberal MPs and supporters were against the war. This alienation from the war started in the Liberal Cabinet. Two members, John Burns and Viscount Morley, and one junior minister, Charles Trevelyan, resigned in protest against the war. Burns, a generation earlier, had been a radical trade unionist and a member of the Social Democratic Federation. But he had been a difficult man to work with. He was not a dynamic or progressive minister, and after 1914 he disappeared from politics forever. John Morley, the biographer and the political heir of Gladstone, was nearly eighty, and took this chance also to withdraw from active politics. From his home in Wimbledon he observed the political scene with detachment, and was benignly interested in the younger generation of progressives, some of whom went to see him and pay homage. Charles Trevelyan was the youngest of the three, and ten years later became one of the men of 1924. In addition, some Radical Liberal MPs declared against the war.

During August 1914 a group of like-minded objectors gathered and set up the Union of Democratic Control (UDC). The title of the organisation was chosen to draw attention to the fact that there had been military and diplomatic agreements committing Britain to war that had not been given parliamentary, and therefore democratic, approval. Their objectives were to campaign against secret diplomacy and for a negotiated peace. Ramsay MacDonald was elected chairman, and E. D. Morel became secretary. Morel was a Liberal but not an MP. He had effectively campaigned against atrocities inflicted on black people in the Belgian Congo and written of pre-war diplomacy. He was an astute organiser and knew how to tap funds from wealthy sympathisers. An early member was Norman Angell, author of *The Great Illusion*, a book that argued that pacifism was in a nation's economic self-interest.

Other founding members included Arthur Ponsonby, Liberal MP and son of the private secretary of Queen Victoria, a former diplomat himself and secretary of the former Liberal prime minister; Sir Henry Campbell-Bannerman; and Charles Roden Buxton and his brother, Noel, both of whom had made a study of the politics of the Ottoman Empire, promoting the interests of the Balkan countries. The UDC represented a radical alternative to international relations.

These people were mostly from the middle and upper classes, a mixture of Cambridge and Bloomsbury. Once a week they met socially at the London home of Lady Ottoline Morrell, at 44 Bedford Square in Bloomsbury. In a large luxurious room on the first floor men and women would gather to talk over coffee and cigarettes. As the evening went on Lady Ottoline's husband, Philip, a Liberal MP, would tickle the ivories of a piano, and the young people would get up and dance, a habit just coming into vogue.[12] Other progressive luminaries would drop in – John Maynard Keynes, Leonard Woolf, Aldous and Julian Huxley, Duncan Grant, and Bertrand Russell, who was one of Lady Ottoline's lovers. Molly Hamilton recalled:

> The dominating mind was Bertie Russell ... it was as a political and social philosopher that we sat at his feet ... For us, unhappily, he destroyed more than he built, and tore the speech of our statesmen to pieces. It was not surprising that he dazzled us: anything more continuously brilliant than his conversation cannot be imagined; his devastating wit played like lightning against the dramatic background of the sombre anguish of the war ... Caustic comments he would emit in his high squeaky voice and with a cackle of curiously mirthless laughter, while his brilliant eyes, like high-powered headlights, bored right into your head.[13]

It was socially a long way from trade union clubs or West Riding nonconformist chapels, but Ramsay MacDonald was completely at home in this circle. In spite of social differences, he had connections, encouraged by Morel.

Membership of the UDC was not solely for individuals. Organisations could affiliate. Trade union branches, local cooperative societies, women's associations, and ILP branches all became members.[14]

Neither was there a single policy beyond the demand for open diplomacy, as suggested by the name of the organisation. Views about war guilt and responsibility varied. Certain notions emerged from the writings of UDC members that were to endure, such as 'the international anarchy'. Other proposals such as setting up the 'League of Nations' were to be widely accepted as pillars of post-war governments' foreign policy. Both terms were attributed to G. Lowes Dickinson.[15] The union issued pamphlets on aspects of the war; some of their ideas filtered through to Parliament, thanks to members such as Arthur Ponsonby and Charles Trevelyan. Dickinson founded the League of Nations Union in 1918, bringing on board two peers, Lord Courtney of Penwith, a former Liberal MP, and Lord Parmoor, a former Conservative MP, both incidentally brothers-in-law of Beatrice Webb. Ramsay MacDonald was initially sceptical about the idea of the League of Nations being a forum that would remove or avert armed conflicts, describing it as 'quackery'.[16] His preferred answer was personal diplomacy, getting to know statesmen of other nations and sustaining constant dialogue.

Serious committee meetings of the UDC took place at Trevelyan's flat in Westminster. They devised a four-point basis for peace negotiations with Germany: Germany had to withdraw from northern France and Belgium and recognise the latter's sovereignty. Germany should pay reparations to Belgium. Germany's colonial Empire should be restored to her. The future of Alsace and Lorraine, taken from France after the 1870 Franco-Prussian War, should be decided after a plebiscite of its people. It is worth noting that the inhabitants of Germany's African colonies were not to be offered a choice.

Another group that responded to the outbreak of the war was the

No Conscription Fellowship (NCF), founded by a young radical journalist, Fenner Brockway. He maintained that it was his wife's idea. The NCF started as a getting together of young men who were resisting the call for military volunteers and were opposed to the idea of conscription into the armed services. The Brockways' cottage in Derbyshire – he was working in Manchester at the time – was a retreat for them. But the numbers grew too large for such informality and the organisation transferred to London, with Clifford Allen as chairman and Brockway as secretary.[17] Supporters of the NCF ranged from Liberals such as the home secretary, Sir John Simon, who resigned in objection to the introduction of compulsory military service, to pacifist opponents of the war. The NCF became the most radical of the anti-war groups.

There was sometimes a paradoxical situation. People were torn between their convictions and their professionalism, as well as the need to earn a living. David Kirkwood, an engineer working in a major munitions factory in Glasgow, opposed the war, but was committed to working in the factory during the week. However, during the weekends he travelled around Scotland and England, campaigning for peace by negotiation.[18]

Conscription was introduced in early 1916 with the Military Service Act. The PLP was divided on the issue. In the early years of the war some Labour MPs joined with politicians of other parties on recruitment drives. Other Labour MPs acquiesced reluctantly in compulsory military service, but the legislation allowed pacifists the right of conscientious objection to military service. Objectors had to face a local tribunal to persuade them that they were genuine. It was easier for men with a religious affiliation to a church, chapel, or the Religious Society of Friends (Quakers). It was much tougher for men with a political objection to the war. The part of Britain with the largest concentration of conscientious objectors was that stronghold of the ILP, the West Riding of Yorkshire, especially around Huddersfield.[19] Those who failed to win over the tribunal were called up to serve in the army anyway. When they refused to comply, they were subject to imprisonment for up to two years with hard labour.

Prison conditions produced a camaraderie among the prisoners. Many were sent to Durham Gaol and had to attend a prison chapel service two or three times a week. The prison governor's daughter used to play the organ at these services. On one occasion the governor and his family were away on holiday for a fortnight. The chief warder was in search of a substitute organist. One prisoner 'volunteered to play the organ and did so for two Sundays. On the last occasion he suddenly struck up "The Red Flag".' The prisoners gradually joined in singing the socialist anthem. 'The warders were yelling at us to stop. They were doing everything to stop us but they could not.'[20]

A third group of war-time dissidents that sprang up was the 1917 Club, which met at 4 Gerrard Street, London. This was not in response to the Bolshevik Revolution in Russia but was rather designed as a meeting place for left-wing Liberals and Labour Party members to meet and find common cause. The leading lights were the radical journalist H. W. Nevinson and the economist J. A. Hobson. Members shared attitudes towards the war and rejoiced at the news of the Bolshevik Revolution. Ethel and Philip Snowden were regular attenders, although even in 1917 Philip disapproved of revolution in general, and the Bolshevik Revolution in particular. The Snowdens withdrew from the club not for ideological reasons but because the club applied for a licence to provide alcohol at their meetings; the Snowdens, especially Ethel, were ferocious teetotallers.[21]

In the opposition to the war, the diverse groupings were to converge towards the end of the war to provide wide support for the Labour Party. This convergence did not mean social mixing. In D. H. Lawrence's novel, Lady Chatterley's socialist middle-class sister, Hilda, explained that 'being on their [the working class's] side makes me know how impossible it is to mix one's life with theirs, not out of snobbery. But because the rhythm is different.'[22]

There were, however, many from the Labour movement who

supported the war. The sons of some of the future 1924 Cabinet ministers – such as Adamson and Henderson – joined up and lost their lives. Others, unexpectedly, showed a military enthusiasm. Will Thorne, a militant trade unionist and MP for West Ham, had retained his membership of the Marxist SDF. He joined the West Ham Volunteer Force and was quietly proud of his honorary rank of lieutenant colonel. His anti-war critics in the borough were horrified.[23]

Labour Enters the Government

Things were not going well for the Asquith government in the spring of 1915. The Gallipoli campaign was turning out to be disastrous. The war was going on far longer than had been anticipated. The prime minister was prematurely aging, drinking too much and besotted by a friend of his daughter, Venetia Stanley. He seemed to be losing his grip. Under pressure, he agreed to extend the base of his government to include Conservatives and Labour. The leader of the Labour Party, Arthur Henderson, was invited to join the Cabinet as president of the Board of Education. Two other Labour MPs took junior posts. William Brace, a miner from South Wales, became under-secretary at the Home Office, and George Roberts, who had worked in the East Anglian sugar-beet industry, became a junior whip.

There was some resistance from the Labour Party at first to the men joining the government, the parliamentary party initially in disagreement. Philip Snowden, who opposed the war, thought Henderson's act was a betrayal of socialism and accused the three of being ready for 'whatever dirty work the Tory masters bid them'.[24]

Labour was brought into the management of the war in other ways. The government was sensitive to the dangers of industrial unrest, and Arthur Henderson was seen as the government's adviser on Labour issues. This was an invidious role and did not make him popular with the rank and file of the Labour Party. Henderson, as leader, had taken the initiative and set up the War Emergency Workers' National Committee (WNC). This broad committee included pro-war and anti-war factions, and even included people outside the Labour Party, such as H. M. Hyndman. It helped to prevent a permanent division in the ranks of Labour.

As leader, Asquith seemed to be conducting war as he had conducted peace. Ministers were responsible for their departmental concerns. In December 1916 Lloyd George, who was seen as more dynamic and purposeful, replaced Asquith as prime minister. Lloyd George introduced a centralised direction of the war. He brought outside interests, such as businessmen, into the government. He tended to see the country as an aggregate of interests whom it was necessary to cajole, flatter, and ingratiate – the press, business, and labour. He took Parliament for granted and was not in the House of Commons as frequently as Asquith had been. He created a small five-man War Cabinet with Henderson as one of its members. It was as if Henderson was to represent Labour as a class, rather than the Parliamentary Labour Party. Labour was less reluctant to join his coalition this time, and the party struck a deal with Lloyd George. Labour agreed to join on the condition that a separate Ministry of Labour was formed. Lloyd George agreed and John Hodge, an iron and steel worker trade unionist, became the first minister. John Hodge made one further demand. He was able to select as his permanent under-secretary David Shackleton, who had been a Labour MP before being persuaded by Winston Churchill to join the civil service.[25] The new ministry took over responsibilities from the Board of Trade. Labour was given status with this move. It was changing from a pressure group to a constituent part of the country's decision-making process.

Other Labour men were brought in. George Barnes, a previous chairman of the Parliamentary Labour Party and a former engineer, was made minister of the newly created Ministry of Pensions. A third Labour minister was J. R. Clynes, a trade unionist and former cotton worker from Oldham who had been an MP from 1906. He had joined another newly created ministry, formed because of the exigencies of the war – the Ministry of Food. The minister was Lord Rhondda and Clynes, his under-secretary, was the ministry's spokesman in the House of Commons.

If putting Labour men in senior positions was becoming acceptable, so were policies of state control. Food shortages led to panic buying, hoarding, and profiteering. The Ministry of Food introduced food rationing. Some people called it war socialism. The economist J. A. Hobson argued that the 'war has advanced state socialism by half a century'.[26]

The other two ministries, headed by Labour men, had a high impact on the lives of ordinary people and accustomed the public to the idea that government posts were not the exclusive preserve of men from the older parties or the privileged classes.

Revolutionary Fervour

Lloyd George's ousting and replacement of Asquith split the Liberal Party bitterly. Some on the Left saw this as an opportunity for Labour. Instead of being a patronised appendage to the Liberal Party, it was able to see itself as a central element in the country's life, and even as a potential government. In 1917 the party produced a document, *Labour and the New Social Order*, ambitiously presenting a programme for a prospective Labour government. Written mainly by Sidney and Beatrice Webb, it stated more specifically Labour's war aims and that one of the consequences of the war was socialistic measures being taken, such as food rationing.

In early 1917 the Labour movement was still divided. Opinions about the war varied: some socialists were in prison for resistance to the war, some Labour MPs were on recruiting platforms. The previous year had been awful, with the mass slaughter on the

Somme and its strategic deadlock. Would the war ever end? And if so, how? Then, in the spring of 1917, brighter news of revolution in Russia reached Britain. The collapse of the tsarist regime in March brought hope to a demoralised Labour movement. For years Labour and many Liberals had campaigned against the oppressive old regime. Jews who fled from pogroms found a welcome in progressive Britain. They joined other political exiles who had found a refuge in London and elsewhere. Pro-war progressives had been embarrassed by finding Britain in alliance with that regime. Any claim that the war was being fought for democratic values sounded hollow. So it was with relief that news came of the fall of the tsar. There was some popular enthusiasm for the new regime, led by Kerensky, a man with liberal beliefs. Secret treaties to which the old regime had been party to were published. The new Russian government called for peace negotiations with no annexations. Although the new rulers were not socialist, many other socialists and revolutionaries returned to the country and were active; the situation was volatile. For those opposed to the war, the fall of the tsar was seen as a sign that the corrupt old order that had got Europe into this mess was vulnerable and crumbling. International socialist solidarity that had been shattered in August 1914 was revived. Socialists in belligerent and neutral countries were reaching out to each other. Towards the end of the year, in Russia, the Bolsheviks were organising workers' and soldiers' soviets that were taking over the country in the name of the people and claiming legitimacy. Some militants in Britain sought to follow suit. Left-wingers and conservatives were in agreement in anticipating a revolution, the former with eagerness, the latter with horror.

In the summer of 1917, three months after the fall of the tsar and five months before the Bolsheviks took over, socialist organisations in Britain arranged to hold a conference to celebrate the Russian Revolution. A secretariat was formed from the ILP and from another smaller socialist body, the British Socialist Party. The event was called not a conference but a convention, an echo of the Chartist convention of 1839, which aimed to take the place of Parliament and met in Leeds. Over a thousand delegates attended; they included trade unionists and delegates from women's organisations, cooperative societies, and other democratic and progressive organisations. There was a feeling of euphoria. It was, as one delegate put it, 'the very greatest that we have seen in this country since the days of Chartism'.[27] Ramsay MacDonald and Philip Snowden were among Labour MPs who attended, as well as the secretary of the ILP, W. C. Anderson. Bertrand Russell was there, and so was the thirty-six-year-old trade unionist Ernest Bevin, as well as prominent suffragettes such as Charlotte Despard, Dora Montefiore, and Sylvia Pankhurst. The London socialist leader, George Lansbury, sent his apologies for his absence; he was convalescing from appendicitis. The miners' leader, Robert Smillie, took the chair.

Four resolutions were proposed and accepted. Ramsay MacDonald's resolution hailed the achievement the Russian Revolution; Philip Snowden called for a new international order in the conduct of diplomacy; and a third resolution called for the affirmation of civil liberties. But the fourth resolution was the most challenging. It called for the establishment 'in every town, urban and rural district of Councils of Workmen and Soldiers' Delegates for initiating and coordinating working-class activity in support of the foregoing resolutions'.[28] This was probably the climax of revolutionary feeling in Britain at this time, and it put the establishment on the defensive.

A similar potentially revolutionary situation seemed to be brewing in western Scotland. Glasgow on the river Clyde was a centre of shipbuilding and armaments production. It was also an area of high voluntary recruitment into the armed forces. The families at home were vulnerable, and landlords started putting up rents. This led to a vigorous campaign by women. 'Street meetings, back-court meetings, drums, bells, trumpets – every method was used to bring the women out.'[29] There was a collective refusal to pay any rent increase. Bailiffs were chased away by militant women. When eighteen munitions workers were summoned to court for non-payment of rent, 10,000 engineers and shipyard workers dropped tools and marched to the court house. Extensive and damaging strike action was threatened. The cases were dropped, and a Rent Restrictions Act was rushed through Parliament.

Glasgow had been a major location for the manufacture of munitions from the early months of the war. A Ministry of Munitions was established with a purposeful Lloyd George as minister. A Munitions Act gave him extensive powers over the direction of labour, but not over the profits made. The government had encouraged the practice of dilution, whereby less skilled (and less unionised) women were brought in to take over men's jobs. They were also paid less for the work, and this led to a fear of a general depression of wages at a time when profits were high.

Glasgow was a volatile city. The local ILP issued a newspaper, *Forward*, edited by a very effective journalist from Kirkintilloch, Tom Johnston. The city was full of immigrant labourers and their families from Ireland and the Highlands. Neither group had any love for or deference towards the wealthy or privileged.

Workers in Glasgow thought that union leaders had made a deal with the government. This deal was symbolised by the inclusion of the Labour leader, Arthur Henderson, in the government. Local trade unionists felt alienated from their leaders, and a vigorous shop stewards' movement emerged speaking the language of revolution. The movement revolved around the Clyde Workers' Committee (CWC) and was chaired by William Gallacher, a future Communist MP. Lloyd George came to Scotland in December 1915, accompanied by Henderson, addressed 3,000 shop stewards, and was booed. The minister's supporters broke into singing 'See the Conquering Hero Comes', but this was drowned out by the singing of 'The Red Flag'.[30] The leader of the shop stewards' movement, David Kirkwood, was arrested and the government followed an uncertain course of alternate coercion and conciliation.

In both these cases there was clearly a class conflict, with landlords and profiteers apparently exploiting the situation. Confrontation continued. Gallacher and Kirkwood among others were arrested. *Forward* was banned. Others were charged with sedition. Repression was not working, and the authorities were more sensitive as the war ended, but the CWC was the breeding ground for the left-wing socialists who were elected to Parliament from the city in 1922. For a few years Glasgow was seen as the city that could be the birthplace of a British revolution.

Responses to the Bolshevik Revolution

As prime minister, Lloyd George responded to the March revolution in Russia with apprehension. He was aware of the lack of morale of Russian soldiers, the possibility that they would fraternise with German soldiers, and that, overall, they were weakening the military alliance with France and Britain. He decided to send his War Cabinet colleague, Labour leader Arthur Henderson, to the Russian capital, Petrograd (after 1990, St Petersburg, and between 1924 and 1990, Leningrad), to assess the situation and to strengthen the revolutionary Russian government's resolve. It was not a happy mission, even though it was fairly open ended and Henderson was told that, if he thought it necessary, he could take the place of the ambassador. The mission was not fruitful, and Henderson returned without having accomplished much.

Meanwhile the Russian government supported a proposed conference of international socialists that was to take place in neutral Sweden. The conference was to include socialists from belligerent as well as neutral countries. At first Lloyd George liked the idea, as did Henderson, but he then faced opposition from the three Conservatives of the five-man War Cabinet. They saw a threat to the whole old-world order. In August a War Cabinet was convened to discuss the idea, but Henderson was told to wait outside 'on the doormat'. The cabinet minus Henderson decided that they would not acknowledge the Stockholm conference. Henderson was humiliated and had no option but to resign from the government. He refused the sop of being appointed a Companion of Honour. He was replaced in the War Cabinet by the more accommodating George Barnes as the Labour representative in the war-time coalition.

Henderson never trusted Lloyd George again. He had been led to consider himself as equal to other Cabinet ministers, and Labour as having been brought into the central direction of the war. He felt he was forced to quit as if he were an under-servant. He had not given up his position of secretary of the Labour Party, and as a direct consequence of the rebuff he spent the next eighteen months working with MacDonald and preparing the Labour Party for power. And, incidentally, the end of Lloyd George's government career.

When the Bolsheviks took over in the October Revolution – actually in November, according to western European calendars – the victory was greeted initially with great enthusiasm in the Labour movement. The workers had actually taken over; the revolution spoke the language of socialism. But in time that enthusiasm became nuanced. There were soon reports of brutality and repression, and arrests of socialists who did not toe the Bolshevik line. Some justified these excesses as the inevitable consequences of a revolutionary situation. Others saw them as a response to the opposition of the White Russians, supporters of the old regime, egged on by ministers such as Winston Churchill, who wanted British intervention to snuff out the Bolshevik peril. There was, however, wide agreement, not limited to the Labour movement, that the British government should refrain from interfering to restore the monarchy and capitalism.[31] This opposition to military intervention owed little to sympathy with Bolsheviks, but rather to the fear of more war in distant lands with no obvious or agreed positive outcome. It could go on for ever. This opposition united the disparate ranks of the Left. Ramsay MacDonald best articulated this view at the time. He opposed military intervention to overthrow the new regime, but he stated firmly his commitment to the possibility of a parliamentary road to socialism. Indeed, he stated this in a small book titled *Parliament and Revolution*, published by the National Labour Press in 1919.

Some enthusiasm for the Bolshevik Revolution survived the Great War and found expression in the foundation of the Communist Party. There was a messianic approach to the Soviet experiment, expressed in explicitly religious terms. For the young Harry Pollitt, mixing allusions to Islam and Judaism, 'Moscow was the Mecca of my dreams,' and arriving in Russia he experienced the elation of 'having reached the Promised Land'.[32] George Lansbury, an anti-war pacifist, went to Russia and found himself surrounded by 'soldiers, not one of whom understood a word we were saying. However, it was a great joy for me to feel myself in a Socialist country, even though the masses were starving.'[33] Other visitors, such as Bertrand Russell, were sceptical, even hostile to the new experiment.

Labour Comes Together

By the beginning of the year 1918 the conflicting strands of the Labour movement were coming together. The massacres on the Western Front from the summer of 1916 affected every neighbourhood and most households. There seemed to be no end to the unremitting carnage. What was the point of it all? The peace camp seemed to be offering acceptable alternatives. Two events strengthened these views. In November 1917 the former Conservative foreign secretary, the Marquess of Lansdowne, wrote a letter to the *Daily Telegraph* calling for a negotiated peace settlement – which is what MacDonald and the UDC had been calling for since 1914. The UDC gave a qualified welcome to the Lansdowne letter, qualified because Lansdowne wanted to restore the situation as it was in July 1914, before the outbreak of war, rather than pressing for a new way of dealing with international affairs.

The second event came from the United States, who entered the war on the side of Britain and her allies, but conditionally. President Woodrow Wilson issued a document outlining the Fourteen Points that should be the basis of a post-war settlement. These included self-determination, no annexations, and proposals for a League of Nations. Again, the UDC and other active groups that had opposed the war felt vindicated. More specifically there was agreement that Belgium should be liberated, and that Poland and the Balkan countries should be free and independent. The Labour Party issued a document, *Memorandum on War Aims*, outlining these points, written by Arthur Henderson, Sidney Webb, and Ramsay MacDonald. It derived most of its ideas from pamphlets and propaganda issued by the UDC.

Henderson, Webb, and MacDonald were also the main authors of a new Labour Party constitution that was ambitious and comprehensive. It set up the framework of the organisation of the party, but there were two specific innovations. The constitution's fourth clause declared the party to be ideologically socialist – stating its policy to be the public ownership of the means of production, distribution, and exchange. This was a statement that the Labour Party had a social and national policy that went beyond being a sectional working-class pressure group. Although the fourth clause was and has always been seen as radical, it began as an extension of war-time crisis policy when state control was extended to public services. Labour, however, made specific demands for public ownership of shipping, railways, armaments, and electric power.[34]

The second innovation was to open membership to individuals who were neither trade unionists nor members of socialist societies. The party was rearranged into constituency (or divisional, as it was then called) Labour parties (CLP). The CLP became a significant weight in the scales of the national party. The idea was not entirely new. For some years there had been a London Labour Party, whose secretary during the war was Herbert Morrison. Glasgow too had a Glasgow Central Labour Party that had been founded in 1911.[35] The new divisional Labour parties were grafted onto these older bodies and were linked with local trades councils. The new arrangement led to a spurt in the membership, especially from disillusioned members of the older parties. Now these local efforts were rationalised and coordinated within the framework of the Labour Party. This was very much an idea driven by Henderson, who retained his position as party secretary as well as being party leader throughout the war. Henderson travelled extensively round the country, jollying along local activists in his avuncular if slightly pompous way. He encouraged the formation of women's groups, and the sale of the party's newspaper, the *Daily Herald*.

There was one unforeseen consequence of the formation of the CLP. In Scotland, Bradford, Norwich, and other cities there had been and still were strong local branches of the ILP. In the immediate post-war years there would be two allied parties, and from 1918 the ILP developed its separate identity, becoming a left-wing ginger group within the Labour movement. Indeed, the number of ILP branches actually grew in 1922 and 1923. The chairman of the ILP, Clifford Allen, a war-time pacifist and activist who had been imprisoned for his resistance to conscription, was dynamic, and for a few years a confidant of Ramsay MacDonald. The ILP stressed the social side of political life, with lectures and outings to Easton Lodge, Essex, the stately home of the socialist and former socialite the Countess of Warwick.

Labour at the End of the War

Labour's standing was very different from where it had been at the beginning of the war. It could claim to be a national party, and no longer spoke for one class. Individuals had served in the Cabinet and occupied high-profile ministerial posts. Socialistic ideas, such as state direction of the commanding heights of the economy, had become acceptable and tested options. At the end of the war

Labour could not be taken for granted. Laissez-faire was no longer the panacea. Nor could it be argued that market forces allocated the rewards of the economy automatically to those who deserved them. Military success had depended on everyone in the community. The class assumptions of entitlement and privilege on the one side and deference on the other were no longer unquestioned. Those from the Labour Party and the radical wing of the Liberal Party – many of whom would join Labour in the next few years – had come up with positive ideas for dealing with a world order that had been shattered by the outbreak of the war. And the Labour Party now had an organisation that met the needs of an inclusive national political party. Hopes and ambitions restrained the factions and differences. Personal rivalries were kept in check for the greater good. The Great War had changed Labour's expectations in ways that could not have been anticipated.

Lloyd George had transformed the political scene, with consequences that were unforeseen and unintended. His coalition with the Conservatives split the Liberal Party, offering opportunities to the Labour Party. Moreover, organised labour was no longer a marginalised class that was required to do the bidding of their social superiors. It had to be appeased or brought into the power structure as an ally or partner. Three general elections in the five years after the end of the Great War, in 1918, 1922, and 1923, enabled the Labour Party to capitalise on these advances and take Labour to Downing Street.

4

Steps to Downing Street

The New Franchise

In late 1917 a Representation of the People Bill was introduced into the House of Commons and passed into law in June 1918. Until then only about 60 per cent of men and 0 per cent of women were entitled to vote. The right to vote had been linked to property, and was thus reserved for male-owned households. Some men were able to have an extra vote in some constituencies where they had business premises. University graduates were able to vote for university seats. But it did not look good for so many of the surviving soldiers coming back from the trenches, having fought for liberty, to be denied the right of exercising any liberty in choosing their government.

Controversy over votes for women had been intense and violent before the war, but there was little opposition to extending the franchise to all men, and to women over the age of thirty. With some upper-class condescension, it was felt that women had 'deserved' the vote after their sterling and patriotic work in munitions factories and on the home front. Crusty old gentlemen may have grumbled into their port, but there was never any attempt to reverse the extension of the franchise.

The 1918 Act was the largest extension of the franchise in British history, almost trebling the number of voters from nearly eight million to over twenty-one million. It added five million men and over eight million women to the electoral register. In the debates on the bill, proportional representation was narrowly rejected. The Act made other changes. Instead of voting taking place over several days, polling henceforth would happen all on one day.

In the 1918 Act women were permitted to vote in municipal elections from the age of twenty-one. The agreement to restrict the franchise in national elections to women of thirty and above was the result of a compromise. Ten years later, votes for women were granted on the same basis as votes for men. Plural voting was abolished in 1948.

Democracy (with qualifications – certified lunatics and peers of the realm did not have the vote) had arrived, and the aspirations of democrats, nineteenth-century Radicals, and twentieth-century socialists were achieved. For the Labour Party there were high hopes. The newly enfranchised men and women had been politically excluded. The great majority of the new voters were working class, and Labour saw opportunities. Were the new voters going to be Labour voters? If class was a marker for voting patterns, then there should be a sure and enduring majority for Labour. Optimistic Labour strategists did not take into consideration the patriotic Tory working man (and woman) and the deference voter. Belief in a hierarchical society with the royal family at the top was strong.

The 1918 General Election

Under the 1911 Parliament Act a general election was due to be held in 1915, but because of the war, it was postponed. The Armistice marking the end of the Great War was on 11 November. Prime Minister Lloyd George immediately called a general election. He wanted to cash in on his personal popularity as 'the man who won the war', and to prolong the coalition government he led. His Conservative chancellor of the exchequer, Andrew Bonar Law, agreed and a 'coupon' – an allusion to the war-time food rationing – was issued to all those candidates, Liberal, Conservative, and Labour, who agreed to support the extension of the coalition government.

In late November 1918 an emergency Labour Party Conference was convened. The eight Labour members of the coalition government, it was resolved, should resign. Four resigned at once, including (reluctantly) J. R. Clynes, who had been a successful minister of food, but not George Barnes, who had been leader of the Parliamentary Labour Party in 1910. He stayed on as a minister and disappeared from Labour politics. The conference called for the immediate nationalisation and 'democratic control' of vital public services, such as the coal mines, the railways, shipping, armaments, and electric power. This was a radical peacetime programme, although in many ways it was only an extension of government controls that had been introduced during the war. The four years of the war had so undermined the received wisdom about the management of the economy and society that Labour's policies were becoming mainstream. After the conference, Labour held a rally in the Albert Hall with dense crowds outside waving red flags.

Labour had a fairly clear political programme and, notwithstanding financial constraints, an organisation that was very different from anything before the war. The Liberals were split between followers of Lloyd George and Asquith, the latter's supporters appearing to be an embittered rump. Lloyd George's Liberal whips made deals with Conservatives in 150 constituencies.[1]

The electoral campaign resembled a plebiscite; are you for or against Lloyd George? The relief resulting from the end of the war did not eradicate sentiments of triumphalism. A sense of revenge took hold of many people. It was George Barnes, in fact, who called for the hanging of the Kaiser.[2] Demands for reparations from Germany were made: 'Squeeze Germany until the pips squeak.' Candidates who had been against the war were denounced as pro-German or traitors. MacDonald, Snowden, Jowett, Trevelyan, and Ponsonby all lost their seats. So did Arthur Henderson, who had opted for a constituency nearer London rather than County Durham. The enthusiasm for Lloyd George extended to partisanship in the Liberal Party. H. H. Asquith and his allies – Reginald McKenna, Walter Runciman, Herbert Samuel, and John Simon – were all defeated.

The result was an overwhelming triumph for Lloyd George's coalition government, which won 520 seats. This was a distortion of the distribution of the popular vote. Just over 5 million votes were cast for the coalition government, and 4.6 million against. Moreover, there was overall a low poll. Fewer than three voters out of five actually turned out to vote.[3] In Ireland, in their last general election as part of the United Kingdom, Sinn Fein, the political wing of the Irish Republican Army, won all (but one) of the seats in Ireland outside Ulster. As the elected Sinn Fein MPs refused to recognise and take up their seats in the House of Commons, Labour was the second largest cohesive group there.

Labour won fifty-seven seats, an improvement on their previous total of forty-two. At this rate it would take centuries before Labour won a majority. Moreover, the distribution of Labour representation in the country was uneven. In this election Scotland and Wales were poorly represented, and there were only four Labour MPs south of a line from the Severn to the Wash, of whom three were elected in London.[4]

In spite of Labour's consistent support for votes for women, the party put up only three women candidates. None were elected; they shared the same fate as Liberal and Conservative women candidates. Only Sinn Fein was successful in electing a woman candidate, but she refused to take her seat on the principle that Sinn Fein did not recognise the London parliament.

The 1918 Parliament

Lloyd George, re-elected prime minister, observed that when he looked across to the Opposition, it was like looking at the Trades Union Congress, whereas behind him was a gathering of the

Chamber of Commerce.[5] The great majority of the Labour MPs were sponsored by trade unions.[6] The supporters of the coalition government were overwhelmingly Conservative. Politically Lloyd George was a hostage.

Labour's leader, Arthur Henderson, lost his seat and the Scottish miner and trade unionist William Adamson, an amiable and loyal man but without dynamism, was elected in his place. He was suffering from ill health and was not an effective performer in the House of Commons; he was replaced in 1921 by J. R. Clynes. Adamson's lacklustre performance resulted in aggressive Labour politics shifting away from Parliament to the industrial wing of the movement.

Before the war syndicalist ideas spread among the trade unions. These suggested that Labour could show its muscle through strong and militant unions, rather than through the ballot. In 1914 the leaders of three of the new largest unions – the Miners' Federation, the National Union of Railwaymen (NUR), and the newly formed Transport and General Workers' Union (TGWU) had agreed to form a 'Triple Alliance'. If one union called a strike, then the others would come out in support. Indeed there were plans for strikes in the autumn of 1914, but after war broke out the unions agreed to an industrial truce and the Triple Alliance was suspended. This was not accepted by all unionists. Some militants did not agree that war invalidated the relevance of syndicalist ideas, and the war years saw some unofficial strikes, not supported by union bosses.

After the war the leaders of the three big unions revived the Triple Alliance, and in 1921 the miners were about to strike, but failed to get the support of the new general secretary of the TGWU, Ernest Bevin, or of the leader of the NUR, J. H. Thomas. The alliance turned out to be brittle. The day of the collapse of the 'syndicalist' policy became known as Black Friday.

As far as most people on the political Left were concerned, hopes of political change switched back to Parliament. Many who were enthusiasts for the Bolshevik Revolution joined with the British Socialist Party, an anti-war breakaway from the pro-war Social

Democratic Federation (SDF), to form the Communist Party of Great Britain. Lenin, now implementing the new order in Russia, followed developments in Britain with informed interest: he had been an exile in residence in London ten years earlier. The Communist Party professed to offer general support to Labour, but as Lenin cynically observed, the support was 'to be the same as a rope supports one who is hanged'.[7] From the beginning the Communist Party received support from the new Bolshevik government in Moscow. And many in the Labour Party saw the new party, in the words of Frank Hodges, the South Wales miners' union leader, as 'taking orders from the Asiatic mind'.[8] Although individual members of the Communist Party were friends and allies of people in the Labour Party, the Labour leadership was always suspicious of the Communist Party. Their suspicions extended to the party as a whole, and the annual conference in 1921 passed a resolution 'that no member of the Communist Party be eligible for membership of the Labour Party'.[9] Labour refused to allow members of the Communist Party to join the party. In 1922 J. T. Walton Newbold was elected Communist MP for Motherwell. His application to take the Labour whip was rejected.[10] Trade union membership rules were more relaxed, and individual Communists became leaders and activists within the trade union movement. Many socialists were sympathetic to the Bolshevik Revolution, and were fellow travellers with the Communist Party, although staying inside the Labour Party. After all, these socialists argued, the Russian experiment had successfully destroyed capitalism and an iniquitous class system. Visitors to Russia made a kind of pilgrimage to Moscow to be flatteringly received by Lenin, who was no slouch in the arts of public relations. But the great majority of the British Left accepted that the British road to socialism was by way of the ballot box.

Outside Parliament, Labour was spreading its influence, especially in local government. Labour was extending its geographical influence too, beyond its strongholds in Scotland, northern England,

and South Wales to London. The powerful figure of George Lansbury, who had been an MP before the war, dominated the East End and became mayor of Poplar. The mayor of neighbouring Stepney was the thirty-six-year-old former public-school boy and retired army officer Clement Attlee. Poplar was the poorest of the London boroughs. The freshly elected Labour councils introduced better local services for the unemployed, better relief for paupers, and for council employees a minimum wage and equal pay for women. Local rates were insufficient to cover these extra costs. These local rates were also expected to contribute to the London County Council (LCC) for common services, and the Poplar councillors refused to pay these on the grounds that Poplar's needs should be an LCC problem and not exclusively a borough concern. Legal action followed, as a result of which thirty councillors were sent to prison. These included George Lansbury himself and members of his family. Among the six women imprisoned was Susan Lawrence, one of the first Labour women MPs.

The official Labour Party leadership disowned the Poplar rebels, who became instead local heroes and heroines. The issue of Poplarism highlighted the inequalities of society but also tensions between Labour's pursuit of respectability within the law and a popular militant base.

The 1922 General Election

During 1922 the Labour Party went from strength to strength, winning fourteen by-elections. The glitter of Lloyd George and his coalition was tarnished. Bonar Law, the Conservative leader and ally of Lloyd George, resigned on grounds of ill health, and was replaced as chancellor of the exchequer and leader of the Conservative Party by Austen Chamberlain.

In October 1922 a significant number of Conservatives who had supported Lloyd George withdrew from the coalition, making it unworkable. The political scene was shifting. Lloyd George had for years been sustained by Conservatives. The Liberals were divided between the supporters of Lloyd George and his ousted rival, H. H. Asquith. Some younger radical Liberals were defecting to the Labour Party.

Lloyd George called a general election in November, and the Labour Party continued to progress from pressure group to national party. The party called for a revision of the Treaty of Versailles and for the nationalisation of mines and railways; for pensions for widowed mothers; and a national housing scheme to deal with the slums.[11]

Labour fought 414 (out of 603) constituencies and gained an unprecedented 142 seats. The support was strong – overwhelming in some areas, but patchy. Mining areas were now solid for Labour, but far less so in regions dominated by textile workers. Birmingham, Bristol, Cardiff, and Liverpool returned no Labour MP, and only nine Labour MPs were returned out of sixty-two London constituencies.[12]

The 1922 Parliament

There were sixty-seven new Labour MPs elected in 1922, double the number that there had been in the previous Parliament. In other words, the new Labour MPs outnumbered the old-timers. The proportion of trade unionists was lower, and there were many eager socialists and intellectuals who were ready to change the world. The intake was as significant as that of 1906. Then, they had triumphed thanks to a secret pact with the Liberals. Now, they had reached the outer portals of power on their own efforts.

Former MPs who had lost in 1918, such as MacDonald and Snowden, F. W. Jowett and George Lansbury, who had all opposed the war, were returned. And so were new converts to Labour who had been Liberal MPs, such as Charles Trevelyan and Noel Buxton.

One of the first acts of the new parliamentary party was either to confirm J. R. Clynes as leader or to elect a new one. Ramsay MacDonald was the man to challenge Clynes, who had been leader for nearly two years. MacDonald had had ministerial experience in the war-time coalition. He had the charisma that Clynes lacked, and had worked on persuading disillusioned radical Liberals to come over to Labour. He also had the support of his fellow Scots from Glasgow. It was one of the Clydesiders, Emanuel Shinwell, who proposed MacDonald as leader. Clynes had the support of the trade union MPs and two senior members who had backed the war, Arthur Henderson and J. H. Thomas, as well as Philip Snowden, who had not. Snowden had been fiercely critical of Clynes for accepting office in the war.[13] The latter was expected to win, but some trade union MPs who would probably have voted for him failed to turn up. MacDonald received sixty-one votes and Clynes fifty-six.[14] Clynes graciously congratulated MacDonald and was unanimously elected deputy leader. Other party officials were also elected, including two vice-chairmen. One was the veteran Lancashire trade unionist Stephen Walsh. The other, more surprisingly, a recent convert to the party, Colonel Josiah Wedgwood. The cleavage between supporters of the war was being bridged. The leader had opposed the war, Clynes and Walsh had supported it, Wedgwood had a distinguished record as a soldier. Although he had lost his seat at the general election – he was soon to be returned at a by-election – Arthur Henderson was elected chief whip.

Overall, the intake of Labour MPs was the most diverse so far. The stereotype of the dour trade unionist or the earnest socialist propagandist was broken. There was a great range of experience among them, not only in industry and local government but also in the professions and foreign affairs. The Labour Party was changing. The nineteen losses could be absorbed in the general euphoria of victory. Of those nineteen, eleven had been gained at by-elections and one was the seat of a defector to the Labour Party. Other losses were by a small margin.

Many of the new MPs were awed by Parliament. The House of

Commons can be an egalitarian club, and some new MPs found themselves passing men in the corridor whose names were familiar and whom they had seen only on cinema newsreels. The pageantry of the State Opening of Parliament with royal and parliamentary officials togged up in Tudor robes was potentially intimidating. As the MPs processed from the House of Commons to the House of Lords, one Clydeside MP said to John Wheatley, 'John, we'll soon change all this.'[15]

The cohesive group of Glasgow MPs, known as Red Clydesiders, brought an unfamiliar, almost incomprehensible broad Glaswegian accent to Parliament. One of them, David Kirkwood, played this up. A hotelier took him for a Portuguese.[16] Kirkwood was full of characteristic Scots wisdom and observations. He recognised that the prime minister, Stanley Baldwin, was a shrewd operator, remarking that he was a man who 'doesna sell his hen on a wat day'.[17]

James ('Jimmie') Maxton emerged as the leading personality of the Clydesiders. A tall, gangling, untidy, chain-smoking former schoolteacher, he was a great orator with a mop of undisciplined black hair that swept down to his chin. When he was not denouncing them, he could be utterly charming to his political opponents. Oswald Mosley became an ally of the Clydesiders when he was a Labour MP during the 1920s. Maxton maintained his relationship with Mosley even after he had become a Fascist, and he was one of the few political figures to visit Mosley in prison when he and his wife were detained during the Second World War.[18]

In March 1923 Labour MPs introduced a motion that was unrelated to any proposed legislation. The motion proposed that, as the capitalist system had failed to provide for

> the necessary standard of life for vast numbers of the population ... this House declares that legislative effort should be directed to the gradual supersession of the capitalist system by an industrial and social order based upon the public ownership and democratic control of the instruments of production and distribution.[19]

Philip Snowden made the case for socialism, but the whole debate, which was adjourned without resolution, was an extraordinary and unprecedented case of a theoretical discussion of social organisation.

In June 1923 the Clydesiders showed their disruptive mettle in the House of Commons during a debate on the Scottish estimates. The budget was being reduced. Cuts included taking off £89,000 from the health budget. Conservative MPs applauded the cuts. Maxton rose to speak. He started calmly and pointed out that there had been a rise in tuberculosis in Scotland. Emergency supplies of food and milk for nursing mothers and infants were being cut, as were hospital admissions for children with whooping cough and measles. Maxton became more heated as he went on and ended by denouncing those who supported the measures as 'murderers'. The speaker told him that this term was out of order and asked him to withdraw it. Maxton refused. The confrontation lasted for half an hour. Maxton turned to his neighbour and fellow Clydesider, John Wheatley. 'You take my place, John,' he said. Wheatley repeated the word, refusing to withdraw or to apologise. Both were suspended.[20]

The Labour Party on the Eve of Office

In the five years since the adoption of the new constitution, the Labour Party came a long way. Membership grew, albeit unsteadily, to 3.16 million. This figure may be deceptive, for it includes the total membership of trade unions affiliated to the party. This included individual trade unionists who may actually have voted Liberal or Conservative.

Labour had been reluctant to have a 'leader'. For many years the nominal leader had been the chairman of the parliamentary party, who was elected each year by MPs. But by 1923, with the scent of possibly forming a government, the leader's post became permanent and was filled by Ramsay MacDonald, who was also treasurer of the party.

The source of authority for the Labour Party was the Annual Conference. There was a precise and formalised arrangement for delegates with voting powers who were eligible to attend the conference. Trade unions and political societies were able to send one delegate for every 1,000 of their members. There was a similar prescribed quota for constituency parties and trades councils.[21] The conference passed resolutions that were theoretically binding on the party; it could amend the constitution and standing orders.

By 1923 there were 603 constituencies, most of which had some kind of party activity. The significant growth of Labour Party branches during 1923 was spurred on by the successes of the 1922 general election. By the end of the year there were 2,653 branches,[22] a 10 per cent increase over the year, with a branch opening every day of the week on average. Constituency Labour parties, referred to as divisional Labour parties, were often merged with pre-existing trades councils. This number had more than doubled over the previous six years. Trade union membership in 1923 totalled 3.12 million, having peaked at 4.13 million in 1920. The drop represented no lack of enthusiasm but rather the impact of unemployment.

The numbers of trade unionists hugely outnumbered the numbers in constituency Labour parties and socialist societies by at least ten to one. It meant a similar domination of the Annual Conference. This was reinforced by the financial contribution to the party. Trade unions, socialist, and cooperative societies paid a fee of threepence (one-eightieth of a pound) per member per annum to party funds. The socialist societies and trade union financial contribution to the Labour Party in 1923 was £48,000. By contrast, the contribution of the local constituency parties and trades councils was under £1,000.

The permanent body for running the party between conferences was the National Executive Committee (NEC), annually elected by the conference. Its role was to ensure that resolutions of the conference were carried out. It met for two or three days each month, and appointed subcommittees with particular tasks who reported to the

NEC. Ramsay MacDonald was chairman of the NEC, but his parliamentary deputy was not vice-chairman of the NEC; that role was undertaken by a trade unionist, C. T. Cramp of the National Union of Railwaymen, in 1923. Apart from the secretary, Arthur Henderson, the chairman (MacDonald), and vice-chairman (Cramp), the NEC had twenty-one members. Five were elected from local constituencies. These were from a wide geographical range: two were from London, one from Lancashire, one from Durham, and one from South Wales.

Trade unionism was generally a blokey business, but the framers of the 1918 constitution were conscious of the imminent enfranchisement of women and the importance of 'women's issues' in politics; accordingly 'women's sections' were set up, from whom a quota were elected to the NEC. In 1923 there were over 1,031 women's sections with a combined membership of 120,000.[23] Dr Marion Phillips was the party's chief women's officer. An Australian, she had come to London in 1903 and did a PhD at the London School of Economics on Australian colonial history. She worked as a research assistant for Beatrice Webb when she was on the Royal Commission on the Poor Law and became a socialist. In Australia she had had a vote and was mystified that women were denied the vote in the mother country. Intelligent, energetic, and enthusiastic, she set up nine regional Women's Offices. Often these women's Labour organisations developed from or were grafted onto local suffrage committees. In certain places membership boomed: in Leeds, for example, the six constituencies had between 1,500 and 2,000 women members.[24]

The membership of the NEC was largely made up of trade unionists. Eight members were MPs. The NEC was a body that straddled the political and industrial wings of the party, but also included people who were neither MPs nor trade unionists. Undoubtedly it represented the Labour movement in the years up to 1923. The trade unions had provided – albeit by affiliation – the bulk of the members, and certainly the bulk of the finances. But in 1923 the

NEC in no way reflected the people who were being attracted to the Labour Party as voters or potential members. The problem for Labour was to win over people who had not voted Labour before.

The Parliamentary Labour Party (PLP) had a separate structure. The initiative for selecting Labour candidates in elections lay with the local constituency party, but candidates had to be approved by the NEC. There was rarely any dispute over this. Once elected, their professional world was completely involved with parliamentary affairs, and their link with the Labour Party was through the PLP.

Coordination of the different wings of political activity was through another layer, the National Council of Labour, which included representatives of the NEC, the PLP, and the General Council of the Trades Union Congress.

Cumbersome and bureaucratic though the machinery of the Labour Party was, it was aimed to formalise democratic procedures, and to ensure fairness and transparency. The human element contributed to the smooth running of the party, while the mechanisms probably minimised personal rivalries and friction. At the centre of it all was the general secretary of the party, Arthur Henderson. He had held the post since 1911, not resigning when he took government office during the Great War. He was efficient and omniscient about the personalities and issues of the party. Sometimes pompous, he was generally known affectionately as 'Uncle Arthur'. He travelled around the country, encouraging local parties. In London his office was in Eccleston Square, a terrace house whose lease – and a £50 carpet – had been purchased from the previous occupant,[25] Winston Churchill. At the office he was supported by a small staff who included the national agent, chief women's officer, and finance officer, with their respective staffs. There was also a press and publicity department that pioneered basic ideas of market research in promoting Labour, stressing matter-of-fact issues rather than making an intellectual appeal.[26] For the 1923 general election the party produced a poster with the slogan, 'Greet the Dawn: Give Labour Its Chance'. The telegraphic address was Labrepcom,[27] a remnant from the Labour Party's earlier identity before 1906 as the Labour Representation Committee.

The 1923 General Election

The Conservative prime minister, Andrew Bonar Law, resigned in May 1923. He was suffering from terminal cancer and died in the autumn. He was replaced by the chancellor of the exchequer, Stanley Baldwin.

The Conservatives had fought the previous election on a free trade programme. Baldwin, who combined a shrewd, politically calculating brain with a reputation for honesty, saw the rising figures of unemployment and concluded that he should impose tariffs on imported foodstuffs to stimulate home production, thereby increasing the number of jobs. For this he thought he needed a fresh electoral mandate, and called a general election for Thursday, 6 December 1923. He later acknowledged that he entertained a fear that Lloyd George – who had left office just over a year earlier – would make a comeback. Lloyd George had been on a tour of the United States and was on his way back. It was suggested that he had devised a programme, also embracing protection. Baldwin feared that this could be a winner, especially if he could secure the support of some coalition Conservatives.[28]

It was Labour's opportunity. They were in a strong position in terms of a recent steady increases in votes and successes at by-elections and in local government elections. By the end of the war Labour was in control of ten local authorities.[29] They were not so strong in terms of fighting a general election, however, lacking the financial resources of the older parties, and the press was overwhelmingly hostile. Apart from news about the leader, Ramsay MacDonald, the main newspapers, or 'the capitalist press', as Labour propagandists called them, largely ignored the Labour Party. It did not have enough money to fight every constituency, and in those it did, there was not the supply of cars to take old and sick electors to the polling booths. But the rate of unemployment was rising.

During the election the major parties were preoccupied with the old issues of free trade and protection. This was the main divide between Liberals and Conservatives. Few strategists appreciated that the next generation would see the divide as being between socialism and capitalism. Labour broadly accepted the Liberal arguments of free trade and so were electorally on the Liberal side of the divide. One Labour election issue that might have united the older parties against them was Labour's proposal for a capital levy, a tax on wealth. It was argued that as people had given their lives in the national interest during the war, it was not too much to ask those who possessed vast resources to give up some of their wealth to the nation. Ramsay MacDonald was, however, reluctant to press the issue.[30]

In 1920 Winston Churchill had made the hurtful jibe that Labour was not fit to govern. This put Labour on the defensive and they were keen to be taken seriously, with carefully thought-out proposals. The party made unemployment its principal election issue, and in its manifesto proposed measures of government sponsored public works such as a national system for electric power, the extension of transport networks, afforestation, town planning, and housing.[31]

The two wings of the Liberal Party came together, with Asquith, now in his seventies, assuming the leadership.

On a poll of 73 per cent, the Conservatives were reduced to 258 seats. Labour came second with 191, and the Liberals third with 158. Labour made gains in London and its suburbs – gaining twenty-two seats (in contrast to nine the year before), but still none in Birmingham and only one in Liverpool. Overall there was no great difference in the distribution of votes among the parties. In 1922, the Conservatives gained 38.5 per cent of votes cast; in 1923, 38 per cent. Labour gained 30.7 per cent as against 29.7 per cent the year before. The Liberal share went up from 28.8 per cent to 29.7 per cent. Labour took seats from the Lloyd George Liberals. As financial constraints meant that Labour could not afford to fight every seat, the party tactically withdrew from some constituencies to assist the Liberals.[32] Party managers, and especially MacDonald, were aware that Labour needed to gain the support of people who had not voted before. There emerged a tension between the leadership and the zealous supporters who were impatient about what they saw as a pusillanimous approach to socialism.

Final Steps to Office

After the results were declared, there was no reason for Baldwin to resign until he lost a vote of confidence in Parliament, which was not due to reassemble for six weeks. Labour felt confident and held a rally at the Albert Hall the weekend after the election. A young audience, the average age estimated at under thirty, was addressed by Ramsay MacDonald. The atmosphere was spiritual and religious, according to the journalist H. W. Massingham.[33]

Outside the ranks of Labour, some of the established classes were alarmed and apprehensive. They were usually ignorant of the Labour Party. Some frantic efforts were made to get the Liberals to combine with the Conservatives. The seventy-three-year-old Conservative MP for the City of London Sir Frederick Bunbury said he would personally lead the Coldstream Guards to Westminster to protect the constitution. The parliamentary key to saving the country from socialism was with the leader of the Liberal Party, H. H. Asquith. On Tuesday, 18 December, Asquith addressed the recently elected Liberal MPs and observed that it was 'a novel experience for me, after being for seven years the favourite target for Tory and Coalition vituperation, that I should now be suddenly acclaimed in the same quarters as a potential Saviour of Society'. He thought a Labour government was inevitable, if not now then at some time in the future. 'If a Labour Government is ever to be tried in this country, as it will sooner or later, it could hardly be tried under safer conditions.'[34] That made things clear, but Asquith continued to receive 'appeals, threats ... from all sorts and conditions of men, women, and lunatics, to step in and save the country from the horrors of Socialism and Confiscation'.[35]

On Wednesday, 12 December, MacDonald had dinner with the Webbs; the other guests were Clynes, Henderson, Snowden, and Thomas. It was agreed that, unfavourable though circumstances were, they should form a government. Snowden had been reluctant, having argued that Labour should stand aside and force a Liberal–Conservative coalition. But free trade solidarity and the imminence of office was too strong. At the dinner it was agreed not to push for more controversial parts of the Labour programme, such as the capital levy or nationalisation.[36] There seems to have been no discussion of the allocation of jobs.

A few days later the National Executive Committee of the Labour Party formally agreed that Labour should accept an invitation to form a government, and also that MacDonald should have the freedom to nominate ministers.

MacDonald left London before Christmas to consider whom to appoint to his government. It is not clear how he made up his mind, or whose advice he sought. Usually the personnel of a government is formed in consultation with the chief whip, who in 1923 was Ben Spoor, a Durham miner. MacDonald chose to keep his own counsel. He was unimpressed by the potential of many of the Labour trade unionists, party stalwarts with roots in industrial Britain. However, he could not ignore them. But a minority government had to be sustained with credible men of experience. MacDonald had been at the centre of Labour and progressive politics for twenty-five years. He was probably more familiar with the personal strengths and weaknesses of potential candidates for office than anyone else. His retreat to Lossiemouth spared him the hassle of being lobbied personally, but his daily postbag was enormous.

He stayed in Scotland until Monday, 7 January. One serious

challenge was the House of Lords. Apart from new allies such as Haldane, Parmoor, and Chelmsford, there were only two hereditary members of the upper house who were members of the Labour Party. One was the twenty-three-year-old ninth Earl De La Warr, who was made a lord-in-waiting. The other was the second Earl Russell, grandson of the Victorian prime minister Lord John Russell and older brother of Bertrand. He was not interested in taking office.

Some appointments were to ministerial posts outside the Cabinet. Emanuel Shinwell, a Clydesider, although born in London, became minister for mines. Harry Gosling, a former Liberal who had been a London trade unionist and a founder member of the Amalgamated Society of Watermen, Lightermen, and Bargemen, was made minister of transport. His principal legal officers, apart from Haldane, were Sir Patrick Hastings who became attorney general, and Henry Slesser, an old Fabian Anglo-Catholic, who was made solicitor-general.

Among the junior appointments were men (and one woman) who were later to play a prominent part in Labour politics. The under-secretary at the Admiralty, representing the first lord, Lord Chelmsford, in the Commons, was Frank Hodges, a South Wales miners' trade union official. Lord Thomson and the Air Ministry were represented in the Commons by William Leach, a Yorkshire businessman and Bradford ILP stalwart. John Wheatley's deputy at the Ministry of Health was Arthur Greenwood, who fifteen years later was to be deputy leader of the party. Margaret Bondfield, the leading woman trade unionist, was parliamentary secretary to the minister of labour, Thomas Shaw.

Parliament reassembled on 21 January, and the Baldwin government lost its vote of confidence. Labour and most of the Liberals voted for the Labour amendment. Ten Liberals voted with the Conservatives.[37]

Labour was poised and prepared to take office. MacDonald wrote in his diary that night, 'so I am to be P.M. The load will be heavy & I am so much alone.'[38]

5

The Leader

The Challenge of Writing About MacDonald

History has not been kind to the memory of James Ramsay MacDonald. The events of August 1931, when he formed a national government, repudiating his former Labour colleagues, were seen as a betrayal of the party, of socialism, and of the work he had done for over thirty years in building up the new party. Clement Attlee, never a man given to overstatement, described his defection as 'the greatest betrayal in the political history of this country'.[1] He has been seen as a villain by the Left but has never been embraced by the Right. The first major biography, by Lauchlan MacNeill Weir, was a sustained assault on his character as a traitor and snob. David Marquand's authoritative biography of 1977 did something to redress the balance. His work up to the 1920s was given due credit, and Marquand examined the options that were before MacDonald in 1931. Expelled from the Labour Party in 1931, he was politically homeless. MacDonald's case was not helped by the mental decay in his last few years combined with his pathetic clinging to office. But his career was one of the most remarkable in British political history.

Born illegitimate to a servant in a remote part of the United Kingdom, MacDonald left school at fifteen and came to London (via Bristol), and was soon at the heart of left-wing politics. He endured great poverty in those early London years. As he later recalled,

> I used to buy myself whatever food I wanted around the slums of King's Cross, but I used to receive my staple of oatmeal, sent to me from home, and I always paid for it. Of course, I could not afford tea or coffee, but I found hot water quite as good as tea ... when once you have grown used to it.[2]

He was a prolific writer of political books, he travelled widely and married well. He was able to get on with anybody, and, although sensitive to slights, presented a social assurance and amiability that defied his obscure origins. In the way he had emerged from nowhere, was able to charm drawing rooms, and showed a single-minded devotion to getting his way in politics, he resembled the young Disraeli.

He had a great command of English, and his books – on his travels, on socialism, and on his wife – are polished, have an easy style, and are based on extensive reading and reflection. He was, in the words of Thomas Johnston, founder and editor of the ILP newspaper, *Forward*, 'one of the greatest descriptive journalists of his generation', with the gift of 'prose poetry' in him. But he lacked humour; there were no laughs in his articles.[3] He was well-organised, with the habit of punctuality,[4] was a good administrator and an outstanding orator. With a gentle but unmistakable Scottish accent, he seemed, like of Sean Connery, classless, with a universal appeal. Hugh Dalton described his voice as being 'exceptionally fine and deep, resonant with a great variety of tone and sufficient of a Scots accent to give it charm'.[5] He was the obvious and appropriate leader in the early 1920s. 'JRM is certainly more than a passable leader,' Beatrice Webb, not always a fan, observed in 1924. 'He is an extraordinarily *accomplished* leader, nothing ragged or obviously defective in him.'[6] In the 1920s he had no rival; although some may have grumbled, his position was unassailable.

One of the greatest assets that contributed to his undoubted charisma was his physical appearance. He was, as Dalton said, 'reasonably tall, slim, well-proportioned, with a noble head and handsome profile, a big and flowing moustache, early greying dark hair, with a big quiff at the front.'[7]

Lossiemouth

James Ramsay MacDonald was born in 1866 in Lossiemouth, a fishing village on the Moray Firth, in the north of Scotland. His mother, Anne Ramsay, was in service at Alves, a village about seven miles away. His father was head ploughman from the Black Isle of Ross, north of the Moray Firth. He was christened James McDonald Ramsay.[8] As a lad he was known as Jamie McDonald. The 'Ramsay' was introduced later, as was the switch from 'Mc' to 'Mac'; both changes added a touch of class. He was brought up by his mother and his maternal grandmother. His parents never married and his father soon disappeared from the scene. He received his education first at a Free Kirk school in Lossiemouth, and then at the parish school in Drainie, requiring a four-mile walk each way. His teacher, or 'dominie', was well-read and encouraging. At the age of fifteen MacDonald became a pupil teacher at the school. His first political activity was as president of the Lossiemouth Democratic Association,[9] and he acted as sub-agent for a Liberal in a parliamentary by-election.[10] An avid reader, he became interested in the physical world around him, inspired by such books as the multi-volume encyclopaedia *Orr's Circle of the Sciences* and Hugh Miller's *My Schools and Schoolmasters*, with its account of the work of an amateur geologist and Scottish pedagogue. When he was seventeen, he founded the Lossiemouth Field Club, which built up a collection of shells, feathers, and fragments of rock.[11] He went into nearby Elgin and spend his pennies on books. Once, in later life, he was at a smart dinner party and was asked what his university had been. 'Cassell's Popular Educator,' he replied.[12]

Lossiemouth was always important to his identity. 'Nobody knows MacDonald,' observed a close political friend, Lord Thomson, 'who has not known him in his native place.'[13] He retreated there as often as he could, not least at critical times in his political career, such as in the weeks before the formation of the first Labour government. It was far from importunate colleagues and gave him detachment. With its mists and the stories of fairy folk he had imbibed from his grandmother, it fed into his own vague mystic approach to the world. Going there always refreshed him. He was, as Hugh Dalton recalled, 'at his best when just back from Lossiemouth'.[14] The village developed during his lifetime. The people of the town were not all proud of the local boy, the 'Lossie loon' who did well. Locally he was known, inaccurately, as 'the anarchist', partly because of the red tie he always wore.[15] The broad stretches of land there were suitable for a golf course and MacDonald was a keen player. (He recorded walking and golf as his recreations in his *Who's Who* entry.) In the first quarter of the twentieth century nearly all the leading politicians played golf, and the golf course was a venue for political horse-trading and fellowship. It was a bitter humiliation when MacDonald was expelled from the Lossiemouth Golf Club during the Great War. He transferred his membership to Spey Bay Golf Club a few miles to the east.[16]

The walking continued throughout his life. He knew much of the terrain between Lossiemouth and Elgin, and a favourite walk with guests was to Covesea Lighthouse on the cliffs three miles to the west.[17]

Bristol and London in the 1880s and 1890s

Despite his love for his hometown, Lossiemouth could not satisfy MacDonald's ambitions. He chose to go south and took a job assisting a Church of England minister to organise a youth club in Bristol. He travelled south in 1884 and spent the best part of a year in that city. Here he encountered a group of socialists, with a branch of the Marxist Social Democratic Federation. He attended their meetings at a workman's coffee tavern at 58 West Street. Here he read a paper on John Ruskin to a handful of socialists.[18]

Bristol was not enough. He moved on to London, living at a subsistence level, working for, among other organisation, the Cyclists' Touring Club.[19] Three years later, in 1888, he became secretary to a Liberal MP. This was a breakthrough. He was involved in politics and the political world at one remove. At the same time he was exploring more left-wing political circles. He joined the Fabian Society in 1886 and was in touch with James Keir Hardie, another charismatic Scot who was also illegitimate. He was a spectator at the socialist rally in Trafalgar Square in November 1887, known as Bloody Sunday.[20] During one of his periodic trips to Lossiemouth to see his mother in 1889, he supported a radical Liberal candidate in a by-election. The candidate's programme included Home Rule for Ireland and Scotland, state aid to fisheries, and free education up to and including university. The candidate lost, but not disastrously.[21]

The Fabian Society was more his cup of tea; he was a member of the society's executive from 1894 to 1900 and gave lectures for them around the country.[22] He overcame his shyness and with bursts of engaging unaffected laughter became well known in the progressive circles of the capital.[23] During these years he showed his skills as a good organiser. He was efficient and enormously hardworking. He aspired to be a lecturer at the newly founded London School of Economics and Political Science, a creation largely of Sidney and Beatrice Webb, but did not meet their exacting standards, even though Beatrice Webb recognised that he was 'a brilliant young Scot'.[24] He continued to live modestly and, for a while, shared lodging with Sydney Olivier, a future 1924 Cabinet colleague.[25]

He also joined the Independent Labour Party and was the ILP parliamentary candidate for Southampton in 1895. He spoke at various public venues, at one of which he told his audience that there were 30,000 people 'in Southampton living in a single room'.[26] It could have been better expressed, but you can see what he meant. He was more successful in municipal politics, and represented

Central Finsbury on the London County Council from 1901 to 1904.

By this time he was at the heart of Labour socialist politics. In February 1900 socialist societies and trade union representatives met at Farringdon Street Memorial Hall and founded the Labour Representation Committee, with the aim of getting more Members of Parliament who would be independent and not an appendage of the Liberal Party. MacDonald became secretary at the age of thirty-five. He was unpaid, and there was no office.

Six years later he became member of Parliament for Leicester. It was a two-member constituency, and MacDonald had wooed the local Liberals. His return was one of the fruits of his negotiations with the Liberal chief whip, Herbert Gladstone, on a series of local electoral pacts. He loved Parliament and was able to get on with MPs of other parties. He was respected for his assiduity and commitment to the parliamentary process. The Conservative leader, Arthur Balfour, described him as 'a born parliamentarian'.[27]

Husband and Widower

There was a gaping void in the life of Ramsay MacDonald in 1924. He had had a blissfully happy marriage, which ended with his wife Margaret's death from blood poisoning in September 1911. She was forty-one. In losing her, as David Marquand put it, 'part of MacDonald died with her.'[28]

Margaret Ethel MacDonald was born in 1870 into a comfortable middle-class London family, academic and religious. Her family name was Gladstone; she was a great fan of the Victorian statesman, but they were not related. Her childhood and youth were filled with European travel and extensive reading in three languages; she also had a burgeoning social conscience. By her early twenties she was active in social work dealing with women's issues, sweated labour, and exploitation. She absorbed information about the conditions of the poor with almost religious zeal. As her husband put it, 'A Blue Book was second in rank of sacredness only to the Gospels.'[29] She supported the Independent Labour Party and sent money to MacDonald to help with his election expenses in Southampton in 1895. She then met the candidate, and they fell in love and married the following year.[30] She was a perfect political wife, with an independent but complementary range of interests. With a mixture of irony, affection, and respect she used to address her husband as 'My dearest Sir'.

Margaret had a private income, and after the marriage MacDonald enjoyed a financial security unique among the early Labour leaders. They were able to have a comfortable home in central London.

The house they took in Lincoln's Inn Fields was the centre for the work of the Labour Party, the front office overflowing with papers. Space could be cramped. One man who attended a meeting recalled that he had to go through a whole meeting sitting on a coal scuttle.[31]

The husband and wife were great travellers, not only to see the sights but also to meet politicians and social activists. They went to America, Canada, India, Australia, and New Zealand, as well as many European countries. In turn, everyone was welcome at their home if they were visiting London. Despite this frenetic whirl of activity, they were able to produce five children. At moments of leisure, Ramsay MacDonald used to read aloud to her – the novels of Dickens and Thackeray, the works of Ruskin, Carlyle, and J. A. Symonds on the Renaissance.[32]

His wife's private income allowed the MacDonalds to take a cottage, Linfield, at Chesham Bois in the Chilterns. This retreat enabled them both to tramp the Buckinghamshire field paths, and visit sites associated with Oliver Cromwell, John Milton, and William Penn. MacDonald loved both history and poetry.[33]

In 1910 one of their children, David, died at the age of five, and Margaret never seemed to recover from the shock. She died the following year. MacDonald wrote a very affectionate and moving memoir – almost a work of hagiography. It was written at speed, within three months of her death.[34] In widowerhood, he employed a Dutch woman as a housekeeper and moved from Lincoln's Inn to Howitt Road, Hampstead.[35] He never remarried. With domestic help he brought up the four surviving children and his eldest daughter, Ishbel, acted as hostess when he was prime minister.

His wife's death occurred at the time of MacDonald first taking the chairmanship of the PLP, effectively party leader. Arthur Henderson took over the secretaryship and was to hold that for the next quarter of a century. Labour had not done well in the two general elections of 1910. MacDonald was the most engaging of the leaders so far, and also the most proactive. He socialised in circles beyond the Labour movement. In 1911 he was the guest of Lord Haldane at a lunch in honour of Kaiser Wilhelm II. Other guests included John Morley, the writer Edmund Gosse, and Lord Kitchener. MacDonald was criticised by some in the Labour Party for accepting the invitation. A socialist leader, in the view of his critics, should always be a propagandist.[36]

Party Leader and War-Time Dissident

As national leader of British socialists he took his international role seriously and was a regular visitor to Europe, meeting socialists. He enjoyed trips to Europe (and beyond) and built up strong personal relationships with socialist leaders such as Jean Jaurès of France, August Bebel of Germany, Émile Vandervelde of Belgium, and Pieter Troelstra of the Netherlands.[37]

The outbreak of war in 1914 was a bitter blow to his international socialist ideas. As most of the party disagreed with him, he resigned the leadership, giving way to Arthur Henderson. His nuanced position led to him being miscast as a pacifist. 'We condemn the policy which has produced the war, we do not obstruct the war effort, but our duty is to secure peace at the earliest possible moment.'[38] His stance was ambiguous and led to misunderstanding. To an audience in his Leicester constituency, he said that those 'who can enlist ought to enlist, those who are working in munition factories should do so whole-heartedly.'[39] He drew the line at joining recruiting platforms.

His political activism, outside the Labour Party, was devoted to the newly founded Union of Democratic Control (UDC), of which he became secretary. This brought him into close contact with Liberal MPs who were war dissidents, some of whom, such as Charles Trevelyan and Arthur Ponsonby, later joined Labour and were in the 1924 government, as well as more independent intellectuals and activists such as E. D. Morel and Norman Angell.

As the war progressed there grew in the country a venomous press campaign against those who were not gung-ho for the war. It affected MacDonald personally to the extent that one close observer thought he was on the brink of suicidal despair.[40] One of the sources of MacDonald's income was journalism. Many papers declined to accept his articles.[41] The war hardened him and increased his personal isolation. Horatio Bottomley, muckraking journalist and proprietor of the magazine *John Bull*, located MacDonald's birth certificate and made public his illegitimacy. Bottomley, who claimed himself to be the illegitimate son of the Victorian atheist Charles Bradlaugh, denounced MacDonald as 'a dirty, pro-German traitor'.[42] It must have given MacDonald some satisfaction eight years later when he was serving as His Majesty's prime minister, and Bottomley was serving time in one of His Majesty' prisons, having been convicted of fraud.

MacDonald's isolation actually endeared him to the pacifists in the party, and he developed comradely relations with individuals on the Left, such as Fred Jowett of Bradford. After a rally in Leeds when socialists wanted to send a delegation to Russia to see the post-revolutionary but pre-Bolshevik situation, MacDonald and Jowett went to Aberdeen to take a boat bound for Petrograd. At Aberdeen the crew of the boat, inspired by the jingoistic leader of the Seamen's Union, refused to carry MacDonald. He had to stay in Aberdeen. MacDonald was under surveillance by the police, and two detectives were assigned to keep an eye on him. MacDonald filled his time by setting out early one morning for a brisk thirty-mile walk into the countryside, pursued at a discreet distance by one of the two detectives. The next day the other detective had to trail MacDonald.[43] MacDonald never got to Russia.

Another left-winger to whom MacDonald was close during the war was Davis Kirkwood, who got to know him so well that they went walking together on the Pentland Hills, south of Edinburgh.[44] MacDonald fascinated the blunt, no-nonsense engineering shop steward from Glasgow.

> His head was a thing of beauty. Black hair waved and rolled over a fine brow, one curl almost touching his straight, strong eyebrows, from under which his eyes glowed. His voice was rugged, but soft, and, as he spoke, there came into it a throb. It was the natural instrument of an orator. Standing upright, he was a splendid figure of a man, and his appearance of height and strength was increased by his habit of rising on his toes and throwing back his head. He was the first man of culture I had met.[45]

When, in 1917, Kirkwood wanted to see the minister of munitions about his exclusion from work in munitions in Glasgow, MacDonald's social skills were such that he was able to phone the minister, Winston Churchill – with whom there can have been very little politically in common, save membership of the House of Commons – to arrange for Kirkwood to see him. An appointment was all fixed up within hours.[46]

But in November 1917 MacDonald felt he was back in the mainstream of politics. A former Conservative foreign secretary, the Marquess of Lansdowne, wrote to the *Daily Telegraph* calling for a negotiated peace, which is what MacDonald had for years been seeking. That same month the Bolshevik government came to power in Russia and published the secret treaties between the Allies, which had been in the Imperial archives: further vindication of MacDonald's stance. Far from being a war to defend Belgium, it was now seen as a war of imperialist expansion. It was revealed that Russia would take Constantinople and that Persia would be partitioned between Russia and Britain. Britain would take Mesopotamia (Iraq) and France, Syria. Before the end of the year, President Woodrow Wilson of the United States issued his Fourteen Points, proposing a brave new international order under the League of Nations, again echoing what MacDonald and the Union of Democratic Control had been advocating. Other voices close to the government were saying similar things. Alfred Milner, who had been an ally of the War Cabinet, that autumn wrote in the *Evening Standard* that peace terms should not be vindictive or punitive, but should be targeted at ending 'Prussian militarism'.[47]

At the emergency Labour Party Conference, just before the 1918 general election, MacDonald was warmly cheered: his stand reflected views of all sections of the party. But things did not go so well in his Leicester constituency. He was opposed by a candidate supporting the Lloyd George coalition, a former Marxist. It was a bitter campaign, and MacDonald was denounced as a 'pro-German'. He received supporting visits from Bernard Shaw and J. H. Thomas. Women over thirty had the vote for the first time, and MacDonald felt their bitter opposition to him. 'The haunting memory', he wrote afterwards, 'is of the women – bloodthirsty, cursing their hate, issuing from the courts and alleys crowded with children, reeking with humanity.'[48] Although Labour increased its overall representation, MacDonald, along with other opponents of the war, was defeated.

MacDonald used his time out of Parliament to travel and attended the Berne Convention of socialists from all European countries, on both sides of the conflict. This was held as the Versailles conference of the victors was meeting.

In 1921 MacDonald contested a by-election at Woolwich, for a seat vacated by the popular local man Will Crooks, who had been Labour MP since 1903. The constituency seemed safe. However, the largest employer was the Woolwich Arsenal, which had benefited, as it were, from the conduct of the war; many former servicemen lived in the constituency. His opponent was Captain Harry Gee, who had obtained a Victoria Cross in the Great War. It was a bitter campaign, with many outsiders pouring in. MacDonald was abused as a revolutionary and a traitor. Bottomley came to speak at Plumstead Baths and was prevented by a large pro-Labour crowd. Bottomley's paper continued its venomous articles against MacDonald. At the poll, Gee won, but only narrowly. MacDonald was scathed and his loneliness was intensified. 'I miss my dear dead companion at such times,' he wrote in his diary. 'Lonely, lonely.'[49]

Leader Again: Charisma and Vulnerabilities

MacDonald was returned to Parliament in the general election of November 1922, when he was elected for the South Welsh constituency of Aberavon. The Labour MPs gathered to elect or re-elect their leader. The self-effacing J. R. Clynes had been leader for two years. MacDonald had the support of the newly elected radical Scottish MPs, the Clydesiders, who saw MacDonald as one of them, an opponent of the war. MacDonald was proposed as leader by Emanuel Shinwell, a Jewish Glasgow MP. The Clydeside MPs thought their group support tipped the balance, and his opponents were more conservative trade unionists. He was elected, and Clynes gracefully accepted the result. He recognised that MacDonald had a charisma that he lacked and could appeal to voters who had not before voted Labour. MacDonald had been unwell in the previous week or two – nerves perhaps? – but on election day, as one who was there observed, he 'sat up at once. All the lassitude and illness disappeared. He was as vigorous as any man in the room.'[50]

MacDonald then selected two MPs to be his parliamentary private secretaries. They were a contrasting pair. One was the

Glasgow journalist Lauchlan MacNeill Weir. The other was a London MP, still in his thirties (just), known as Major Attlee.[51]

The void in MacDonald's life left by his wife's death manifested itself in a number of ways. He was seen as aloof, and that detachment enabled him to show considerable personal courage. But in his social relations, his inability to memorise people's names did not always help.[52] With his well-stocked mind and his eloquence, his aloofness led to him being seen as a 'superior person' by trade unionists.[53] But that superiority did win people over. He impressed the young Fenner Brockway 'immensely':

> He was then very handsome, with waving black hair, a heavy moustache, strong features, and a fine figure. He expressed his opinions with the manner of a god and I felt at least that I was in the presence of a great man ... his organlike voice and oratory captivated me.[54]

After the death of Keir Hardie in 1915, he spoke at a commemoration of the dead leader at St Andrew's Hall Glasgow the following Sunday. 'If there were doubts about MacDonald in the minds of Scottish Socialists,' recalled Fenner Brockway, 'this speech removed them.'[55]

His aloofness was coupled with an acute personal touchiness. One Labour MP, Tom Dickson, had the gift of mimicry and used to entertain friends with his take-off of some of the mistier rhetoric of MacDonald's oratory. ('Ah, my friends, dear friends, we must go on, and on, and on, this way, that way, and the other way.') One of the Clydesiders, David Kirkwood, reacting to MacDonald's preachiness, dubbed him 'MacChadband', alluding to the sanctimonious preacher in Dickens's *Bleak House*.[56] MacDonald was far from sharing in the general amusement.[57]

As leader he took on an enormous amount and determined the direction of the party. At the same time he was indecisive, and there was no one among the leadership of the party with whom he could unbend or who could steer him. He relied on Clifford Allen, a young pacifist who had been a conscientious objector during the war, to be his eyes and ears within the ILP.[58] When he was prime minister, Allen lunched with him at Number 10 regularly. Other intimates included the middle-class journalist and Cambridge graduate Mary Agnes Hamilton.[59] More formally, the secretary of the ILP would arrange periodically to see MacDonald, who was not cordial: 'Well, Brockway, what commands have you brought me today?' 'Not commands, but considerations,' Brockway replied. But he found the prime minister testy.[60]

He was also drawn to appearances, to the superficial glamour and glitter of power, position, and authority. Lloyd George dismissed him as 'a fussy Baldwin'.[61] When he became prime minister he loved the position, even though he may not have had clear ideas about what to focus on apart from foreign affairs. He spoke of 'the exhilaration of office'[62] and was sentimental about the House of Commons, describing it as 'this dear old place'.[63] John Morley, the veteran Liberal who had resigned from Asquith's Cabinet on the outbreak of war in 1914, used to say, wagging his finger, that MacDonald 'had the front bench mind'.[64] His attraction to the high life during the evenings annoyed his party, who thought he should be briefing himself on political issues. MacDonald also made use of the prime minister's country resident at Chequers. This was good for his relaxation but further distanced him from his core support.[65] Josiah Wedgwood thought MacDonald's widowerhood made him vulnerable to the aristocratic embrace: 'J. R. M. has no woman, which makes it all the more dangerous.'[66] (The wives of Philip Snowden or J. H. Thomas, however, did not pull their husbands back from being seduced by high society.)

Nonetheless his apparent snobbery may have had, consciously or unwittingly, a strategic advantage for the Labour Party. MacDonald was aware of the millions of people who did not vote for a Labour government. For Labour to be seen as an accepted government, the party had to make electoral inroads into those millions. It was a working-class party, but not all the working class supported it. MacDonald was keen to break the idea of Labour being exclusively class-based. It had to form national government. The aristocracy may not be converted into Labour voters, but MacDonald's socialising helped to make a Labour government tolerated, if not loved, by a powerful and influential class.

There was one way in which MacDonald emulated aristocratic entitlement. In 1924 he sought to get his son, Malcolm, while still an undergraduate at Oxford, into the House of Commons. He was not the only senior Labour politician to follow this practice. Two sons of Arthur Henderson were elected as Labour MPs in 1923.

In some ways MacDonald's weaknesses were reflections of his strengths. His loneliness made him self-reliant but also lacking in self-awareness and self-criticism. His self-assurance gave him authority as a captivating orator, able to charm and mesmerise large crowds of sympathetic supporters. This did not immunise him from flattery, and he could be a poor judge of people and situations. His isolation and his ferocious hard work fed each other, and he grew to think he was indispensable. He was able to escape to the unquestioning affection of his children. After the death of his wife he had no ally of his own generation – be it a brother, sister, or a friend from childhood – who could offer frank and friendly advice.

Reaching Number 10

Lord Haldane, who had served in the Cabinets of two previous prime ministers, found MacDonald a good Cabinet chairman. He prepared an agenda in advance with the Cabinet secretary, Sir Maurice Hankey, and was business-like. He 'knew how to let a colleague run on without checking the length of his statement prematurely'.[67] Haldane thought MacDonald had read his briefing papers. The Cabinets were relaxed and good-humoured, partly helped by

MacDonald allowing the men to smoke their cigarettes, pipes, or, in the cases of Haldane and J. H. Thomas, their cigars.[68] MacDonald was unfailingly courteous to his colleagues.[69]

His industry was noted. A hall porter at 10 Downing Street was reported as saying that no prime minister had worked so hard since Archibald Primrose thirty years before. He used to work far into the night to be on top of his paperwork and be up at seven in the morning.[70]

His obsession with work had its downside. As prime minister, he seemed sometimes to lack what one who knew him well described as 'spontaneous geniality',[71] and often seemed preoccupied. When a delegation of Labour MPs called on him, he gave the impression that they were unwelcome; his mind was torn between the business on which they had come to see him, and the government documents on his desk.

In public affairs he was cautious, but he enjoyed the sense of danger that came from being driven at speed and flying in bad weather. Once he attended a party conference and persuaded his chauffeur to go at breakneck speed. His police escort was left trailing behind. He also, observed one who later became close to him, enjoyed a 'tense exhilaration' in confronting a hostile crowd.[72]

MacDonald could always rise to the occasion with an eloquent set speech. With many ordinary people he was popular. Postcards of him and the members of the first Labour Cabinet circulated, and when the Labour government fell in October 1924, Beatrice Webb, often a stern critic, wrote in her diary that 'in spite of Court dress ... he has again become the idol of the left and the respected leader of the right.'[73]

Many of the senior members of the party either wholly or partially distrusted him. Philip Snowden did not vote for him as leader in 1923. Henderson felt underappreciated. Only J. H. Thomas, the railwaymen's leader, seemed to be close to him. This was strange, for MacDonald was refined and Thomas was vulgar and indiscreet. Both accepted aristocratic invitations and Thomas was often the worse for drink the following morning, a charge never made against MacDonald. But Thomas could make MacDonald laugh and brightened up his dour, sober Scottish bearing.

In forming his government MacDonald appointed himself as foreign secretary. MacDonald had travelled more than any other possible rivals for foreign secretaryship, with the exception of Josiah Wedgwood, and had met many international statesmen, and all the leading European socialists. He had, in the words of J. H. Thomas, 'great personal knowledge of practically all the prominent political figures in the world' and had 'an intimate knowledge of world affairs'.[74] It is perhaps only his immediate predecessor, Lord Curzon, who was as well-travelled a foreign secretary. He had consistently encouraged the party to think internationally, and was always a courteous host to foreign socialist delegations to party conferences.[75]

MacDonald: Socialist and Socialite

What were Ramsay MacDonald's political beliefs when he became prime minister? In the fifteen years before 1921 MacDonald published a dozen books on politics. Some arose from his foreign travels.[76] He used the word socialism in the titles of many of his books. He was fairly clear about the philosophy of socialism but far less so on specifics. He was a gifted writer and a good communicator, even if his style was sometimes pervaded by a Celtic mysticism. In his early manhood he had made a start on writing a novel. His journalism, for the ILP paper *Forward* and for the *Daily Herald*, was once collected and produced in book form. His most authoritative account of socialism is in *The Socialist Movement*, published in 1911. It was part of a series on politics: the companion volume on Conservatism was written by Lord Hugh Cecil. For MacDonald socialism was, he sometimes said, 'his religion'.[77]

Although MacDonald repudiated Marxism, he saw a progression

in political and social history from feudalism to capitalism. Capitalism was a failed system and unable to provide for all. Just as Whiggism gave way to Liberalism in the nineteenth century, so Liberalism was bound to yield to socialism in the twentieth. Liberalism represented 'individualism' as opposed to conservatism, which represented 'aristocracy'. During the nineteenth century the state had intervened to protect a standard of living for the poor and vulnerable:

> The state had to protect the child from the factory, then the woman, then the young person; it had to provide education; it had to impose responsibilities like Employers' Liability and Workmen's Compensation upon the 'free' employers; it had to regulate hours and conditions of labour; it had to legislate on matters of housing and public health. At the same time municipalities had to provide their own water, gas, and tram services, their own houses, their own works departments … libraries, museums, art galleries, and arrange for concerts and recreations for their citizens.[78]

This extension of public involvement in social matters was not the exclusive concern of one political interest. All parties supported aspects of public enterprise. Lloyd George's state insurance and the Conservative Party's support of public corporations were evidence of this.[79] Indeed, in Parliament, MacDonald rarely referred to socialism as an ideology.[80]

MacDonald and many of his progressive contemporaries had a great faith in science. It was two generations since the publication of *The Origin of Species* by Charles Darwin, and ideas of evolution permeated society. Mankind was an organism that evolved. MacDonald harnessed the scientific spirit to socialism.

> The reason why Socialism and the scientific mind should be congenial to each other is not far to seek. The scientist loves order and is repelled by disorder. The same intellectual promptings

> which lead him to invent a water tap which will not drip, will make him take an interest in proposals to do away with the industrial wastage of unemployment.[81]

Socialism was 'the method of evolution applied to society ... Socialism alone is worthy now-a-days of scientific politics.'[82]

Just as scientists need to get their data right, so issues of public health, family needs, and school hygiene need to be investigated and shortcomings identified and diagnosed for remedy. 'In short, the Socialist sees a machine that will not work, an engine which is always slowing up and breaking down, and he studies its mechanism to discover its faults.'[83]

The idea of society as an organism was consistent in MacDonald's political behaviour as well as his political philosophy. This was a Burkeian conservative idea, and MacDonald welcomed members from a conservative background – Liberals such as Ponsonby, Trevelyan, Buxton, and Wedgwood, and Conservatives such as Parmoor and Mosley – into the Labour Party. They had, it seemed, discarded their own class interests to join the Labour Party and added to the notion that it was a truly national party. Trade unions, MacDonald thought, were only part of society and represented sectional interests. This may have influenced his reserve towards working-class trade unionist colleagues. To many of the Labour core support, it sometimes seemed that MacDonald was more at ease with the middle- and upper-class converts.

The events of the war helped to reinforce MacDonald's evolutionary socialism. During the war the British government hesitantly managed a command economy, with the objective – although it did not always succeed – of overseeing controlling prices, wages, and standards of quality. The government controlled the import of foodstuffs. There was a widespread acceptance of the limitations of laissez-faire individualism in a national crisis. In 1919 the Sankey Commission recommended the state ownership of the mines, part of the programme of the Labour Party. Even the Conservative leader, Bonar Law, 'was prepared to adopt the [Sankey] Report in the spirit as well as the letter ... without delay'.[84]

MacDonald saw himself as prime minister for the whole organism of society and of the country. He had a strange respect for old aristocracy and a disdain for the more recently ennobled, saying:

> On the shoulders of our ancient aristocracy tippets hang naturally, and the coronets sit quite properly upon their brows, but on the shoulders of our newer nobility, of those who have just left holidaymaking on Blackpool sands, the tippets do not hang naturally. They are not an aristocracy. They have purchased their way into the other House, and whatever respect ... we have for the old aristocracy, we have absolutely none for the new.[85]

To do MacDonald justice, even in the sad dotage of his declining years, he refused to accept an earldom or the Order of the Garter, the normal reward for a former prime minister. But he had accepted the symbols of authority and position, court dress, the deference to royalty, and the association with classes outside his political base. He was the custodian of the whole of society, not the leader of the sectional Labour Party. The hobnobbing with aristocracy annoyed other ideological socialists and was held against him. In their view his most notorious friendship was with the Marquess and Marchioness of Londonderry. She was a right-wing hostess, whose husband was a leading Ulster Conservative. He was a frequent guest at the Londonderrys' Mayfair mansion. For her, he was a 'curiosity'.[86] The Londonderrys were seriously rich with extensive properties in Northern Ireland and coal-rich lands in County Durham, where the Marquess had the reputation in Labour circles as a reactionary and heartless mine owner. When MacDonald tried to justify his infatuation with the Marchioness by saying they had a spiritual relationship, one Labour activist commented, 'I thought the bugger was daft.'[87]

He first met Lady Londonderry soon after becoming prime minister at a dinner at Buckingham Palace. He was asked to escort her to the dinner table – such was the custom of the upper classes at that time. Discussion of politics was eschewed and they chatted about their joint affection for the Scottish Highlands. 'He loved beautiful things,' Lady Londonderry recalled, 'books, pictures, beautiful women, and lovely jewels and colours.'[88] MacDonald had a cloyingly flirtatious relationship with Lady Londonderry, addressing her in notes as 'My Dear Ladye',[89] and showing off the official uniforms he felt obliged to wear on royal occasions.[90] As the journalist and Labour parliamentary candidate Geoffrey Garratt observed, it was as if he was 'the hero of his own romance'. The romance was underlined when he would refer to a simple life and a diet of herrings and oatmeal.[91]

Cabinet colleagues were miffed that the Londonderrys were invited as guests at Chequers while they were not.[92] This kind of behaviour undermined their loyalty to MacDonald, who also failed in small courtesies such as showing appreciation or encouragement to his colleagues.[93] The only way for them to get close to their leader was, according to Henderson, to 'feed him with admiration and adulation'.[94] While he was prime minister, he lived at 10 Downing Street and the deputy leader, J. R. Clynes, lived at Number 11. Although there were connecting doors, MacDonald was secretive and the two would meet, not over an intimate drink – be it whisky or even cocoa – at Downing Street, but only at the House of Commons.[95]

The friendship with the Londonderrys was politically unwise. Even his cousin, Winston Churchill, fell out with Lord Londonderry over the latter's attitudes to the miners during and after the general strike of 1926.[96]. One of their several opulent homes was in County Durham in the heart of a mining constituency, which MacDonald took as his own in 1929. His friendship with the class enemy did not go down well with his working-class constituents.

To go back to MacDonald's socialist ideas: in his mind, socialism was allied to evolution – he had no doubt that socialist ideas would prevail. Society as a whole would become socialist. There was no need to go down the revolutionary path. 'The Socialist method avoids such disasters. The approach to Socialism is always by the parliamentary method. Step by step we shall go …'[97]

When he came to specific measures, they were palliatives, tinkering with society and dealing with matters such as 'factory and mine regulation and inspection, the feeding of school children, old age pensions'.[98] These measures would have been accepted by the advanced Liberal of 1911. MacDonald had an international approach and saw other countries nationalising public services, such as telephone systems and railways, for the sake of efficiency.

The vehicle for socialism in Britain was the Labour Party, which, he said, 'is not Socialist. It is a union of Socialist and trade-union bodies for immediate political work.'[99]

MacDonald, in touch with European socialist movements, attended gatherings of the International Socialists. He also knew the unpromising situation of socialism in the United States, and saw socialism as an international movement that would ensure peace. The German journalist Egon Wertheimer saw MacDonald in the later 1920s as 'beyond question the outstanding figure of International Socialism'.[100]

The Socialist Movement was published in 1911. It is a confident book, full of hope. Such hopes had a major setback with the outbreak of the Great War.

After the war, in 1919, MacDonald produced a short book, *Parliament and Revolution*, published by the ILP. In it he reaffirmed his position. He criticised revolutionary Russia, where socialists were in power and locking up former comrades. He warned against dogmatism. Whilst 'the Socialist conception of Society remains fixed, its creeds and methods must never sink into infallible dogma and its gospels become closed books'.[101] There was a British road to socialism.

> The Independent Labour Party is a product of British history and British conditions. It is neither Russian, nor German, nor

> American. It found the Radical movement as one ancestor, the trade union movement as another, the intellectual proletarian movement – Chartism and the earlier Socialists thinkers like Owen, Hall, Thompson – as another; the Continental Socialists – especially Marx – as still another.[102]

Overall, he had a way with words. As an orator he was inspiring. One of his biographers contrasted his approach with that of Snowden: MacDonald was the man of heart, Snowden the man of reason.[103] With his matinee idol looks (as people might have said at the time) and his enthralling voice, he could weave words of promise and encouragement to the large crowds who would flock to set eyes on him. His progresses around the country during the general elections of 1923 and 1924, ending at his (then) South Wales constituency of Aberavon, were like the course of a revivalist preacher.[104] The Aberavon Constituency Labour Party was well organised. It was said that in the 1923 general election MacDonald ran it 'like a chess player'.[105] The fact that he was hissed at by political opponents in Malvern only added to his appeal to the working class.[106] A sympathetic journalist was with him and described how 'the car could hardly move. We had to shut off the engine, and allow the crowds to push us along. The people swarmed on every inch of it, and clung to every bit of MacDonald they could touch.'[107] At party conferences, critics from the left of the party were to rise to their feet at the end of a MacDonald speech and cheer him.[108]

Foreign Secretary

Ramsay MacDonald appointed himself as foreign secretary. Within the Labour Party, one possible contender for the post had been E. D. Morel. Morel, who had a French father and was born in Paris, had also been active in the UDC and edited their journal, *Foreign Affairs*. Morel had made his name as a campaigner. He had opposed

Britain's entry into the Great War and had been imprisoned for anti-war activities. He joined the ILP in 1918 and, as Labour candidate, defeated Winston Churchill at Dundee four years later. There was a coolness between MacDonald and Morel. In his regular contributions to *Foreign Affairs*, Morel was violently critical of the Versailles Treaty and quite abusive about France. The French occupation of the Rhineland with the use of troops from French African colonies aroused an extraordinary racist diatribe from Morel:

> In ones and twos, sometimes in parties, big, stalwart men from warmer climes, armed with sword-bayonets or knives, sometimes with revolvers, living unnatural lives of restraint, their fierce passions hot within them, roam the countryside. Woe to the girl returning to her village home, or on the way to town with market produce, or at work alone hoeing in the fields. Dark forms come leaping out from the shadows of the trees, appear unexpectedly among the vines and grasses, rise from the corn where they have lain concealed. Then – panic-stricken flight which often availeth not.[109]

MacDonald agreed with Morel on the iniquities of the Treaty of Versailles, but he was measured in his criticisms of other countries. He was aware of the importance of good relations with France and thought they would not be improved with the outspoken Morel in charge of British foreign policy.

There were other potential candidates for the foreign office. In terms of political outlook, the former Liberal MPs Josiah Wedgwood, Charles Trevelyan, or Noel Buxton were all qualified. MacDonald seriously considered J. H. Thomas, good-natured and able to get along with anyone, especially over a drink. News of MacDonald's idea was leaked to the press and a campaign against such an appointment made MacDonald abandon the idea.[110]

He did, however, appoint another former Liberal MP, Arthur Ponsonby, as parliamentary under-secretary for foreign affairs, and effectively deputy foreign minister. In his absence Ponsonby would be the foreign affairs spokesman in the House of Commons. In the House of Lords a former Conservative MP, now Lord Parmoor, was appointed lord president of the council in the Cabinet, and to be Foreign Office spokesman in the House of Lords.

Ponsonby was the son of Queen Victoria's private secretary and was himself a page of honour to the queen. He studied at Eton and Balliol College, Oxford, before becoming a diplomat serving in Constantinople and Copenhagen. Following the death of Sir Henry Campbell-Bannerman, the Liberal prime minister, in 1908, Ponsonby was elected Liberal MP in his Scottish constituency. He opposed Britain's involvement in the war in 1914 and became a member of the Union of Democratic Control. Along with other anti-war MPs, he lost his seat in 1918, joined the Labour Party and became Labour MP for the very working-class constituency of Sheffield Brightside in 1922. As under-secretary it was his job to run the day-to-day business of the Foreign Office, but the prime minister laid down the policies and launched the initiatives.

Within the Foreign Office itself, MacDonald was warmly welcomed as foreign secretary. His immediate predecessor had been the Marquess Curzon.

My name is George Nathaniel Curzon,
I am a most superior person.

Curzon was accustomed to treating his staff, even the most senior, as if they were servants. By contrast MacDonald was (almost) always courteous in dealing with officials.[111] In his diary, MacDonald noted that 'Curzon apparently treated them [the officials] badly and the F.O. was on the edge of revolution. Gentlemanly treatment will do much.'[112]

In Number 10

The salary of the prime minister was £5,000 a year. He had many expenses to pay from this salary, including entertainment and household items such as linen and china. His eldest daughter, Isabel, acted as hostess and housekeeper, and the family groceries were ordered from the local Co-op and brought to the house in a van. The family would take meals not in the private flat, where coals had to be bought to keep the rooms warm, but in the official banqueting room that was centrally heated at government expense.[113]

6

The Big Four

J. R. Clynes

John Robert Clynes is the least known of the leading figures of the early twentieth-century Labour Party.

He was born in 1869 in Oldham, Lancashire, to a family that had migrated from Ireland to work in the cotton textile industry. His father later worked as a gravedigger for Oldham Corporation.[1] As Irish immigrants the family had to live in the worst slums; children had to be tough to survive rickets, diphtheria, or pneumonia.

At the age of ten Clynes began working as a 'piecer' in a textile mill, two miles from his home. His work was to run, barefoot, between the spinning machines clearing up broken threads. It was potentially dangerous work. For this he was paid two shillings and sixpence a week (12.5p).[2] He worked six hours a day, receiving some schooling in the afternoon. From the age of twelve he was working full-time for ten shillings a week (50p), but spent such spare time as he had educating himself at the Oldham Equitable Co-operative Society library. By his early teens he had read and become entranced by the plays of Shakespeare. Like other working-class autodidacts, he also read works by Thomas Carlyle, Charles Dickens, and John Ruskin. Clynes acquired a small library from purchases at second-hand bookstalls in Oldham, saving up his pennies for the purpose. One treasured purchase was a dictionary that cost him sixpence (2.5p).[3] He studied this by the light of a candle. Another work that he read and reread was William Cobbett's *Easy Grammar of the English Language*. (In 1923 he wrote an introduction to a new edition of this work.) A lot of Shakespeare and poetry was committed to memory. As he worked, he later recalled, he 'used to repeat appropriate passages of poetry in time with the glide and thrust of the jennies. Had anyone heard me I should have been thought mad; but the everlasting noise was my safeguard, and my small voice was swept away.'[4] On one occasion the foreman caught him reading John Milton's *Paradise Lost*. 'Books'll never buy thee britches,' he observed contemptuously.[5]

He became interested in politics at the age of fourteen. The large Irish community in Lancashire was politicised, with the Irish National League campaigning for Irish Home Rule. Clynes and a friend attended one such campaign, and later they set up a debating society. This helped Clynes with public speaking and to think on his feet. He was only fifteen when he started to write articles anonymously for the local newspaper about conditions of work in the mill.[6]

As if this was not enough, he was still in his teens when he started to organise the piecers into a union. Piecers often graduated to being spinners, who were well unionised, but were not unionised themselves. In this work Clynes encountered opposition from the Spinners' Union as well as mill owners, but he persisted and spread his net to other Lancashire towns. This meant correspondence, organising meetings, and public speaking. A speech made when he was nineteen was described by another trade unionist: 'He was nothing to look at – a frail lad, pale and serious in ungainly clothes. For three quarters of an hour the piecer-orator spoke with well-measured sentences of sincerity and grammatical precision.'[7] In later years the German journalist Egon Wertheimer wrote of his speaking style as having 'a poise, articulation, and richness of language, compared with which the Oxford diction of certain young men of the Party sound unbearably affected.'[8]

His promotion of trade unionism brought him in touch with

other trade union workers, including the gasworkers. The National Union of Gasworkers and General Labourers was founded in 1889 by Ben Tillett and Will Thorne. The latter was the general secretary, and he spotted Clynes's talent. In 1892 Thorne came to a recruitment rally and heard Clynes speak. He saw a crowd 'was gathered about a mere slip of a lad, hardly more than a boy. Having come to be amused I remained to be amazed.'[9] Immediately Thorne invited him to be the Lancashire organiser for the union. From this time onwards Clynes was a full-time trade union official, travelling around the country and getting a reputation beyond Oldham and southern Lancashire. He never lost his base and was active in the new Oldham Trades Council, a local combination of trade unions, and was its president in 1897.

As a young trade unionist he left south Lancashire for the first time to attend a conference at Plymouth. The train journey made a profound impression on him.

> To look through the carriage window and see grass and bushes that were really green instead of olive, trees that reached confidently up to the sun instead of our stunted things, houses that were mellow red and white and yellow, with warm red roofs, instead of the Lancashire soot and slates, and stretches of landscape in which the eye could not find a single factory chimney belching – this was sheer magic.[10]

In 1893 Clynes was present at the inaugural meeting in Bradford of the Independent Labour Party, and later that year went as a delegate for his union to the International Socialist and Labour Congress in Zurich, where he met and got on well with Bernard Shaw, whom he found 'sincere and vital, still full of satirical ... truth and justice'.[11] He was not, however, impressed by what he called the 'inflammatory verbal orgies' that he encountered at the congress. This trip probably reinforced his insular approach to the world and his devotion to his own country. He was always suspicious of bombastic rhetoric.

Shy and unprepossessing in appearance, he was determined, conscientious, and hard-working. His thoughtfulness, however, also sometimes made him slow to reach a decision, and prone to procrastinate. 'When in doubt, do nowt,' it was mockingly suggested, was his practice.[12]

Clynes was also a delegate of his union at the foundation meeting of the Labour Representation Committee, the immediate precursor of the Labour Party, in London in February 1900. From 1904 he was on the National Executive Committee of the party – and was to be re-elected for the next thirty-five years.

He stood unsuccessfully for Parliament for Oldham three times and was finally elected for Manchester North East in 1906, defeating the sitting Conservative. The newly elected Liberal MP for Manchester North West was the thirty-one-year-old Winston Churchill. Clynes and Churchill were both invited to a football match at the old ground of Manchester United at Bank Street. Clynes kicked off the first half, Churchill the second half. Manchester United won.[13]

He joined twenty-eight other newly elected Labour MPs, thirteen of whom were from Lancashire and Cheshire.[14] He took a seedy bed-sit in Lambeth, returning to Lancashire at the weekend to join his wife, Mary, and two children. But London was expensive, and late-night sittings meant having to pay cab fares.

The parliamentary group organised themselves initially under the chairmanship of James Keir Hardie, who was not universally popular with the trade unionists. The cult of leader was not encouraged, and the chairmanship rotated. Clynes became vice-chairman of the group under George Barnes. He grew to love the House of Commons; he regularly attended and listened, and was particularly impressed by the former Conservative prime minister Arthur Balfour.[15] He asked questions and spoke regularly, generally on issues relating to trade union interests. The Labour Party pressed for social reform, including the provision for school meals and medical inspection of schoolchildren, and Clynes supported the campaign to extend the vote to women.

Between the two general elections of 1910, Clynes accepted an invitation to be a delegate to the conference of the American Federation of Labour (AFL). Mary accompanied him, and they sailed first to Canada to study trade unionism there. The Clyneses attended a gathering of Lancashire immigrants, and Mary was greeted with the lusty singing of 'For she's a lassie from Lancashire'.[16] At the AFL conference they listened to its president, Samuel Gompers, speaking for four hours, marching up and down the platform, chomping a cigar. Clynes spoke for a modest ninety minutes.[17]

Back in London, Labour's impact continued, albeit hesitantly. The 1911 Parliament Act introduced payment for MPs, which eased Clynes's own financial situation. He combined parliamentary duties with union activity and was elected president of the Gas Workers Union – although he had never actually been a gas worker. As a trade unionist he was a conciliator, seeing strike action as a failure in the negotiating process. He liked to identify common ground with the other side, and then press further for trade union interests. The years before 1914 saw several strikes and a rise in ideas of syndicalism that challenged parliamentary sovereignty. Clynes was not sympathetic to this ideology.

When the Great War broke out, Clynes supported Britain's commitment to war, aligning himself with both majority trade union opinion and feelings in Lancashire.[18] He spoke at rallies to encourage voluntary recruitment, but when conscription was introduced in January 1916, he opposed it. Compulsory military service would mean the loss of the main wage earner in a working-class household. There was a difference in principle and in consequences.

Like other Labour MPs who supported the war, he was not uncritical of its management. The Labour Party continued to emphasise the consequences of the war's privations on the working class, such as the rising price of food and fuel.[19]

In May 1915 Prime Minister Asquith transformed his exclusively Liberal administration into a national coalition, bringing in Conservatives and offering places to the Labour Party. Arthur

Henderson became president of the Board of Education. Clynes was offered a place on a committee dealing with the health of munitions workers who were exposed to acid. His union experience regarding issues of health and safety at work was relevant. Lloyd George took over from Asquith in December 1916 and Henderson became part of a five-man War Cabinet. In 1915 Clynes had been outvoted when he opposed Labour joining Asquith's coalition, but he supported Labour joining up with Lloyd George. The new prime minister offered the necessary 'vigorous guidance' demanded by the critical military situation.[20]

Other Labour men were brought into the government, and Clynes was appointed parliamentary secretary at the Ministry of Food. The minister was Lord Rhondda, who was in the House of Lords, so Clynes was the ministry's spokesman in the House of Commons. He became a privy councillor. He relished the role, even though worry, he said, turned his hair white.[21] Food supplies were threatened by enemy action against ships crossing the Atlantic Ocean and rationing was introduced for some essential foodstuffs, such as sugar, lard, flour, and butter. In the last year of the war, subsidies on bread were introduced. These controls mitigated the effects of shortages and profiteering. The experience gave him lessons in practical socialism. When resources were scarce, there needed to be controls in place so that everybody had fair access to essential foods. As he wrote later, 'Never was it more clearly shown than in the work of the Food Ministry that the State is a better shop-keeper, a better employer and a better salesman than the private owner and the capitalist.'[22] Clynes felt that the controls imposed by the ministry prevented profiteering, which re-emerged after the war when those controls were lifted.[23]

In early 1918 Rhondda died and Clynes was promoted to replace him. His replacement as parliamentary secretary was the Honourable Waldorf Astor, a Conservative MP and husband of Nancy, the future first woman to take a seat as an MP. As minister of food, Clynes introduced Consumers' Councils, composed of producers, consumers, and representatives of cooperative societies. They were in contact with local authorities and offered the government constructive advice. At a local level there were food committees that were required to include at least one woman.[24] There was a ban on the wasteful throwing of rice instead of or in addition to confetti at weddings.

During the war Clynes developed a regard for the royal family for their public spirit, and especially for King George V. Lawns at Windsor Castle were dug up and turned into vegetable plots.[25] The regard was reciprocated, and Clynes was invited to the wedding of the king's daughter, Princess Mary. For this he faced criticism from some Labour MPs; Clynes argued ingenuously that he was there representing the working class.[26] He also had a respect for the energy of the war-time prime minister, David Lloyd George.

Minister though he was, Clynes was always self-effacing. There is a story that, while at a conference at Blackpool, he was served a minute portion of fish in the canteen. He asked the waitress for a second helping, to which she replied, 'I'm afraid I daren't. They say the Food Controller is present.'[27]

At the end of the war Clynes was in favour of Labour remaining in the coalition, but the party was for disengagement, so reluctantly he resigned from the government. He retained his seat in the 1918 general election and became deputy leader of the Parliamentary Labour Party, the leader then being William Adamson. Adamson suffered from ill health and was not seen as effective, so Clynes took over as leader in 1921. He could be pugnacious and incisive in debate, but his authority was hampered by his having been in the coalition.[28] His national standing was recognised in 1919 when he was awarded an honorary degree at the University of Oxford – along with Field Marshal Earl Haig and the French Marshal Joffre.[29] At the same time he was immersed in trade union activities, and his union was merged with a number of smaller unions to ultimately become the General and Municipal Workers' Union.[30]

Although rooted in working-class politics, Clynes's war-time experience led him to see Labour 'not as a detached section of the nation [but] came near being the country itself'.[31] That was in a speech in January 1922 to the Imperial Commercial Association; it shows how the Labour leadership was reaching out, beyond the usual Labour support base.

In the 1922 general election he spoke at Cambridge in support of the Labour candidate. Some young Conservative undergraduates heckled him. He was undeterred. 'I am well aware', he said, 'that there is a great mass of educated ignorance in this place.' He impressed one Old Etonian, Hugh Dalton, as a man of 'natural dignity and courtesy, sincerity, loyalty to colleagues, and a command, in speech, of good and simple English'.[32] The study of the English dictionary and of Cobbett's *Grammar* as a teenager paid off.

That general election saw the return of an increased number of Labour MPs, a triumph for Clynes's leadership. Many ILP members who had opposed the war, including Ramsay MacDonald and Philip Snowden, returned to Westminster. When the enlarged number of Labour MPs assembled there was an election for leader. Pale and frail, although honest and popular, Clynes lacked the commanding presence of MacDonald. Clynes by contrast was seen as 'small, unassuming, of uneven features, and voice without colour'.[33] MacDonald was elected. Clynes was the only leader of the Labour Party to have been voted out of that office. He was aware of his limitations and graciously accepted being deputy leader again, urging the party to reunite behind the new leader.[34] At a rally held that evening at Kingsway Hall, MacDonald did not turn up, and Clynes spoke in his place, 'a magnificent speech, ringing with loyalty and unity'.[35]

With MacDonald, Snowden, Thomas, and Henderson, he was regarded as one of the 'big five' of the Labour Party, each with his own power base, Clynes's being Lancashire and trade unionism. Often those five were wary of each other. Clynes was loyal to all but was particularly close to Henderson.[36]

Henderson and Clynes were the only two Labour men of 1924 to have had ministerial experience, although the former Liberals

Haldane and Trevelyan had served in Asquith's pre-war government. When Ramsay MacDonald formed his administration in January 1924, Clynes was appointed lord privy seal and deputy leader of the House. Having had departmental responsibility during the war, he was initially disappointed not to have a ministry to run. He was in effect deputy prime minister and, to the chagrin of Philip Snowden, had 11 Downing Street as his official residence, although he and his neighbour at Number 10 did not see a lot of each other.[37] Unlike his job at the Ministry of Food, which he had enjoyed, being lord privy seal brought with it a lot of tiresome ceremonial duties. But in the House of Commons, because of MacDonald's absences as foreign secretary, Clynes often had to speak on behalf of the government.

Mary Clynes rose to the responsibility of being a fine hostess, able to hold her own with well-educated guests. She was unimpressed by 11 Downing Street: it lacked both a piano and a sewing machine.[38] It also became a financial burden, for the Clyneses were personally responsible for paying up to seven or eight of the domestic staff as well as fuel and electricity bills; these wages consumed 40 per cent of his ministerial salary.[39] On official receptions at Buckingham Palace he was expected to pay for a chauffeur and a footman.[40] Beatrice Webb, not always easy to please, approved of Mary. 'She reads GBS with appreciation and delights in good music,' she recorded with condescension in her diary, '[and] has no desire to escape her class'[41] (this tells us more about Beatrice Webb than it does about Mary Clynes). Mary outlived her husband by just one month after nearly sixty years of marriage.

Arthur Henderson

Arthur Henderson was popularly known as 'Uncle Arthur' among party activists. He was the key trade unionist in the first Labour government, and always a potential challenger to MacDonald as leader of the party – as he did become on three occasions. He was regarded as the most representative Labour leader of our time.

Although territorially associated with north-east England, he was in fact a Scot, born in Glasgow in 1863.[42] He left school at the age of nine to work in a photographer's shop. His father died when he a boy and his mother remarried, the family moving to Newcastle-upon-Tyne, which became his geographical political base. He went back to school for a year or so but left at the age of twelve. In 1906, when asked what book or books had influenced him he replied, 'The book of life.'[43] He was apprenticed to an iron founder. When he was sixteen his life was transformed by a profound religious experience. He found religion, converted by a revivalist preacher, Gipsy Smith, and became a committed and lifelong Wesleyan Methodist. He foreswore alcohol, smoking, gambling, and blasphemous language. Before the conversion, he was, in the words of his elder brother, 'just the ordinary boy'.[44] In due course he became a regular lay preacher, was active in temperance organisations, and campaigned to dissuade trade unions from holding their meetings in public houses.[45] He did, however, play cricket, and was also a founder of St Paul's Football Club, which later was a contributing part of Newcastle United.[46] At the Methodist Mission in Newcastle he met his wife, Eleanor, whom he married when he was twenty-five. They soon had three sons. His Christian faith became the most important part of his identity.

He embarked on a long trade union career in 1883 with the Iron Founders Union, and was always a moderate, keen on reconciliation and arbitration, and was appointed secretary of the North-East Conciliation Board in 1894, in which year he attended his first Trades Union Congress.

His first political allegiance was to the Liberal Party, and he was elected to the Newcastle-upon-Tyne City Council in 1894. He shared political platforms with John Morley, Gladstone's biographer and then a Newcastle MP. The following year he was initially chosen as Liberal candidate in the forthcoming general election, but he had to withdraw because some Liberals objected to a candidate of working-class background. One local newspaper said he was a socialist in disguise.[47] Nonetheless the following year he was made a justice of the peace.[48] This started a process of radicalisation, although he retained his loyalties, albeit waning, to the Liberal Party for several more years. He acted as agent for the Liberal MP for Barnard Castle, Sir Joseph Pease, a wealthy mine owner. Meanwhile he and his family moved to Darlington where he became active in local government, both on the Durham County Council and on the Darlington Town Council, where he was its first Labour mayor in 1903.[49]

Although he kept his Liberal credentials in local government, there was a different emphasis in his trade union activity. He supported the Iron Founders' Union being affiliated to the Labour Representation Committee at its foundation in 1900. Party identities were not fixed, and Henderson continued to be the Liberal agent in Barnard Castle, while supporting the idea of separate Labour representation. Riding two horses simultaneously was tricky, and in 1903 he became unsaddled. Sir Joseph Pease, the Liberal MP for whom he had been working, died suddenly. His son invited Henderson to be the Liberal candidate in the forthcoming by-election. But the Iron Foundry Workers' Union had already promoted his candidature under an independent Labour banner. It was highly unusual in modern politics for one man to be a potential candidate for two conflicting parties. Henderson won the election. It was the first time Labour won in a three-cornered contest.[50] He became one of four Labour MPs, and held this constituency until 1918. He increased his majority in the 1906 general election and the family moved from Darlington to Clapham Park, in south London, which was to be his home for the rest of his life.

At first he was the quintessential Lib–Lab, initially slightly detached from the main Labour group. In his early years in Parliament he saw Labour as a trade union pressure group, similar to the Irish nationalist party representing Irish interests. He claimed that the Labour Party had inspired the Trade Disputes Act that reversed the Taff Vale judgment, the Workmen's Compensation Act, and the Education (Provision of Meals) Act.[51]

Henderson was slow in shifting his position to Labour, but once he did so he was totally loyal to the cause. He took a while to declare himself a socialist, was not a member of the Independent Labour Party and only joined the Fabian Society in 1912. With his experience in local government and trade unions, he was a good organiser, pragmatic and trusted. He worked with Liberals on issues such as the minimum wage and was active in promoting women's trade unions. He campaigned for temperance and supported the non-militant women's suffrage movement.

He was elected as treasurer of the party. Within the Labour group in the House of Commons he became their chief whip,[52] and in 1908 succeeded Keir Hardie as leader, giving way to Ramsay MacDonald in 1911. Until then the Labour Party had been run from the MacDonalds' house in Lincoln's Inn Fields, but when Henderson replaced MacDonald as secretary of the party, the headquarters took new premises nearer Parliament. He served the party as secretary for twenty-three years, until 1934. He did not give up his trade union links and was elected president of the Iron Foundry Workers in 1910.

His relations with MacDonald were never smooth. Henderson recognised the charisma and leadership qualities of the (slightly) younger man and readily gave way to him as leader in 1911. But there was friction. Both were sensitive to slights, and it was suggested, on one occasion before the war, that if 'MacDonald had had a gun, he would have shot Henderson'.[53]

As general secretary, he moulded the character of the administration of the Labour Party. Initially the offices were at 1 Victoria Street, and then the party bought the lease of 33 Eccleston Square. He was methodical and well-organised but was seen sometimes as bossy. He had a loud commanding voice but, in contrast to Ramsay MacDonald, was good at remembering faces and putting a name to them. More than any of the other leaders of the party, he travelled around the country extensively. He took by-elections seriously and developed an instinctive feel for rank-and-file opinion, and also for the Labour Party emerging as a national movement.[54] He recruited his son, William, into the office, as well as a schoolteacher, Arthur Greenwood, to be head of research. Greenwood was later to be deputy leader of the party.[55] Henderson used to arrive at the office early and always had a tidy desk. He answered letters at once.

By now Henderson was totally committed to a Labour movement that was more than a pressure group for the organised working class. It is reckoned that he coined the phrase to describe the movement as composed of 'workers by hand and brain'. He encouraged younger people to be active and was not in awe of intellectuals such as R. H. Tawney, G. D. H. Cole, and Harold Laski. No one could accuse Henderson of being an intellectual. His politics were instinctive rather than cerebral. His reading outside of politics was the perusal of sermons. 'I can handle these chaps,' he would say. He seemed to think collectively, rarely used the first person singular, preferring to talk from the perspective of the 'Socialist Movement' or the 'Party Conference'. Listeners could hear these emotive collectives as if they had capital letters.[56]

Henderson had travelled in Germany as a trade unionist on two occasions before the war, meeting his counterparts. Indeed, it was when he was shepherding a fraternal Labour Party delegation to Germany in 1912 that one of the party, Pete Curran, reassured him, 'All right, Uncle Arthur, We'll all be there.'[57] The nickname stuck. However, although widely respected and generally popular, his avuncular image could slip. He could be pompous and even a bully to party subordinates until he got his way. As party secretary, he was a centraliser. Constituency Labour parties had to toe the line, and he was resistant to there being any distinctive Scottish or Welsh Labour Party.

In 1914 Henderson was one of the leading Labour supporters of Britain's entry into the war, although he deplored jingoism and had opposed the Boer War.[58] He was persuaded that Britain had a moral obligation to Belgium when that country was invaded and was committed to guaranteeing its independence. When Ramsay MacDonald opposed entry into the war and resigned the parliamentary leadership of the party, he was replaced by Henderson. Henderson actively campaigned for men to enrol into the army. In 1914 he negotiated with the chancellor of the exchequer, Lloyd George, a Treasury agreement to restrict the right to strike. His loyalty was rewarded by being made a privy councillor in the 1915 New Year's honours list and becoming a right honourable.[59] Four months later he was brought into Asquith's coalition Cabinet as president of the Board of Education. The following year, in September 1916, his eldest son, David, was killed at the Somme. This tragedy gave him a greater sense of obligation to public service.

His appointment to government office was only made after receiving the consent, reached with some controversy, of the Parliamentary Labour Party and the party's national executive. Many members of the ILP were opposed. But Henderson carried on doggedly. He was obliged to support conscription. The following year he was made paymaster-general, acting also as adviser to the government on labour issues. This put him in a difficult personal position, especially since he was seen by some trade unionists as too close to the class enemy. Lloyd George was less tactful. Both men visited Glasgow together in December 1916 and were vigorously heckled with shouts of 'Traitor!'[60] Lloyd George had just become prime minister and had brought Henderson into his five-member War Cabinet.

As a minister his hands were tied, and he was unable to bring in any progressive measures. The Liberal MP Walter Runciman observed that Henderson 'has tumbled into LG's basket, tickled by the flattery of Curzon and company.'[61] He was unable to select his parliamentary private secretary, and had to oversee cuts to the education budget. He was accused by Ramsay MacDonald in the House of Commons of being 'unenlightened'.[62]

Henderson was sent on an ambiguous official mission in 1917 to the Russian capital, Petrograd, to meet members of the post-tsarist and pre-Bolshevik revolutionary government. The purpose of this mission was to encourage Russia to stay in the war. Henderson was to liaise with the British ambassador, Sir George Buchanan, but was put in the extraordinary position of having to decide whether to supplant him as British representative, following the example of France, who had replaced their ambassador with the 'patriotic' socialist Albert Thomas.[63] He did no such thing, but reported back and returned to London.

Later that year the Labour Party, with Henderson's support, was advocating attending at Stockholm an international conference of socialists including delegates from countries with whom Britain was at war. Initially the prime minister, Lloyd George, supported the idea but, under pressure from Conservative colleagues such as Bonar Law and Lord Curzon, he changed his mind. The Cabinet discussed this in Henderson's absence – he had to hang around humiliatingly outside the Cabinet room, on 'the doormat'. The rest of the Cabinet opposed any British participation in the conference and Henderson resigned one week later. Lloyd George offered him the Companionship of Honour, but Henderson declined. He felt that not only he but the whole Labour movement had been used and humiliated by the prime minister. It led to a deep and enduring distrust of Lloyd George in Labour ranks.

Until then Henderson had been loyal to Lloyd George, and it seemed as if he needed an older brother, a figure to whom he could defer. He transferred this deference for the next decade, despite frequent irritations, to Ramsay MacDonald, who was actually three years his junior.[64]

During his war-time government service Henderson continued to be the nominal leader of the party, and chairman of the Parliamentary Labour Party, the actual duties being carried out by the acting chairmen. Henderson's departure from the Cabinet gave a boost to his personal reputation in the Labour movement.

Henderson in the next few months threw his energies into reorganising the Labour Party. He actually resigned from the chairmanship of the PLP, being replaced by the lacklustre William Adamson. With the anticipated end of the war there were the prospects of a general election, the first since 1910. Prospects for the Labour Party seemed rosy. Sidney Webb and Henderson drafted a manifesto, *Labour and the New Social Order*; this was published in January 1918. With Webb and Ramsay MacDonald, he drafted a new constitution for the party, with its declaration of socialist objectives in Clause Four and the arrangement for people who were not either trade unionists or members of a socialist society to join the Labour Party. A new network based on constituencies was created.[65] Henderson was successful in integrating the trade unionists into the party, and gradually convincing them that the Labour Party could be more than a pressure group; it could form a government.

Henderson's life was now based in the capital, and he switched constituencies for the general election of December 1918. He stood for East Ham South but lost heavily. His electoral history was henceforth chequered. He seemed to be good at by-elections and bad at general elections. Such was his standing in the party that he had no great difficulty in quickly finding a new constituency after a setback. He was stoical about these constant reverses. Indeed he always had a shrewd idea about election results. At one general election, after having won a by-election, he anticipated his loss. 'There are houses in these streets that had my picture up last time, and have not got it this.'[66] After his defeat he extended his international experience and visited the United States, meeting American trade unionists. He was returned as MP for Widnes in a by-election in August 1919, but he was not enthusiastic about serving under the leadership of the amiable but underwhelming Willie Adamson.[67] He lost his seat at the next general election in 1922. Hapless as he was in elections results, he was a vigorous campaigner and platform speaker. 'He uses a cast-iron voice and a bull vitality', two American journalists observed, 'to pound in the sensible central interpretation of a plain man, and he does it with all the energy and noise of an exhorter of the extreme left.'[68]

Again, he bounced back at a by-election in his Newcastle-upon-Tyne homeland and strongly supported Ramsay MacDonald as leader of the Parliamentary Labour Party. He lost again at the 1923 general election that heralded the Labour government. He soon found a new constituency, Burnley, and was returned at a by-election in February 1924. His two surviving sons had been luckier in the general election, both being elected. The two sons – perhaps uniquely – formally introduced their father into the House of Commons.[69]

In January 1924 Ramsay MacDonald, after some negotiation, invited Henderson to be home secretary. Relations with MacDonald were not completely fraternal, but Henderson recognised that MacDonald was 'the indispensable leader'.[70] Conversely, MacDonald underestimated Henderson's abilities and envied his familiarity with Whitehall, gained from his war-time ministerial experience.

He accepted the senior position of home secretary, but it was not a happy spell in his career. He seemed to accept the conservative advice of his officials, and had to defend positions that drew criticism from the Labour rank and file, such as seeming to be opposed to strike action. In order to maintain the distribution of supplies of essential goods he seemed to be ready to invoke the Emergency Powers Act. But it is in the nature of the role of home secretary to uphold the law as it is, and not as one would like it to be.

He did not resign from being secretary of the party, but he did not take the salary. Office and the political limelight had, in Beatrice Webb's words, made him pompous, albeit with a 'ponderous common sense', but a little later she acknowledged that 'the more I see of that man, the more I respect his sterling character.' [71] Hugh Dalton, who was to work closely with him and developed an affectionate respect for 'Uncle Arthur', found him 'slow, pompous and self-important, but very much a politician'.[72] Dalton recalled a League of Nations official in Geneva saying of Henderson that 'he is slow to start, but when he does, he is like an elephant going through jungle.'[73]

One party supporter wrote that he was 'so efficient, so genial, so accessible, that you would feel that you knew him better in an hour than you could know MacDonald in a year'.[74] Beatrice Webb also noted with approval that he was not liked by King George V: he would not kowtow to royalty.[75] After he died, she summed Henderson up with ambiguous appreciation: he had

> no intellectual distinction, no subtlety, wit or personal charm. Nevertheless he was an outstanding personality, because of his essential goodness, absence of vanity and egotism, faithfulness to causes and comrades, and a certain bigness, alike of soul and person, which made him continuously impressive in all the circles he frequented.[76]

Philip Snowden

'He is the greatest man in our Political Labour Movement,'[77] wrote the South Wales miners' leader, Frank Hodges, of Philip Snowden in 1925. Snowden had been campaigning and writing for socialism for thirty years. His Cabinet colleague J. H. Thomas recalled that there had been 'no more brilliant platform exponent of the aims and principles of Socialism'.[78] He honed an expertise in public finance and became, almost inevitably, chancellor of the exchequer in January 1924. The events of 1931 have eclipsed his reputation, after which he was seen as a traitor to the movement he had helped to build up. The charge of treason was compounded by some vicious attacks on his former colleagues. But his public speaking had always had an element of venom. 'He looked like Robespierre,' recalled Mary Agnes Hamilton, 'with his paper-white face, burning eyes, and the sharply cut, simplified features that were a positive gift to the caricaturist; not least when, as in speaking, his long tongue would come out from between his thin lips like a serpent and sting.'[79]

Snowden was born in 1864 in the Pennine village of Cowling, near Keighley, Yorkshire, a village that sent two other men to Westminster.[80] His parents were cotton and worsted workers. Austere, bright, and disciplined, he was brought up in the shadow of a Wesleyan chapel and was a bright boy in the village school, where he graduated and became, like Ramsay MacDonald, a pupil teacher. He first worked in an insurance office and then entered the civil service, becoming a junior officer in the customs department, a job that took him all over the country, from Plymouth to Aberdeen. An injury and a delicate bone structure disabled him for life. After extended sick leave, he was obliged to leave the civil service. He returned to Cowling and was nursed by his now-widowed mother, and for the rest of his life he was often in pain, and needed two sticks to move around.

He was initially a Liberal and was preparing for a debate to refute the new notions of socialism. Conscientiously, he read up on the subject and became a convert. He then became a propagandist for the cause, joined the Independent Labour Party and spent years travelling the country, speaking in all sorts of venues, being boarded by ILP hosts around the country, especially in the north of England. He was well informed and used logic and facts with sarcasm and biblical references to win people over. He was a powerful self-controlled controversialist. One of his audience observed that his brain 'was packed with ice'.[81] Raymond Postgate, son-in-law of George Lansbury, said he did not listen to people.[82] But over the years he probably converted thousands to the cause. The Clydeside firebrand James Maxton was one of his converts – he had previously been a Conservative.[83] He became a member of his village council and, after moving to Keighley where he built up a political base, becoming a member of the Town Council. He became a member of the executive of the ILP and by the beginning of the twentieth century was, with Keir Hardie, Ramsay MacDonald, and Bruce Glasier, regularly re-elected. In 1902 he became chairman of the ILP in succession to Keir Hardie.

His single-minded devotion to the cause was tempered by his marriage to Ethel Annakin of Harrogate, who was a political figure in her own right, as a campaigner for teetotalism, women's rights, peace, and socialism – in that order. She was of striking good looks, tall, golden-haired, with elegant features and enveloping eyes.'[84] She was sixteen years younger than Snowden when they got married; she had actually taken the initiative and proposed to him.[85] Within a few years she became a successful lecturer in the United States, for some years the more successful earner of the two. Snowden's mother could not stand her, and did not attend the wedding. Nor did anyone from her family. Snowden was chairman of the ILP at the time, and one of the few who attended was Fred Jowett, the Bradford activist. Ethel was socially ambitious and occasionally tactless, but she was wholly protective of her husband. One Labour activist recalled that it was 'amazing the way she looked after him ... if you had a bright idea that you'd just like to go and say hello, you'd have to get past her first.'[86] Beatrice Webb reports a conversation with her in which Ethel suggests she and Philip Snowden had not had sexual relations, or, as she put it, she had never 'lived with' him.[87] But Beatrice Webb never liked her, seeing her as an arriviste.[88] According to his eldest son, Lloyd George may have given her some satisfaction.[89] But Ethel was an inspirational speaker.[90] In 1919 she was part of a delegation sent to see the new Russia and returned totally and virulently hostile to the Bolshevik regime. She was at ease in social circles that went beyond the Yorkshire Pennines. Beatrice Webb seems to have had a particular animus against her, calling her 'a "climber" of the worst type, refusing to associate with the rank and file of plebeian members'.[91] Were they rivals for the role of senior Labour wife?

After two failed attempts, he was elected to Parliament in 1906 for Blackburn, holding that seat until 1918. On the first Sunday of May after the election he addressed 10,000 supporters in Blackburn market place. Over the next few years he was, with Keir Hardie and Ramsay MacDonald, one of the most assiduous of the new Labour MPs. He had, as one journalist said, 'the bitterest tongue and the sweetest smile in the House'. He was always well-prepared and was 'an omnivorous reader of newspapers and periodicals'.[92]

Snowden gradually built up his parliamentary expertise as the economic expert in the Labour Party. In 1909 he published *A Socialist Budget* as a rival to Lloyd George's People's Budget. His views were limited to strict balancing of the books, not moving beyond Gladstonian finance in this respect.

Snowden opposed Britain's entering the war in 1914. He and Ethel were on tour in America when war broke out. They rushed back and were articulate in the pacifist cause. Snowden was bitterly hostile to those Labour men who joined the war-time coalition. They were 'office seekers', ready to do any 'dirty work at the bidding of their Tory masters'.[93] Like other war dissidents, he lost his seat in the general election of 1918. This was in spite of support he received from the poet Siegfried Sassoon.[94] He was returned to Colne Valley in 1922. The war did not change his fiscal views. Governments had to borrow money, and the notion of deficit management became part of successive governments' financial management.

Snowden was never close to Ramsay MacDonald. Indeed, he grew to hate the man. Snowden was one of the few people MacDonald was afraid of. He acknowledged Snowden's expertise in finance and economics, but saw him as a prude in relation to his other concerns – free trade and temperance.[95] But there was an inevitability in Snowden's appointment as chancellor of the exchequer in January 1924. He became close to William ('Willie') Graham, his financial secretary to the Treasury, effectively his deputy. A diminutive Lowland Scot, he was a master of detail, dedicated to his work. Snowden tried to get him to relax and 'read a detective story as a change, but that was too frivolous an indulgence.'[96]

As time went on, and when in power, it seemed that his socialism was subordinated to two other causes: the old radical creed of free trade and adherence to the Gold Standard. Neither had anything to do with socialism.

J. H. Thomas

If Ramsay MacDonald had an intimate among the old guard of the Labour Party, it was James Henry ('Jimmy', but 'Jim' to those who were closest to him) Thomas. This was strange, for MacDonald was a refined and sophisticated Scot whereas Thomas was a brash and uninhibited Welshman. Each was loyal to the other. MacDonald was amused by Thomas's outrageousness, and they both shared a taste for the social world of London 'society' and cigars. Both were also great public performers with a strong sense of occasion. Thomas accepted a junior role to MacDonald, who tolerated his buffoonery and occasional incompetence.[97] He respected MacDonald, who by 'his organising ability had done more than any other single individual to create the Labour Party'.[98]

There was another bond. Both MacDonald and Thomas were illegitimate. Thomas for many years thought he was the youngest son of a sailor's widow in Newport, Monmouthshire. In fact, he was the son of that widow's eldest daughter, who was sent out to service after Thomas's birth in 1874.[99] The family were Conservative and members of the Church of England.[100]

There was another side of Thomas that was less obvious to observers and cartoonists. Lord Birkenhead saw him as 'by far the ablest politician among the Labour members of the Cabinet' of 1924'.[101] He could be an astute operator and was also known as 'Slippery Jim'.[102]

After leaving school at fifteen he was employed by the Great Western Railway as an engine cleaner. A voluble speaker and organiser, he soon became active in union politics and was president of the Newport Trades Council by the age of twenty-three. Moving to the railway town of Swindon, he was elected to the town council shortly afterwards. He became chairman of both the Finance and

Law Committee, and of the Tramways and Electricity Committee of the Council. 'This meant', he recalled, 'that although I was now receiving a salary from the Great Western Railway of 24s. a week, I was actually responsible for the town's finances, and introducing several budgets which embraced anything between two and three hundred thousand pounds.'[103] In his early thirties he became president of the Amalgamated Society of Railway Servants.

When he was thirty-five he was elected as Labour MP for Derby, another railway town, displacing the Lib–Lab railway trade union leader, Richard Bell, who had held the seat since 1895. Derby became his political base for the next quarter of a century. Like many other Labour MPs before the war, he was a member of the teetotal fellowship, the International Order of Good Templars.[104] That was to change. One of his patrons in the new Parliament was the veteran radical Sir Charles Dilke, a hereditary baronet who interested himself in trade unionism.[105] He took to the House of Commons, spoke well, and was the first Labour MP to have a child christened in the House of Commons crypt.[106]

Parliament was important, but Thomas's other base was the railway trade unions. The decade 1910 to 1920 was a crucial period in the development of trade unionism in Britain. Class deference was fading. Membership of trade unions expanded, and men (trade unionism was mostly, but not exclusively, male driven) were beginning to become aware of their growing power to make demands to secure acceptable working conditions and adequate pay. The creed of syndicalism that favoured political power through trade unions became popular. The railwaymen before 1914 had been divided. Employment practice and culture had been influenced by military patterns, with uniforms and a hierarchy. The private railway companies were slow to recognise the unions. Railway employees were divided into four major unions before 1913, when three of them, the Amalgamated Society of Railway Servants, which was Thomas's union, the General Railway Workers' Union, and the United Pointsmen's and Signalmen's Union amalgamated in 1916 to form the National Union of Railwaymen (NUR). The Associated Society of Locomotive Engineers and Firemen (ASLEF) remained separate. The NUR had a membership of nearly 400,000 and, with the National Union of Miners (NUM) and the Transport and General Workers' (TGWU), were to form the Triple Alliance at the end of the war.

Thomas was to become general secretary of the NUR. He was popular with them, at the same time as rubbing shoulders with members of railway boards. He treated the bosses as his personal equals, joshed with them, and accepted their hospitality while fighting for his members' rights. The directors came to the view that it was better to cooperate with the unions than to confront them. For the rest of his life, even after he was formally repudiated by the union, he retained a sentimental attachment to railwaymen. He knew hundreds individually and would make a point of looking them up when travelling, greeting them by name, and asking about the welfare of their families.

On the outbreak of the war in 1914 Thomas was in the United States – as was Philip Snowden. Thomas rushed back and supported Britain's involvement. During the war he was brought into government consultation and was sent on a government mission led by the former Conservative prime minister Arthur Balfour to the United States. On his return he was made a privy councillor. He was invited to become a minister but thought he could do more for the war effort without a departmental responsibility.

If there was a principle in Thomas's career, beyond self-promotion, it was the emancipation of his own class. He had no time for the theories of socialism. 'I am not a socialist,' he said, 'and I don't read any of those bloody books.'[107] Nonetheless he wrote his own bloody book, *When Labour Rules*, published in 1920, and a very good book it is too. The word 'socialism' does not appear, but the book has two themes. It is an attempt to reassure people who may be persuaded by negative propaganda and scare stories about Bolshevist Labour. It also presents quite a detailed programme of what a Labour government might do when in power. It is far more specific on legislative details than most of Ramsay MacDonald's more voluminous writings. Thomas was a pragmatist. Much of what he argued for might be seen as an extension of the Liberal Party's great reforms of a decade earlier. But another persistent theme was his identity with Labour and the working-class movement. Labour in the previous thirty or forty years had been increasingly admitted to the council chambers of decision-making – municipal councils, Parliament, and Royal Commissions. This was only fair and reasonable. Thomas's book was pervaded with good humour. It is clear and assertive but not strident. He made efforts to understand (if then to dismiss) alternative views. It was a charitable book and does much to explain Thomas's character and subsequent career, for he was always ready to see the best in other people. James Maxton, politically no friend of Thomas's, said he 'never had an ounce of malice in him'.[108]

The word socialism hardly appears in his memoirs either and only as applied to other people. He had a sense of nation and empire with the monarchy at its head, and he shared with MacDonald a notion of gradualism. National emergencies needed collectivist solutions. Mines, railways, and other key industries came under state control during the war. His sense of nation would have been his justification for accepting the aristocratic embrace. He never lost his sense of being from the working class, whom he believed should have access to the good things of life, and these included cigars and champagne. The mocking saying 'Nothing's too good for the working class' might have been coined with him in mind. He was a regular guest in the private box of the Earl of Derby at the Grand National,[109] and was often invited to Cliveden, Lady Astor's mansion on the Thames near Henley.[110] In 1920 he received, alongside Lloyd George, Bonar Law, and Austen Chamberlain, an honorary doctorate from the University of Cambridge.[111]

Four months after Labour came to power MacDonald and Thomas and his wife were invited to a very smart dinner dance in honour of the king and queen of Romania. According to Henry Channon, a wealthy young American social climber who was dressed for the evening as little Lord Fauntleroy, Thomas was invited by an equerry to escort the Duchess of Atholl into dinner. 'Rather,' replied Thomas, immediately dumping his wife to fend for herself.[112]

His affability meant that he was charitable to people whom his Labour colleagues may have seen as 'class enemies'. This cordiality perhaps has its origins in an incident in 1916 when Thomas was libelled in the press and felt obliged to issue a writ. Sir Edward Carson, viewed as a cold-blooded and hard Ulsterman, approached Thomas and offered his services, casually saying, 'Don't worry what my fee will be.'[113] Thomas accepted but the case never came to court.

As a young man he had opposed the Boer War.[114] He believed strongly in compromise, 'one of the most precious words in the language'.[115] He thought that 'whatever your ideals may be, you must deal with things as they are and not as you would wish them to be.'[116] His lack of ideology extended to fiscal policy. Most of the men of 1924 accepted free trade as a dogma inherited from nineteenth-century Liberalism. Thomas accepted the idea of tariffs more readily.[117]

The image he cultivated may well have concealed a shrewd quick wit and canny calculation, attributes sometimes ascribed to Welsh people. At one meeting, another negotiator observed, 'You forget that I am also a Welshman.' Thomas also had the reputation of being an excellent bridge player.[118]

As a union negotiator Thomas was highly effective. He realised that the strike option was a failure for the workers and he would push negotiations to the limit. Jaunty and good-humoured, he was liked on both sides of the industrial divide. In 1921 the miners were challenging a reduction in wages, and the three major unions formed a 'Triple Alliance'. Thomas held out against a general strike. He could use humour against himself. When accused by militants of compromising and of selling out, he shouted back, 'Yes, I tried to sell *you* but I couldn't get a price.'[119] Nevertheless, in spite of the humour, the accusations of betrayal did hurt, and 'bit into the very soul'.[120]

In the 1920s, and especially after the formation of the Labour government, he took to the life of the capital, accepting any invitation from a society hostess. He became a compulsive gambler and card-player.[121] Partying in the evening, he was not an early riser,[122] and had to commute into central London from his home in Thurlow Park Road, Dulwich. He became known to the cartoonist, David Low, as the 'Right Honourable Dress Suit'. He accepted this mockery 'with philosophy', but 'the hurt has been there all the same.'[123] This did not inhibit him from collecting the original cartoons.[124] He was a popular after-dinner speaker. No respecter of people, he would address peers by their first names as soon as he met them.[125] As Philip Snowden wrote, 'His wit and irresponsibility and his inexhaustible fund of anecdotes never failed to provide amusement and enjoyment for his audience.'[126]

He dropped his h's with defiance. One story reports a morning meeting at the Garrick Club with Lord Birkenhead.

> 'I've an 'orrible 'ead-ache,' said Thomas.
> To which the sophisticated Birkenhead replied,
> 'Why not take a couple of aspirates.'[127]

It may be that he deliberately cultivated this image of a vulgar braggart. It may be that he had complete control of his aitches. Just as he was an excellent raconteur, so he knew how to create an impact. His act lowered people's expectations of his intelligence and gave him a psychological advantage. On one occasion he had colleagues and staff mystified when he kept going on about the Haddock Committee. Was this some committee about empire fisheries that they should know about? They eventually realised that he was referring to an ad hoc committee.[128]

He had a comfortable middle-class home in Dulwich, with a grand piano. His heavy consumption of whisky had no effect on his negotiating skills or his command of an agenda.[129] Although he became an alcoholic, some old habits died hard. When he visited his constituency he used to stay at a temperance hotel and read the lesson at St Andrew's Church, Derby.[130]

He did not moderate his coarseness even with the royal family. He and King George V got on well. Thomas would tell bawdy jokes to the king, making him roar with laughter. This kind of behaviour did not go down with the righteous and censorious Beatrice Webb, who, much later, recorded in her diary that Thomas 'was the quintessence of gross vulgarity in appearance and speech, in his liking for low company, in his appalling sycophancy to royalty, and to high life, in his boozing and gambling, in his ignorance of all that made wisdom in home administration.'[131]

He was able to tell stories against himself. When he was appointed in 1924, he turned up at the Colonial Office before his appointment had been officially announced.

'I am the new secretary of state,' he told the man at the reception desk who turned to his neighbour.

'Another shell shock case, I'm afraid,' he said to his colleague. Or so the story goes. But Thomas was such an anecdotist that he could well have invented the story.

Whereas his predecessors at the office used to summon staff by a bell, he would go to their offices, put his head round the door, and say, 'Come 'ere, you bugger.'[132]

Curzon's approach to his senior staff was different.

7

Old Labour

William Adamson

William Adamson, known in the 1920s as 'Old Willie', was born near Dunfermline in 1863. He started working in the coal mines as a pit boy at the age of eleven and continued working as a miner for twenty-seven years. His full-time education had previously been at a dame's school run by the wife of a mining engineer.[1] He became active in union affairs and worked his way up from a local official to a regional post. Because of the local and scattered nature of the mining industry, miners' union organisations were made up of virtually autonomous units. The Fife and Kinross Miners' Association (FKMA) was relatively strong. The mine owners preferred negotiation to confrontation, and this suited Adamson. By 1908 he had become general secretary of the FKMA. Over the next decade, under the influence of new unionism, there were amalgamations with other localised Scottish miners' unions, and by 1914 the umbrella National Union of Scottish Miners was affiliated to the Miners' Federation of Great Britain.

A committed Baptist and a staunch teetotaller he was active in local branches of the Temperance Union, being the founder of the Dunfermline Temperance Society. Here he learnt how to speak persuasively in public. The society also encouraged self-improvement and reading. Adamson had an enthusiasm for poetry and loved the work of Robert Burns.

As well as trade union activity, he extended his public service to municipal politics and in 1909 was elected to Dunfermline Town Council. Initially he was a Liberal, but he recognised the validity of a party that represented labour interests and early in the new century he shifted his allegiance to Labour. However, he repudiated the idea of the party being socialist.[2] He was the Labour candidate for West Fife in the general election of January 1910, but he lost in a three-cornered contest. The neighbouring East Fife constituency was held by the prime minister, H. H. Asquith. In Fife elections were contested more on ideological issues than according to ethnic or religious divisions. Adamson fought the constituency again in the December 1910 general election, and this time he won. He was the first Scottish miner to be an MP for a Scottish constituency. He held the seat for the next twenty-one years.

He supported Britain's engagement in the Great War. By 1914 he was married, with two daughters and two sons, one of whom was a casualty in the war. He was opposed to compulsory military conscription and voted against the Military Service Bill in January 1916.

During the war Adamson served the party loyally as a backbencher under the leadership of Arthur Henderson, who also served in coalition governments. In the general election of 1918 Henderson, along with other high profile Labour leaders such as MacDonald, Snowden, and Lansbury, lost their seats. Adamson retained his. The newly elected Labour MPs had to choose a leader. The two front-runners were J. H. Thomas and J. R. Clynes, for each of whom support was more or less evenly balanced. Adamson was picked as the compromise candidate and was elected.

It was a strange choice. Adamson saw the Labour Party still as a pressure group for labour and working-class interests rather than as a significant national party. The Liberal Party was imploding, splitting between followers of the new prime minister, Lloyd George, and followers of the ousted H. H. Asquith. Lloyd George Liberals were in coalition with the greater number of Conservatives. The Asquith Liberals formed a cohesive opposition group, but their numbers were fewer than Labour, who thus became the largest single opposition group, and Adamson found himself the leader of His Majesty's Opposition, on the strength of which he was made a privy councillor. It was not a happy time for him, and he was dogged by ill health and anxiety. He held the post until 1921. He was seen as a decent man, respectable but dull-witted;[3] not the man to seize the opportunities of a fast-moving political situation.

He made a poor impression on one eager recruit, Charles Trevelyan, a new convert from the Liberal Party who attended his first Labour Party conference in May 1919. 'Adamson came down,' he wrote to a friend, 'and made as he would, a stupid speech wearying them with irrelevance and feebleness. No one, except himself, regarded him as a leader.'[4]

He was overwhelmed with the responsibility. According to Beatrice Webb, he was 'a squat figure ... with an instinctive suspicion of all intellectuals and enthusiasts'. In spite of this suspicion, he sought the Webbs' advice. He gave the impression of being out of his depth, more concerned that the Parliamentary Labour Party should be provided with messengers and clerks than with policy about technical questions of foreign affairs and finance. He also told Beatrice Webb, with a wink and a smile, in his sing-song voice, 'We mean to make use of your husband.'[5]

He did expand his horizons in 1920 by being part of a Labour Party commission of inquiry into the Irish Troubles. He visited Ireland with Arthur Henderson and F. W. Jowett, with the younger Arthur Greenwood acting as secretary.

Meanwhile there were troubles nearer home. In Fife, Adamson as a trade union official was seen as cautious and autocratic. He opposed any form of militancy, and one militant, William Gallacher, regarded him as a 'close friend of the coalowners and of every Tory in Fife'.[6] One miner, Philip Hodge, who had a more explicitly socialist programme and, if not an intellectual, was certainly an enthusiast, set up a Reform Union challenging Adamson, and sought the ILP candidature in the 1923 general election. The bid failed, as Hodge was not himself universally popular among younger members of the union.

MacDonald relied on trade union support. Adamson was one of the leading figures of Scottish trade unionism. Beatrice Webb suggested that the appointment of trade union bosses in a Labour government was equivalent to the need of eighteenth-century prime ministers to have a duke or two in an administration.[7] In January 1924 Ramsay MacDonald appointed Adamson secretary of state for Scotland. At the despatch box he was famous for avoiding direct questions, saying that he would give the matter 'due consideration'. It became his catchphrase.[8]

As secretary of state, he was in favour of devolution, and spoke at a meeting of the Scottish Home Rule Association, held at Elderslie. But in office he was unable to do anything about it.

Thomas Johnston, a later secretary of state for Scotland who worked closely with him and knew him well, saw him as 'the soul of loyalty and good comradeship.'[9] He was calm and always courteous, even when declining requests. As he put it himself, 'If ye canna gie a man what he wants, we can aye gie him a kind word. It costs damn a.'[10]

Vernon Hartshorn

'No member of the Labour Party ... could speak on trade union matters with such authority and expertise as Mr Hartshorn,'[11] observed Philip Snowden in his memoirs.

Vernon Hartshorn, like J. H. Thomas, came from South Wales. In the nineteenth century the miners of South Wales were loosely federated, and in the last decades of the century were under the spellbinding although waning influence of the poet William Abraham, better known by his bardic name of Mabon. He personified the tradition of Liberal–Labour alliance and had been an MP as early as 1885. There was also a militancy in the mining valleys. In the 1906 Parliament miners' MPs stood aloof from other Labour MPs, and it was under the pressure of the South Wales miners that they added their strength to the party in 1908.[12] Militancy was maintained, indeed provoked, by confrontations with an aggressive police chief in Glamorgan and the mobilisation of military troops. A sense of alienation was exacerbated by the 1913 Senghenydd mining disaster, when 439 were killed in an accident.

Hartshorn was born in 1872 in Pont-y-waun, a Glamorgan mining village that produced six Labour MPs.[13] He started to work in the mines at the age of fourteen. Because of ill health he took a break from working underground and worked as a junior clerk in Cardiff Docks, where he honed his numeracy and acquired some business skills. He returned to the pits and embarked on a public career. He joined the ILP, and was elected to the Risca Urban District Council, becoming chairman in 1908.

He was also active in trade union affairs. In 1905 he was elected miners' agent for the Maesteg district of the South Wales Miners' Federation. In this capacity he was an effective leader of 5,000 miners, with a great social and political influence.[14] Hartshorn represented politically a middle path between the conservatism of Mabon and the radicalism of fiery younger men such as Noah Ablett. The importance of Mabon's Welsh identity was eroded by demographic shifts during his career. In 1871 34,000 miners were employed in the Glamorgan coal field. In 1911 that figure had risen to 150,000, many of the newcomers being immigrants from England. They were unconcerned about the disestablishment of the Church of Wales or temperance – Mabon issues – but rather with wages and conditions of work.[15]

Hartshorn was articulate and able to represent the views of the people he stood for. One who worked with him described him as a 'man of great capacity, and of intellectual ability far above any of the older leaders'.[16]

In the general election of 1906 a Liberal–Labour candidate was returned unopposed for the Mid-Glamorgan constituency. The Mabon influence persisted, but a Labour organisation was set up in

Maesteg – Hartshorn was elected its president – and Labour prepared to displace the older Lib–Labs.

Hartshorn stood as an Independent Socialist at a by-election in 1910 and again at the December 1910 general election. In so standing he was defying some elements of the leadership of the South Wales Miners' Federation who were still trying to woo the old Liberal and nonconformist voters.[17] The two elections were bitterly contested. Hartshorn set out his position in an open letter to the Reverend Towyn Jones, seen as a 'giant of the pulpit' and a strong Liberal. The Liberal machine attacked Hartshorn ferociously, claiming he was not sufficiently Welsh and questioning his nonconformity[18] – although he was indeed a member of the nonconformist Primitive Methodist Church. Hartshorn's own rueful comment was that the 'Labour Party in Mid-Glamorgan is faced with the deadweight of generations of Liberal tradition and prejudice.'[19] His activist reputation got him elected to the executive of the South Wales Miners' Federation. That was the peak of his militancy. He was opposed to the ideas of syndicalism, and also to the Cumbrian Commune strike in early 1914. He was becoming more moderate and pragmatic.

His distancing from militancy was shown in his support for British engagement in the Great War. For this he was bitterly opposed by others. Nonetheless thousands of miners flocked to join the army creating a shortage of manpower in the pits. Another South Wales miners' leader, William Brace, who had been an MP since 1906, was appointed a junior minister in Asquith's coalition of May 1915. Hartshorn became a member of the Home Office committee. The prime minister from December 1916, Lloyd George, appointed him, as the South Wales Labour representative, on the Industrial Unrest Committee. In the major South Wales miners' strike of 1915 Hartshorn urged the men to return to work. The Royal Navy, he argued, still needed coal for their ships and the war effort. Hartshorn visited the Western Front with a delegation of miners and, for his support for the war effort, became among the first batch of people to be awarded the OBE.

He kept in close touch with what was going on in South Wales, writing a column for many years in the *South Wales News*, later the *Western Mail*.[20] In 1918 he succeeded in being returned unopposed as MP for Ogmore. He gave evidence to the Sankey Commission on the mining industry, impressing the commission and also Parliament with his detailed and articulate presentation of matters dealing with the industry. But he faced criticism from some in South Wales who mocked him as 'Lord of Maesteg'. He was at pains to stress his own strong stands against the mine owners.

Hartshorn was a keen chess player and a Primitive Methodist Sunday school teacher. When asked what the influences had been that had swayed his mental and moral development, he replied, 'My wife; Primitive Methodism; and the writings of Robert Blatchford.'[21]

He was chairman of the Welsh group of Labour MPs and Ramsay MacDonald appointed him postmaster general in January 1924. He was one of three miners brought into the Cabinet, each representing different regions of the coal industry.

A shadowy figure outside Glamorgan, Hartshorn personified the centrist tradition of trade union leaders in South Wales – along with his colleague, Arthur Jenkins, father of Roy, a Labour Cabinet minister of the 1960s and 1970s. Such men preferred patient negotiation to impulsive confrontation. They believed in community as well as class, and progress through local government, trade union office, and adult education.[22]

F. W. Jowett

Few of the men of 1924 – apart from Josiah Wedgwood – were as closely associated with one place as Frederick William Jowett was with Bradford. It was his permanent home, and he died within a few hundred yards from where he had been born eighty years earlier. In his twenty years as an MP he did not have a London family base, instead returning each weekend to Bradford.

Fred Jowett was born, one of eight children, in 1864. At the age of eight he was working part-time in a textile mill, switching to full-time at the age of thirteen. When he was eighteen he was made a supervisor and then a partner in the business of William Leach. Meanwhile he attended classes at Bradford Technical College, but more significantly read the works of William Cobbett, Thomas Carlyle, John Ruskin, and William Morris.[23] This reading helped to formulate his political ideology, adding to what he learned from his father with whom he used to tramp the Yorkshire moors on Sundays, talking politics.[24] His father had been active in the Cooperative Movement and the son became chairman of the local Cooperative Association at the age of twenty-four. He had already joined William Morris's Socialist League while in his teens. In addition to Morris, another great influence was Robert Blatchford, editor of *The Clarion* and author of *Merrie England*.[25]

Politically Bradford in the 1880s and 1890s was dominated by the Liberals, who were well established and represented the boss class. Between December 1890 and April 1891 the city was in turmoil, with a prolonged strike of textile workers in the suburb of Manningham. Samuel Lister, the mill owner, had cut the wages of the workers, mostly women, by 30 per cent. The City Council showed no sympathy, with both Conservatives and Liberals backing Lister. The strike ultimately collapsed, with the women being forced by starvation to go back to the mill. But a major consequence was that the workers were politicised. The socialist case was that the Liberals and the Conservatives were united against Labour and that any hopes of an alliance with or concessions from the Liberals were illusory. The Manningham strike was a trigger for the creation of the foundation of the Independent Labour Party two years later. The inaugural meeting, significantly, took place in Bradford. Fred Jowett was present and there was support from all over the country.

At the time of the ILP's birth, Jowett was already a member of the City Council. He stood successfully as a Socialist in 1891, and the

City Council was his principal political arena for the next fifteen years. He was particularly interested in housing and children's health.[26] As a result of his efforts, slums were cleared and children received school meals. Bradford claimed to be the first local authority to provide such care to children. The first dinner was served by the headmaster of one school, the father of J. B. Priestley.[27]

A long-term friendship with Philip Snowden, a fellow Yorkshireman, grew in the 1890s. Jowett was one of only four friends invited to the wedding of Philip and Ethel Snowden in 1905.[28] The friendship was to survive political differences, as Snowden moved to the right and became a pariah to the rest of the Labour Party. The two men were exchanging warm letters until the end of Snowden's life.[29] For Jowett, Philip Snowden was one of the two greatest men of British socialism. The other was Robert Blatchford.

His political ambitions were extended beyond the West Riding in 1900 when he stood for Parliament for the constituency of Bradford West. He lost by forty-one votes but gained the highest percentage of any losing Labour candidate in that year's general election. Six years later he was more successful in Bradford East, a constituency he held through the war to 1918.

His maiden speech in the House of Commons was about the extension of school meals. Jowett kept in regular touch with his popular base by writing about parliamentary affairs in *The Clarion*.

Jowett had a striking appearance – Philip Snowden wrote that it was as if a German professor had strayed into the House of Commons.[30] He was one of the more active of the Labour MPs elected in 1906, taking up a number of issues. He was unimpressed by the amateurism of parliamentary politics, and argued against the traditional confrontation style, and proposed that committees should be set up to supervise the implementation of legislation, in the way that was done in local government. For a period he was chairman of the Public Accounts Committee.[31]

Another issue he pursued with persistence was secret diplomacy. He was, with justification, suspicious that military commitments were being made without democratic accountability. When war broke out in 1914, he was strongly opposed to Britain's involvement. He was national chairman of the ILP when its governing body, the National Council, met at a hotel in Blackfriars Street, Manchester, to register opposition to the war. He was not a pacifist but carried his campaign against secret diplomacy into the Union of Democratic Control (UDC), on whose executive he served. Ramsay MacDonald was secretary of the UDC, which was largely a middle-class, London-based group, dominated by dissident Liberals. Jowett opposed conscription and Labour's participation in the war-time coalitions.

Jowett welcomed the Bolshevik revolution and remained loyal in his allegiance, aware of faults and mistakes but ready to make excuses. Like others who had opposed the war, he lost his seat at the 1918 general election, bouncing back two years later at a by-election. In his time out of Parliament he kept busy. He went on an ILP mission to Hungary in 1920 to report on the White Terror following the suppression of the post-war Communist government. One of the others on the mission was Josiah Wedgwood, who had experienced a very different war. The following year Jowett was on a similar mission of inquiry, this time to Ireland, with Arthur Henderson, William Adamson, and Arthur Greenwood.

The war had split the Bradford ILP, but it was held together by the genial personality of the ILP-supporting businessman William Leach, who became a junior minister in 1924. The local party thrived, with a membership of 1,600 and the ownership of its own hall, its own paper, and even a cinema in Morley Street where Sunday evening meetings were packed out.[32]

When MacDonald was bringing together his ministry in January 1924, he first wanted Jowett to be a minister outside the Cabinet. But he was appointed first commissioner of works, an administrative rather than a policy-initiating post. Jowett was, with Wheatley, one of the most left-wing members of the Cabinet. Jowett respected MacDonald's skills, but the two men were not close – apart from a period during the Great War when they opposed Britain's engagement in the war, although for different reasons. In later years his judgement of MacDonald was severe. He 'has abilities enough', he wrote to Snowden in 1936, 'but he is insincere, he is a snob, loves power and is quite unscrupulous as to what he does or who sinks if he swims.'[33]

Jowett's Cabinet post had responsibility for state buildings and royal palaces, as well as London statues. This gave little opportunity for the promotion or implementation of socialism, but Jowett was able to make his mark. In spite of his republicanism, he carried out his duties with courtesy. He was persuaded to wear a dress suit for formal occasions, after colleagues argued that it was the job's working clothes, equivalent to the engineer's dungarees. He noted that some Crown property overseas, notably in China, was leased very cheaply to British business. He raised the rent, and the extra money raised was used to improve lower-grade housing on royal estates.[34]

He was also able to introduce some ideology into his job. He was responsible for the erection of the statue of Nurse Edith Cavell outside the National Portrait Gallery, a few yards north of Trafalgar Square with its statues of military heroes. On its plinth are the unwarlike words of another war-time nurse, Florence Nightingale: 'Patriotism is not enough; there must be no hatred or bitterness to anyone.' They echoed Jowett's sentiments. 'Cut the words deep,' he instructed his officials.[35]

Sydney Olivier

At first sight Sir Sydney Olivier, knight commander of the Order of St Michael and St George, commander of the Order of the Bath, would not be regarded as among the ranks of Old Labour. But despite his distinguished life of public service and honours, he was, in fact, a pioneer, among the earliest who had toiled in the vineyard of British socialism.

Olivier had a varied career before he entered politics. He was a contributor to the collection *Fabian Essays in Socialism*, edited by George Bernard Shaw, published in 1889. Shaw had something of an editorial challenge in dealing with Olivier's elliptical text on the ethics of socialism.

Olivier was from a Huguenot family, the son of a Church of England minister, and born in Colchester in 1859. Educated at Tonbridge School in Kent and at Corpus Christi College, Oxford, his political philosophy combined Christian socialism with Comtean positivism. Like other socialists of his generation, he was strongly influenced by the writings of Henry George. At Oxford he co-authored a volume of poetry and became a close friend of another of the early Fabians, Graham Wallas, a political philosopher, historian, and teacher. He entered the Civil Service by competitive examination and joined the Colonial Office on the same day as Sidney Webb.

Work at the Colonial Office in 1882 was not terribly onerous. His boss was 'one of the old stagers', and used to 'drive to the office from a remote suburb every day in a dog-cart tandem, arriving at about half past twelve, after which he consumed a considerable lunch and went to sleep until tea-time.'[36] Work could continue, however, in the evening.

This relaxed regime gave Olivier time to undertake social work of different kinds. At the London Working Men's College he taught Latin, yes, Latin, and researched sewage systems in the slums. Shaw was also interested in slum conditions, as reflected in his play *Widowers' Houses*, which explored slum landlordism. The shared interest brought the two men together.

Olivier had no imperial ethic. There was nothing of the Rudyard Kipling or the Joseph Chamberlain about his approach to empire. He thought that the task of the Colonial Office and its staff was to intervene in the interests of the 'natives' against settlers, plantation owners, and commercial interests. The title of one of his books, *White Capital and Coloured Labour*, hints at an assessment of empire that was not typical of colonial servants (although the language reflects the times). This was based on a series of articles and was first published in book form in the Socialist Library, edited by Ramsay MacDonald in 1906. The book is an analysis of capitalist exploitation of colonial peoples, and argues that colonial possessions were trusts and the imperial authorities were trustees, and that the interests of the 'natives' should be paramount. Olivier worked on a revision, and an enlargement of the book was reissued in 1931, published by the Hogarth Press, the publishing house owned by Leonard and Virginia Woolf.

As well as the Colonial Office, he and Sidney Webb joined the Fabian Society together in 1885. He also joined the Rainbow Circle, a progressive discussion group, where he got to know another member, Ramsay MacDonald.

Olivier was secretary of the Fabian Society from 1886 to 1890 and it was said that all the records of the society were kept in a drawer at the Colonial Office.[37] He was seen as a handsome, grave, and distinguished young man, with a sartorial sense of style. During this time he was regarded, along with Shaw, Wallas, and Webb, as one of the Fabian Society's 'four musketeers'.[38] The friendship with Sidney Webb lasted for over sixty years. In 1898 he accompanied Sidney and Beatrice Webb on a tour of the United States.[39] Olivier combined active radicalism with a more conventional progressive upper-middle-class way of life. In 1885 he married Margaret Cox, the sister of Harold Cox who became a Liberal MP and editor of the *Edinburgh Review*.

Olivier steadily rose in the Colonial Office, and served overseas in Honduras, the Leeward Islands, and Jamaica. After a home posting in London he returned to Jamaica, serving there in three different posts, ending up as governor for five years, and coming home for good in 1913. He was noted as governor for his interest in public works, especially clearing malarial swamps and extending a network of roads. Public works for social benefit was for him a kind of socialism in practice. Olivier was very attached to Jamaica and wrote books about the island, going back there several times in his sixties and seventies.

Back in Britain he occupied senior civil service positions, including permanent secretary at the Board of Agriculture, until he finally retired in 1917. Olivier never lost his radical networks. Throughout his career he retained his membership of the Fabian Society, and kept up a regular correspondence with H. G. Wells. Even on home leaves from Jamaica he had the time and inclination to go to Cambridge and address the university's Fabian Society.[40] When in Britain, the Oliviers lived at Limpsfield in Surrey with their four daughters. One neighbour was the critical theorist of imperialism J. A. Hobson, and visitors included Shaw, Wells, the Liberal journalist Henry Nevinson, and the Russian anarchist (and prince) Peter Kropotkin.[41] In Olivier's older years he was still nattily, if shabbily, dressed. According to Philip Snowden, he had 'a voice and articulation which made him almost unintelligible'.[42]

He was, however, not totally free of racial prejudice or the unquestioning acceptance of racial stereotypes, as evident from comments on the viceroy of India, Lord Reading, a Jew and formerly Sir Rufus Isaacs, whom he saw as suffering from the 'racial defect' of 'being always out for a deal.'[43]

In January 1924 he was appointed secretary of state for India – he had wanted the Colonial Office – and was elevated to the peerage. MacDonald in 1924 did not want to create hereditary peers and was assured that, as Olivier had only daughters, the title would die with him. Josiah Wedgwood had wanted the India post and Olivier encountered some criticism from Wedgwood in the Cabinet. His old friend Bernard Shaw observed that Olivier was eminently presentable and much more aristocratic looking than most of the hereditary nobles.[44] His daughters went to the progressive independent school Bedales in Hampshire, to which Ramsay MacDonald and Josiah Wedgwood also sent their children.

Lord Olivier had a nephew who in 1924 started as a student at the Central School of Speech and Drama. His name was Laurence, and he too ended up in the House of Lords.

Thomas Shaw

Tom Shaw was born at Waterside, Colne, Lancashire, in April 1872, the son of a miner. He was working part-time in a textile mill at the age of ten, going to school in the afternoon. This was the pattern of many of his working-class contemporaries; they were referred to as 'half-timers'. He was working full-time from the age of twelve but supplemented his education with evening classes. Interested in languages, he taught himself French and German.[45] He was also a voracious reader of books in English. Shaw married when he was twenty-one and fathered four daughters. He became an active trade unionist and was secretary of the Colne Weavers' Association; he proceeded to extend his activities by setting up the Northern Counties Textile Trades Federation of which he became the first secretary.[46] His enthusiasm for languages accompanied an interest in international trade unionism. This led to him becoming secretary in 1911 of the International Federation of Textile Workers, and to travel extensively in Europe where he was happy to practise his language skills.

He supported Britain's engagement in the war in 1914. 'War between country and country is a bad thing,' he acknowledged, 'but in case of such a war any attempt at a General Strike to prevent the people defending their country would result in civil war which was ten times worse than war between nation and nation.'[47] He undertook war work, being director of national services in the West Midlands.[48] For this work he was made a commander of the Order of the British Empire (CBE).

Shaw was elected as member of Parliament for Preston in 1918. He met some opposition from the local ILP because of what they saw as his enthusiasm for the war. A bluff John Bull kind of figure, he campaigned for the nationalisation of the railways, and was particularly popular for his promotion of the interests of demobilised soldiers. He was made a junior whip in the 1918–22 Parliament, and although not a fan of the Bolshevik Revolution, made a stand against British military intervention in Russia.

He was also a supporter of the League of Nations and the newly established International Labour Organisation. He took part in the reconstruction of the Labour and Socialist International. Of this body, Arthur Henderson became chairman and Shaw was one of two secretaries – the other being the Austrian socialist Friedrich Adler.

Shaw visited the Ruhr region in 1923, recently occupied by France. He opposed this reoccupation, and was also apprehensive of the provocation of reparations imposed on Germany, fearing that it could lead to another war in twenty years' time.[49]

His international outlook also manifested itself in his call for British ratification of the Washington Convention that stipulated that working hours should not exceed forty-eight a week. The 1923 British Conservative government would not agree to this.

In January 1924 he was appointed minister of labour. He took on the task and expectation that a Labour government could do something about the rising unemployment. He was able to introduce palliative measures. He was also working on a Bill to ratify the Washington Convention when the government fell.

One junior minister, Emanuel Shinwell, described him as 'somewhat portly' and 'inclined to be indolent'.[50] Shaw saw the Labour Party's purpose as promoting the interests of trade unions and, like some other trade unionists, disliked the influx into the party of ambitious middle-class men and women, and 'missionary socialists'.[51]

Outside politics he had few interests, but one was collecting working-class Lancashire dialect stories, 'tackers' tales', as he called them, referring to one of the processes of the textile industry. He was a good raconteur.[52]

Shaw was somewhat eclipsed by his deputy, the first woman to hold a government office. Margaret Bondfield was from Somerset and was active in organising women into trade unions, especially exploited shop workers. Although it had a good record in supporting votes for women, Labour was beaten by the Conservatives in actually getting women into Parliament. The general election of

1923 returned the first three Labour women MPs. A Conservative had been elected in 1918. Of the three, Margaret Bondfield was the only one with a trade union background. J. H. Thomas described her as 'a woman of rare charm, dignity and administrative ability.'[53]

Stephen Walsh

Stephen Walsh was a Lancashire miner, known to his constituents as 'Little Steve' or 'Wee Stee' because of his diminutive stature – he stood at just five foot. He was unimpressive in appearance until he mounted a platform, at which point he would be transformed into a great orator.[54]

Walsh was born in a Liverpool suburb in August 1859 to an Irish immigrant family. His father died before he was born, and his mother followed when he was an infant; he retained no memory of her. His first actual memory was being picked up by a policeman as a foundling, on the steps of a church, and then being carried to a home for waifs and strays.[55] He was brought up as a foundling in Kirkdale Industrial School and Orphanage.[56] He recalled that he was 'happy and well-cared for' here. Although he was born of Irish immigrant parents who were presumably Roman Catholic, he chose at the age of twenty to be an Anglican. He was particularly good at mathematics and wanted to be a schoolteacher, but he was told that this was impossible because he was 'too small'.[57]

When he was eleven he went to live at Ashton-in-Makerfield near Wigan, and started work as a pony boy in the mines. He was paid ten pence for a ten-hour day, which was given to him every fortnight. He was an avid reader; the first book he bought was a copy of John Bunyan's *Pilgrim's Progress*. He also became a great fan of the works of Mark Twain, Victor Hugo, and John Stuart Mill, but above all of Shakespeare and Dickens. In later years he would pepper his speeches with literary quotations.

From an early age he was active in trade union affairs, organising the Ashton branch of the Lancashire and Cheshire Miners' Federation. He became chairman of the Wigan Labour Trades Council and was, in 1894, elected as a Labour member of the Ashton-in-Makerfield Council.

He was a trusted trade unionist and was elected as miners' agent and as checkweighman. His mathematical talent made him deft at intricate calculations, and he acquired expertise in wage negotiations. He was also active in the Cooperative Movement, and was made a justice of the peace and deputy lieutenant of Lancashire.

In 1906 Walsh was elected as MP for Ince in Lancashire, sponsored by the Miners' Federation. In the words of Philip Snowden, he was 'the most intellectual of the miners' members'.[58] He was the first of the new Labour intake to make his maiden speech. 'He spoke clearly,' recalled J. R. Clynes, who was present, 'dispassionately and convincingly, with some quotations from Shakespeare and Milton, which must have surprised those uncomprehending Tory Members who had explained with some care that they supposed the new Labour MPs would rant instead of making speeches.'[59] Walsh spoke regularly on mining and industrial issues.

Like many trade unionists – in contrast to the ILP – he supported entry into the Great War and had no time for pacifists. He strongly backed the recruitment campaign and voted for conscription in 1916. He gave support to the war-time coalition and was invited to be parliamentary private secretary to the minister of national service, Neville Chamberlain, whom he served loyally.[60] Walsh argued that in war-time the claims of citizenship went beyond sectional, class, or trade union interests.[61] Lloyd George appointed him a junior minister at the Local Government Board. He was well-respected by his parliamentary colleagues and, in 1922, was elected as vice-chairman of the Parliamentary Labour Party. In the same year he was appointed as vice-president of the Miners' Federation of Great Britain.

He married the daughter of another Lancashire miner, and they had ten children, four boys and six girls. One son was killed in action in 1918.[62] Another became a graduate of Manchester University and of the Sorbonne, and, unlike his father, was able to become a professional teacher.

Ramsay MacDonald had a challenge in finding ministers for the military departments in 1924. So many contenders for high office had opposed or been lukewarm about the war. MacDonald first offered the job to Arthur Henderson, who turned it down. Walsh's record as a 'patriot' made it easy for him to be appointed secretary of state for war. During the Great War he had raised a pioneer battalion in Lancashire.

Among the senior military there was some trepidation about a Labour government; they were conscious of the anti-war rhetoric of the prime minister, Snowden, and others. They need not have worried. Walsh's predecessor in office, the Earl of Derby, who wielded enormous political and social influence in Lancashire, wrote to General Lord Rawlinson, commander-in-chief of the Indian Army. Walsh was, he wrote, 'a very honest, straightforward little miner, whom I have known all my life, and am certain will work most harmoniously with the soldiers'.[63] It was a Lancashire cross-party endorsement.

On his first day in office, he was visited by Field Marshal Frederick Rudolph Lambart, the Earl of Cavan, chief of the Imperial General Staff. Walsh was overawed and rose from his desk.

'My Lord, this is an honour,' he said.

'None of that, Secretary of State,' Cavan replied reassuringly. 'You see that bell on your desk? When you want me you just ring it.'[64]

This does credit to Lord Cavan, who was seen in the army as inefficient, and as out of place in the War Office as 'a nun in a nightclub', as one general said.[65]

There was little scope for implementing socialism in the War Office. One humane measure that was introduced was the reduction in the number of offences for which soldiers were subject to the death penalty.[66]

Although Stephen Walsh took life seriously, he could unbend, and in the Smoking Room of the House of Commons or at a Miners' Club, he could be a most genial raconteur.[67]

His under-secretary was Clement Attlee, a forty-one-year-old former army major and former mayor of Stepney. He was one of the first public school alumni who was not a convert from one of the older parties. Seen as a bit of an enigma by other Labour MPs, he had been critical of the army and of expenditure on armaments in the 1923 Parliament. But he had depths, including a gift for satirical verse. On his appointment, he wrote:

> No more I'll take the platform
> With my comrades tried and true
> And talk for twenty minutes
> To three men and a dog or two
> I've got a government job now
> I've got a government job now
> That sort of thing won't do.[68]

Attlee acquired the reputation of being a master of detail and found Walsh an excellent chief and very popular with the army.[69] Walsh received his Cabinet post, in Attlee's view, because of his 'status in the party'.[70] The other under-secretary was, by contrast, Jack Lawson, a Durham miner. Under Walsh, a friendship was forged between Lawson and Attlee that was to last for the next four decades.

Sidney Webb

Like Ramsay MacDonald, Sidney Webb made a good marriage. Because of the prolific personal output of his wife, Beatrice, we know more about Sidney Webb than any of the other men of 1924. Their marriage was an amazing partnership. They were devoted to work, primarily studies in British social history, trade unions, and local government.

Although G. D. H. Cole sneered at them, saying that they had 'the courage of their obsolescence',[71] the institutions they set up for clearly ideological reasons have endured. George Bernard Shaw, Sidney Webb's oldest friend, called Webb 'the ablest man in England',[72] and Philip Snowden, not always liberal in bestowing compliments, said that his 'power to quickly grasp the bearings of a problem was exceptional'.[73]

Sidney Webb was born in London – off Leicester Square – in 1859. His mother had a hairdresser's business. His father was a keen Liberal and campaigned for John Stuart Mill when he stood for the Westminster constituency in the general election of 1865.[74] He seems to have been somewhat feckless, but he was keen that his three children obtained a good education, which included sending Sidney to France and Switzerland, where he mastered the French and German languages.

After a spell as a clerk in a commercial office, Webb entered the civil service by competitive examination. He first worked as a clerk in the Inland Revenue Department, and then in the Colonial Office, joining at the same time as Sydney Olivier. Webb was also called to the Bar at Gray's Inn and took a Bachelor of Law degree from the University of London. Scholarships, hard work, and application made him an example of what Shaw called a member of the 'intellectual proletariat'.[75] In 1879 Shaw was a twenty-three-year-old music critic and aspiring novelist, and an immigrant to London from lower-middle-class Dublin. Shaw and Webb met that same year, the beginning of a friendship that lasted nearly seventy years. Shaw became an early member of the Fabian Society in 1884, introducing Webb to it the following year. Shaw and Webb started writing pamphlets for the society. Shaw wrote the Fabian manifesto *Tract No. 2*, and Webb wrote the Fabian Tract *Facts for Socialists*, which went through numerous editions in the next half-century.[76]

Webb contributed to the seminal *Fabian Essays in Socialism*, published in 1889, a volume that made socialism if not fashionable, at least a subject of serious discussion in political circles. According to the Fabians, socialist ideas should permeate the whole of society, including the established political parties. As Sidney Webb put it in 1929,

> We put our proposals, one by one, as persuasively as possible before all who would listen to them – Conservatives when we could gain access to them, the churches and chapels of all denominations, the various Universities, and Liberals and radicals, together with the other Socialist Societies at all times.[77]

Over the next forty years Webb did just that.

He married Beatrice Potter in 1892. She was the eighth of nine daughters – one son died in infancy – of a prosperous businessman. Through her sisters she was well connected socially and politically. One sister married a well-to-do Conservative barrister, Alfred Cripps, who became an MP and the father of Stafford Cripps, who served in the War Cabinet of Winston Churchill and was one of Clement Attlee's chancellors of the exchequer. Another married Leonard Courtney, a West Country Liberal MP. Other sisters married men who were successful commercially and socially. Beatrice herself was courted by Joseph Chamberlain and could have been his third wife; she certainly fancied him but was determined to pursue her own career in a way she knew would not be acceptable to the patriarchal Joseph. Beatrice Potter was bright and became interested in social issues in the East End of London and Lancashire. When she met Sidney Webb, she had already published a book on the Cooperative Movement and was committed to researching and writing about unfashionable social matters.

The marriage was mutually advantageous. He argued that, 'One and one, placed in a sufficiently integrated relationship, make not two but eleven.'[78] Beatrice's private income allowed Sidney, who had just retired from the civil service, to pursue his writing and political propaganda work without financial worries. Together they devoted themselves to scholarship, socialism, and each other. Beatrice used to refer to Sidney as 'My boy' – she was eighteen months older than him.[79] Sidney gave Beatrice an emotional anchorage, and together they worked in harmony. She thought she was too old for children – she was thirty-four when they married – and they always had separate bedrooms. They spent their honeymoon in Dublin researching the history of trade unionism in Ireland. Sidney's Fabian contacts, such as Shaw and Graham Wallas, and Beatrice's social world that extended from her family to the Conservative prime minister Arthur Balfour, all came together at the Spartan dinner table at the Webbs' house in Grosvenor Road on the Embankment, not far from the Houses of Parliament. Everyone of social or political importance was included. One young social worker who called on them was unimpressed by the catering standards. 'Seldom', wrote Mary Stocks in her memoirs, 'have such insufficient teas been offered by so few to so many.'[80]

Beatrice Webb had acted as her father's hostess, entertaining the great and the good. She knew how influence could be traded across the dinner table, regardless of the quantity or the quality of the fare.

The two of them acted as a partnership, wielding a profound influence on the Labour movement during and after the Great War. They were often perceived as passionless. Their first biographer, Mary Agnes Hamilton, saw them as basically undemocratic. 'Neither was by temper, instinct, or training democratic. Sidney was a born bureaucrat; Beatrice a born aristocrat.'[81] They almost thought as one mind. Almost, but not quite. They differed on Britain's involvement in the Great War. They resolved their differences by not commenting publicly on the issue.[82]

From her teens to her eighties Beatrice Webb kept a diary, which has been one of the richest sources for information about her circles. She knew everyone of significance in the intellectual and progressive world before, during, and after the Great War. She wrote well and there are unforgettable pen portraits of Herbert

Spencer, Bernard Shaw, H. G. Wells, and Bertrand Russell. She writes frankly of her infatuation with Joseph Chamberlain and her relationship with Sidney Webb. She writes about the political scene in the 1920s, but sometimes her comments on people have to be treated with caution. She got on best with people of her own class, and never appreciated the qualities of some politicians whose roots were outside her upper-middle-class world, such as Arthur Henderson or J. H. Thomas. She patronised the wives of the working-class members of the Cabinet and arranged social gatherings for them. Some preferred to stay in their north-country homes. In her diaries Beatrice was particularly scathing about Ethel Snowden, whom she saw as a social climber with appalling taste in clothes. It was as if, with MacDonald being a widower, she saw Ethel Snowden as a rival for her assumed role as first lady of Labour. She did have a respect for the conscientiousness of the members of the 1924 Cabinet. A fortnight after the formation of the government, the novelist Arnold Bennett met the Webbs taking a constitutional along the Embankment. She said approvingly of them, 'They *do* work. You see they have no silly pleasures.'[83]

In the years before and after the turn of the century, Sidney Webb had little to do with the ILP. He shared their pro-Boer position during the South African War, but he kept his views to himself.[84] He was busy as a progressive member of the new London County Council (LCC), particularly interested in secondary and tertiary education. He was chairman of the London Schools Board and of the Technical Education Board. The powers that had been granted to these boards had been underused. Webb, working with the Liberal MP and future Liberal (and Labour) lord chancellor R. B. Haldane was active in the inspection of secondary schools, and made the LCC secondary education system a model for the whole country. He built on technical higher education and was active – again with Haldane – in the establishment of the Imperial College of Science and Technology, which was inspired by German higher education. Higher education of the social sciences was also professionalised by the foundation, in 1895, with a legacy of £10,000 left to the Fabian Society, of the London School of Economics and Political Science.[85]

In 1899 he was invited by the Liberal Party to stand for the parliamentary constituency of Deptford, without any obligation to pay for any expenses. He declined.[86] He was happier, and probably more effective, in the backroom.

During the 1890s he met Ramsay MacDonald, but they did not get on well personally. Their views on politics, however, were not dissimilar. Both believed that the study of society was a science and just as the human body may be sick and needed science to identify a cure, so social ills should be scientifically diagnosed and a remedy discovered. Poverty was to be abolished, not alleviated. Both were supremely confident that history was on their side. Their view of society was that it resembled a machine that could be monitored and operated from without. A demonstrable example of this approach could be seen in 1919, when the Sankey Commission, which looked at the future of coal mines, recommended that the mining industry be brought under public ownership. Webb, a member of the Commission, saw it as an external instrument to monitor the ownership of a major public enterprise.

By the end of the Great War, relations between MacDonald and Webb had improved and they worked together on gearing the Labour Party up to be a national political party. With his competence in French and German, Webb was useful to the Labour Party's international interests and able to act as interpreter with foreign delegations.[87] Webb was one of the principal authors, along with Arthur Henderson, of the Labour Party manifesto *Labour's War Aims*, which, alongside the document *Labour and the New Social Order*, was an agenda for a Labour government. MacDonald and Webb both prepared for the anticipated post-war general election. Webb was a leading contributor to the devising of the new Labour Party constitution, which extended membership beyond trade unionists and members of specific socialist societies.[88] Clause

Four of the constitution stated the socialist policy of the common ownership of the means of production, distribution, and exchange. This did not mean comprehensive nationalisation, but included co-ownership, cooperative enterprise, and municipalisation of public services. By the end of the war the Labour Party was equipped to be a governing party. This transformation was largely due to MacDonald, Henderson, and Webb.

Webb was a reluctant parliamentarian. He stood unsuccessfully for the London Universities constituency in 1918, but he was more successful in 1922 when he was returned for the Durham mining constituency of Seaham.[89] After this election MacDonald was elected leader, but not with Webb's vote. He may have regretted this, for just over a year later his wife recorded in her diary that 'on the whole he [MacDonald] has done remarkably well – he has altogether surpassed our expectations as a brilliant politician and a competent statesman.'[90]

Webb was not a good House of Commons speaker and was mocked by facetious young Conservative MPs with cries of 'Sit down, Nanny.'[91] He became, however, one of MacDonald's most trusted colleagues, and on the formation of the Labour government was made president of the Board of Trade.

Short but with a huge head and a wide forehead, bearded, and wearing rimless spectacles, Webb never lost his reedy genteel nasal London accent or his unflappability.[92] Beatrice Potter, before she married him, described him brutally as 'an ugly little man with no social position and less means.'[93] She certainly did not marry him for his looks. But, more favourably for her, he was a workaholic, calm, caring, placid, and modest, with an encyclopaedic knowledge.[94]

John Wheatley

John Wheatley, in the words of a former Conservative MP who defected to the Labour Party in 1924, was 'the only man of Lenin quality the English Left ever produced'.[95] (Wheatley was in fact Scottish–Irish.) He was seen as cold, steely, and incisive, a contrast to the emotionalism of his Glaswegian colleagues such as James Maxton. The Conservative Cabinet minister William Joynson-Hicks also saw in him dictatorial tendencies and compared him to Mussolini.[96] On the other hand, the future left-wing Labour MP (and life peer) Fenner Brockway saw him as 'Pickwickian with his pebble-glasses'.[97] And a Liberal MP saw him as 'a sympathetic country solicitor whom the most reticent would be glad to confide their darkest secrets.'[98] Lenin, Mussolini, Mr Pickwick, a country solicitor – Wheatley certainly made an impact in his eight years in the House of Commons. Generally, he was seen as the most effective of MacDonald's 1924 ministers. In fact, although his rhetoric could be uncompromising, in practice he was pragmatic and cautious.[99]

The 1922 general election brought Labour gains in Glasgow. Most of these new Labour MPs spoke the language of revolution. During the war the city had been a centre of strikes and militancy. As prime minister Lloyd George went to the city but was unable to appease the revolutionary spirit, which was strengthened by the inspiration of the Russian Revolution of 1917. The language of socialism in Glasgow was fiery and threatening to the bourgeoisie, who looked at the city in alarm.

On 19 November 1922 the newly elected Glasgow Labour MPs – 'the Clydesiders', as they were dubbed – travelled by train to London together. There was a rousing send-off at St Enoch's station. The surrounding streets were thronged with tens of thousands of supporters. The most charismatic of the Clydesiders was a former schoolteacher, James ('Jimmy') Maxton, gaunt-faced and chain-smoking, with long black hair sweeping to his chin. John Wheatley was, by contrast, 'a fastidious dresser'.[100] Maxton was an avowed admirer of Lenin, whose biography he wrote. There was a real fear of Glasgow soviets being established, which the Clydesiders and their critics saw as harbingers of revolution. John Wheatley was their leader.

The Clydesiders gave their support to their fellow Scot, Ramsay MacDonald, in the election for leadership of the party and, consequently, prime minister in waiting. MacDonald was no revolutionary, but it was important for him to include a left-winger in the Cabinet.

John Wheatley was born in County Waterford, Ireland, in 1869, one of ten children. The family moved to Lanarkshire as part of the large wave of Irish migration into Scotland from the middle of the nineteenth century. Irish immigrants usually had to accept the worst jobs at the lowest wages and to put up with the most basic living conditions. The Irish brought with them their culture, religion, and politics to their new home. Wheatley and four of his siblings were brought up in Braehead, later known as Bargeddie, seven miles east of Glasgow. They lived in a one-roomed house, known as a 'twa faced raw', part of a back-to-back unit of accommodation.[101] The room had recesses in the walls for beds, but no cupboards or storage space. Coal was bought from their employers and stored under one of the beds. Sugar bags took the place of rugs. Water was brought from a communal supply a hundred yards away, and one lavatory supplied the needs of twelve families. It was with a background of such conditions that Wheatley was driven to a hatred of landlordism, leading him to become a pragmatic and effective authority on housing reform.

Wheatley's father was a miner, and John joined him underground, working from the age of thirteen. After ten years or so down the mine, John and his brother, Patrick, set up a retail business, running a grocery shop in Shettleston, an eastern suburb of Glasgow. In 1899 he employed an eleven-year-old boy to run errands. Thirty years later that boy, John McGovern, followed Wheatley as the Independent Labour Party MP for Shettleston.[102] The grocery business lasted until 1901, after which Wheatley started writing for the *Glasgow Observer*. Wheatley always had an entrepreneurial instinct, and combined journalism with acting as a salesman for the paper. He also ran a billiard saloon.[103] His most successful business venture, however, was managing the printing firm Hoxton and Walsh. The company printed promotional material for small businesses, calendars, and Catholic devotional literature. All these activities brought Wheatley in close touch with an extensive public. In 1923 Hoxton and Walsh produced a weekly newspaper, the *Glasgow Eastern Standard*, which survived until 1960.

John Wheatley was the only capitalist entrepreneur among the men of 1924. His secure and successful business allowed Wheatley to get involved in public work. He was first active in the United Irish League (UIL), a radical group pressing for Home Rule in Ireland. The UIL organised lectures and sustained an expatriate Irish culture – music and the Irish language. Wheatley was chairman of the Shettleston branch.

Meanwhile, during the first decade of the century, he became committed to socialism. His belief in socialism was allied to his Catholic faith, both of which, he believed, were collectivist in ideology, committed to the eradication of social injustice. Wheatley founded the Catholic Socialist Society (CSS). He was influenced by an Italian writer, Francesco Nitti, who had written a book in 1891 on Catholic socialism that was translated into English four years later. Wheatley's socialism was also reinforced by his reading of *Merrie England* by Robert Blatchford and by his personal memories and experiences.

He hosted visiting Irish speakers including James Connolly, who combined Christianity and Marxism, and the trade union leader Jim Larkin. The CSS published its own paper, but Wheatley extended his influence by writing for the Scottish ILP journal *Forward*.

Wheatley was a believing and practising Roman Catholic, even refraining from eating meat on Fridays,[104] but his relationship with the local church hierarchy was shaky. He took on the challenge of debating socialism in public with a Jesuit priest in 1907. Two years later the CSS organised a public debate on socialism at the Pavilion Theatre in central Glasgow between Wheatley and Hilaire Belloc, then a Liberal MP.[105] It was only after 1910 that he extended from sectarian politics into mainstream Glasgow socialism, joining allies such as Pat Dollan, Emanuel Shinwell, and James Maxton. But his geographical base was always Shettleston.

In the years before the Great War Wheatley was elected to Lanarkshire County Council. His first act was to demand inspection of the water supplies of Shettleston. Inspection revealed serious health hazards. In 1912 the City of Glasgow boundaries were extended to include Shettleston, and Wheatley duly became a member of the Glasgow City Council, then dominated by the Liberals. Wheatley was soon championing housing and health issues.

He faced some criticism from Catholic priests. One outspoken opponent who denounced him from the pulpit was Father Andrew O'Brien. Wheatley responded in his journalism and vilified pawnbrokers and usurers for their exploitation of the poor and vulnerable. It was well known locally that some of O'Brien's family practised these occupations.[106] In 1912 Father O'Brien condemned socialism and Wheatley by name from the pulpit; Wheatley was in the congregation. Undeterred, he responded in the columns of *Forward* and had copies distributed locally. Father O'Brien, he wrote, poses 'as the friend of God's poor. When God's poor are prepared to act like slaves and sycophants they are flattered, but independence is treated as a deadly sin.'[107] Soon after that a hostile crowd, loyal to Father O'Brien, marched on Wheatley's house singing the Catholic hymn 'Faith of our Fathers'. Wheatley and his wife had gone out for an evening stroll, leaving their children at home with a friend. When they came home the crowd was burning an effigy of him in front of the house. Wheatley, pipe in hand, confronted the crowd and with his wife walked through them. He was unmolested and, indeed, his coolness enhanced his reputation.

Glasgow City Council had extensive authority. From a sumptuous City Hall it managed the city's water, gas, electricity, and telephones. It also ran the tramways on a successful commercial basis. The Public Health Department could arrange for the clearance of slums but had limited power to rebuild. In the council chamber Wheatley drew attention to the privately owned tenement blocks, calling them 'slaughter-houses of the poor'.[108] He advocated the construction of workmen's cottages to be rented at £8 a year. Wheatley proposed a scheme whereby funds would be raised by loans and surpluses from the running of the municipal trams.

Wheatley opposed Britain's engagement in the Great War. He took up the cases of the families of soldiers. The army provided for thousands of the poor men of Glasgow, but the wives and families were often destitute. A soldier's pay was insufficient to meet increased rents, and with the support of many women he organised a Rent Strike in 1915. The scandalous eviction of the families of serving soldiers led to government legislation disallowing rents being raised above pre-war levels.

By the end of the war Wheatley was an experienced political operator. Labour did well in the municipal elections of 1920, and Wheatley became leader of the Labour group in Glasgow. He was familiar with the possibilities for improving housing in the corridors of municipal power. He was well briefed about national legislation and was emerging as the major Labour politician in Glasgow.

He had been selected as the parliamentary candidate for Shettleston in the 1918 general election. His coalition opponent was a rear admiral who supported Lloyd George in his campaign to hold Germany to account for the war. Wheatley concentrated on local issues. The rear admiral won, but four years later Wheatley stood again. He was a meticulous campaigner and coordinated the campaign with other Glasgow ILP candidates, including Maxton, George Buchanan, George Hardie (brother of the late Keir), and the Reverend Campbell Stephen. They regularly ate a meal together – sober, since they were all teetotallers. The rear admiral withdrew at a late stage, and Wheatley faced a National Liberal and a Communist. This time he won comfortably, and Labour did well in the whole of the west of Scotland, winning ten of the eleven Glasgow seats. The eleventh, Glasgow Central, was won by the Conservative leader Andrew Bonar Law.[109] Eight thousand Labour supporters attended the victory rally in St Andrew's Hall.

At Westminster Wheatley was accepted as the leader of the Clydesider MPs, most of whom were younger. He was also better off. While they shared digs, he stayed at the Cosmo Hotel in Southampton Row and travelled to the House of Commons by bus. Morally upright, his only weakness was an occasional flutter on the horses.[110]

Once in Parliament, Wheatley extended his interests. He joined the Commonwealth Group after the French occupation of the German Ruhr. He went there on an ILP visit of inquiry, accompanied by Maxton and David Kirkwood.

Labour was now the official opposition. In his maiden speech, Wheatley spoke about the failure of capitalism to deal with the acute housing crisis. A fiery, even vituperative orator, he nonetheless impressed his hearers by his command of the subject. He had a characteristic manner of speaking. He had a high-pitched voice and used to hold out his left hand, palm uppermost, and strike the open palm periodically with two fingers of the right hand. A colleague observed:

> As the argument develops, the hand moves proportionately quicker, until reaching its climax. The last movement is the most interesting of all. He seems to feel that his opponents are in the hollow of that left hand, and when the last argument is shattered, the two fingers are swished along the open palm with a movement that gives the impression that both opponents and arguments are being swept to the floor and finally disposed of.[111]

Wheatley was comfortably returned to Parliament in the general election of December 1923. The following month Ramsay MacDonald appointed him to the Ministry of Health, which then included issues of housing and local government. He was not MacDonald's first choice. MacDonald had wanted Charles Trevelyan for the post, with Wheatley as under-secretary. But he was unable to overlook the claims of such a vocal group as the Glasgow MPs, even though he was anxious about there being too many Scots in the government.[112] Wheatley's under-secretary was Arthur Greenwood, a future deputy leader of the party. Greenwood was a leading light in a lodge of Freemason Labour MPs, a lodge with the name New Welcome.[113] He chose as his parliamentary private secretary Haden Guest, a medical doctor and former Liberal.

It was a judicious appointment, for Wheatley, of all the Cabinet appointments, was the most professional and best informed about the range of his duties. Like others, he was unhappy about going to Buckingham Palace to receive the seals of office wearing court dress, and got away with wearing a ten-year-old lounge suit.[114] After the audience he told people what he said to King George V: 'Your Majesty, I would never lift a finger to change the country from a capitalist Monarchy to a socialist Republic. Of course, when capitalism goes, the Monarchy will go too. But I hope there will be no ill-feeling on either side.'[115]

So wrote Hugh Dalton, but the king recorded in his diary after the first private meeting: 'Received Mr Wheatley, the Minister of Health. He is an extreme Socialist and comes from Glasgow. I had a very interesting conversation with him.'[116] L. MacNeill Weir, who was MacDonald's parliamentary private secretary in 1924, recorded something of the conversation. The king asked Wheatley why he was a revolutionary. Wheatley told him something of his early years, born and brought up in conditions of the most sordid poverty. He was one of eleven persons who lived, not merely for a month, but for years in a single-roomed house in Lanarkshire. When he was twelve, he was taken from school and sent to work in the coal mines. The king listened with incredulous sympathy, and said later, as Wheatley left, 'I tell you, Mr Wheatley, that, if I had to live in conditions like that, I would be a revolutionary myself.'[117]

Wheatley was also firm in resisting 'the aristocratic embrace' – refusing invitations to upper-class house parties. His wife, who only occasionally came to London, was also immune to these approaches.

She received a letter from a countess, announcing that she would be 'At Home' on Tuesday. Mary Wheatley wrote back, 'I'll also be at home that day, in the family house at Shettleston.' It was suggested to Mrs Wheatley that she should also have informed the countess that Tuesday was washing day in Glasgow.[118]

8

New Labour

Noel Buxton

Noel Buxton was probably the bluest blooded of the men of 1924, with family connections to more members of the peerage than anyone else. But his immediate family was marked by successful business ventures and practical humanitarian activity. One of the Liberal converts to Labour, he was conscious that he was the great grandson of Sir Thomas Fowell Buxton, 'the Liberator', successor of William Wilberforce in the campaign for the emancipation of slaves. The family tradition was Evangelical and Liberal. A great, great aunt was Elizabeth Fry, the prison reformer; a cousin was Conrad Noel, the 'Red Vicar' of Thaxted in Essex. More immediately, his family owned and managed a large brewery in Spitalfields in the East End of London.

Born in 1869, Noel Buxton spent most of his childhood at the family estate in south-west Essex and was educated – like Stanley Baldwin – at Harrow and Trinity College, Cambridge. In 1889 he went to work at the family brewery, combining that with social work. In his early manhood he was influenced by a Christian commitment of social responsibility. In the early 1890s, he was hosted by Beatrice and Sidney Webb, through whom he made further contacts in progressive London.[1] At the end of the century he was a contributor to a collection of essays on progressive political issues, *The Heart of the Empire*, written by a number of young men from well-to-do families, many with a Cambridge connection – G. P. Gooch, G. M. Trevelyan, and F. W. Pethick-Lawrence (later Lord Pethick-Lawrence, a Labour peer).[2] In 1904 he stood unsuccessfully as a Progressive for the London County Council. He also had an interest in and a curiosity about the world beyond Britain. His wealthy family background enabled him in his early manhood to travel extensively to New Zealand and Japan, and also to the Balkans. Here he became absorbed in the affairs of the Christian nations and their liberation from the Ottoman Empire. This launched a concern that lasted for the rest of his life. In this cause, he saw himself as carrying on the tradition of W. E. Gladstone's campaign against the Bulgarian atrocities committed by the Turks in the 1870s.

He was elected Liberal MP for Whitby at a by-election in 1905 but lost the seat in the general election the following year. He spent the time after his defeat undertaking more travel in the Balkans. He was re-elected to Parliament for the more familiar territory of North Norfolk in the general election of December 1910. He soon became recognised as an expert in Balkan politics and ethnography, particularly of Bulgaria and Macedonia. Bulgaria had been partly liberated from Turkish control but Macedonia, a hotch-potch of different communities, was still part of the Ottoman Empire. Hopes for liberation were raised by the Young Turk Revolution of 1908, which had been led by army officers many of whom had been serving in Macedonia. But the hopes of Noel Buxton were dashed. During this time the Balkan Committee was founded, aimed at the liberation of the Christians in Ottoman Europe. It drew its support from radical Liberal MPs and progressive journalists. Its president was the veteran Liberal statesman and historian James Bryce.

Buxton's constituency after 1910, North Norfolk, was largely rural. This was a county where agricultural trade unionism developed. Joseph Arch, the radical organiser of farmworkers, had been a Norfolk MP, and Noel Buxton got to know his successor as general secretary of the National Union of Agricultural Workers, George

Edwards – a Norfolk man and, like Arch, a Primitive Methodist. He became a well-informed student of agrarian politics.

In Parliament, by contrast, Buxton became chairman of the Liberal Foreign Affairs Group. The vice-chairman was Arthur Ponsonby. They were joined by Ramsay MacDonald in submitting a memorandum to the foreign secretary, Sir Edward Grey, about his alleged hostility to Germany.

The attempt to lower the diplomatic temperature was unsuccessful. When war broke out, Buxton supported it, hoping for an early victory. The government – and particularly the first lord of the Admiralty, Winston Churchill – made use of his expertise in Balkan affairs and his closeness to the Bulgarian government to send him to the Bulgarian capital, Sofia, to persuade the country to repudiate its neutrality and to join Britain and her allies. He went, accompanied by his younger brother, Charles Roden Buxton. They felt they were hampered in their mission by being unable to offer any specific inducement from the British government.[3]

From Sofia they travelled to the capital of Romania, Bucharest. There an attempt was made to assassinate them. Noel Buxton was shot in the chin by a Young Turk and spent a month in a Bucharest hospital. For the rest of his life he sported a beard to conceal disfigurement caused by the injury.[4]

Overall his mission failed. Lack of Balkan interstate unity was such that Bulgaria allied itself with Germany and Turkey rather than with Serbia and Britain. Buxton attributed the alignment with Germany to the influence of King Ferdinand I of Bulgaria, himself a Saxe-Coburg, who was known for his sympathies with his German compatriots.

As the war went on and there was no early victory, Buxton campaigned for a negotiated peace. He worked with other Liberals such as Charles Trevelyan and Hastings Lees-Smith (both of whom later switched to Labour), as well as Ramsay MacDonald. Gradually and inexorably, Buxton's own political sympathies shifted towards the Labour Party, and in the general election of 1918 he stood as

'Liberal–Labour'. The election campaign had roused popular feeling against Germany, and to be seen as 'pro-German', as Buxton was, was an electoral liability. Like many who had been either opposed to or detached about the war, or did not share popular enthusiasm for Lloyd George, he lost his seat.

The move to Labour, he wrote, 'was an alarming plunge, being regarded by one's relations and friends as a betrayal, and I hesitated long'. But, he argued, 'Radicalism and Labour have the same views on Free Trade, Conscription, the campaign against Public Waste and Profiteering, Ireland, and Russia. The supposed antagonism between the Parties is fiction.'[5]

By the time of the general election in 1922, he had joined the Labour Party. He thought doing so was an 'extreme action', but he followed the example of his younger brother, Charles.[6] He stood as a Labour candidate for his former Norfolk constituency and won it back.

Buxton had known and admired Ramsay MacDonald for fifteen years or so. He had a genuine personal affection for the man. In 1920 they had travelled to Germany together. Hotel accommodation was in short supply, and they shared a room in Berlin. 'I was for the first time made aware of the extent of his industry. About six in the morning he was already dressed and writing at the table.'[7] He noted how MacDonald resumed friendships with German socialists whom he had known before the war. For Buxton, MacDonald was 'magnificently athletic' and had a 'cool nerve'.

When the Labour government was formed, Buxton hoped that his expertise would qualify him to be foreign or colonial secretary. He was disappointed, and instead was given the Ministry of Agriculture, for which he was also qualified. There were not many Labour MPs who represented rural constituencies, and his friendship with George Edwards was an asset.[8]

As minister in a minority government his room for manoeuvre was limited, but he did introduce county Agricultural Wages Boards, which were designed to raise and standardise the wages of farm labourers. He also prepared a Bill to nationalise land, which he argued would benefit all who worked on farms. Most farmers were tenants-at-will, their tenure dependent on the will of large landowners. State ownership would guarantee the farmers' security. For the farm labourers it would make no difference.

He had a commanding presence. 'Tall and distinguished-looking with a long lugubrious face and pointed beard',[9] he must have stood out at party meetings and conferences. Beatrice Webb thought he was a 'charming gentleman, but mediocre in intellectual calibre'.[10] But he was loyal to his adopted party.

Viscount Chelmsford

Frederic John Napier Thesiger, the third Baron and first Viscount Chelmsford, was the most improbable Labour minister. There had been no consultation with senior Labour colleagues, and his appointment came as a surprise to observers of the political scene. It was also received with disbelief and scepticism by the bulk of Labour loyalists. Chelmsford was described by Lord Curzon as 'an orthodox pillar of Conservatism',[11] and had been chairman of the Dorsetshire Conservative Association. He had an impeccably establishment background. His grandfather had been lord chancellor in the Earl of Derby's Conservative governments. The family connection with the county town of Essex was tenuous. The first baron's reputation as a lawyer was based on a successful action at the Chelmsford assizes.

Our Lord Chelmsford was educated at Winchester and Magdalen College, Oxford, where he got a first-class degree as well as a Blue for cricket. He represented the university at cricket and also played for Middlesex. He was a fellow of All Souls, Oxford. He had been an imperial public servant, serving as governor first of Queensland and then of New South Wales. After a break in London, he was appointed in 1916 to the grandest of imperial posts, viceroy of India.

As viceroy he steered a path between liberalism and the upholding of British authority. The secretary of state for India, Edwin Montagu, visited India and the two worked out a policy of increasing delegated powers to Indian institutions. This policy became known as the Montagu–Chelmsford Reforms. At the same time, he introduced repressive measures against what was seen as nationalist agitation. These measures were used by General Dyer to suppress a gathering of Sikhs at the Jallianwala Bagh Temple in Amritsar. Soldiers fired on the Sikhs, leading to the killing of 379 people and the wounding of over a thousand. At first the viceroy gave his support, but when the details of the outrage became clear, he censured the measure and disciplined Dyer.

Chelmsford's imperial career led to him being knighted no fewer than four times. Some of the titles went with the job of being viceroy, but by the time he joined the first Labour government, he was a knight grand commander of the Order of the Indian Empire (GCIE), a knight grand cross of the Order of the Star of India (GCSI), a knight grand cross of the Order of St Michael and St George (GCMG), and a knight grand cross of the Order of the British Empire (GBE).

Sir Edwin Lutyens's design of New Delhi was still under construction when Chelmsford's nephew, the future Arabian explorer Wilfred Thesiger, then aged seven, came to visit India with his parents. 'From the moment I arrived,' that nephew recalled, 'I was immensely impressed by the pomp and the ceremony which surrounded my uncle as Viceroy, fascinated by the splendour of the bodyguard, and the varied liveries of the doorkeepers, messengers, coachmen, household servants and other functionaries.'[12] When he met him later as an undergraduate at Oxford he found his 'uncle Fred' an 'austere and impressive figure'.[13] His looks were as aristocratic as his pedigree. He married a first cousin of Winston Churchill.

Yet there were one or two indications in his CV that suggested that he was not a knee-jerk Tory. At the beginning of the century, as the Honourable Frederic Thesiger, he had been a London county councillor, serving as a Moderate, which meant Conservative, but he interested himself in public education and was on the London Schools' Board along with Sidney Webb, who had a high regard for him. (Beatrice referred to him as 'a good fellow but a timid Conservative.'[14]) He was entertained by the Webbs, meeting George Bernard Shaw.[15] And in December 1923 he was chairman of an Oxford delegation visiting Cambridge, where he made a speech calling for endowments for the poor. 'Quite a Labour speech!' observed a future Labour chancellor of the exchequer who was present.[16]

Moreover, when he was governor of New South Wales he helped the local Labour Party to take power there in 1912. If not one of them, he knew how to work with socialists.

Above all he was imbued with a sense of public service. The Labour government in 1924 was legitimate and badly needed support in the House of Lords in order to function effectively in the bicameral parliamentary system. Chelmsford explained his position in the House of Lords in February 1924. He had negotiated his role with Ramsay MacDonald.

> I came in not as one who took the Labour label, but as one detached from politics, who was prepared, as a colleague, to help to carry on the King's Government on a disclosed programme ... It was distinctly understood between ourselves that, if occasion arose where I was unable to follow the politics of the present Government, it would be regarded as fair on both sides that I should give in my resignation.[17]

The occasion never arose.

The post of first lord of the Admiralty, in charge of the Royal Navy, the 'senior service', was normally given to someone with private means. Admiralty House, a very stately home in Whitehall that went with the post, required the occupant to pay for the domestic staff who maintained it.

It seems likely that Lord Haldane suggested Chelmsford's name to MacDonald. Haldane had known Chelmsford in the House of Lords and was familiar with his progressive educational attitudes on the London Schools' Board, as was Sidney Webb.

But his appointment was 'the greatest surprise' and was kept a secret from most colleagues until it was announced.[18] Chelmsford's appointment created helpless astonishment in the House of Lords, but he was more acceptable to the first sea lord, Lord Beatty, who had contemplated resignation rather than take orders from trade union appointees or 'socialist agitators'.[19] Lord Beatty need not have worried. Chelmsford accepted the post on the condition that there would be no reduction on naval expenditure, and that the air force would be supported to keep pace with that of the French.[20]

The Admiralty's spokesman in the House of Commons was Frank Hodges, who was civil lord of the Admiralty. He was a trade union leader of the South Welsh miners, a very different personality. Hodges was an intellectual, a fluent French speaker, a Primitive Methodist, and had been secretary general of the Miners' Federation in his thirties. As a union leader he had proved himself not only very able but also good at compromising. J. H. Thomas thought he was 'much too sensitive of nature to withstand the turmoil of political battle'.[21]

Viscount Haldane

It is not easy to pigeon-hole Labour's first lord chancellor, the first and last Viscount Haldane. He was a former senior Liberal Cabinet minister and had been a close friend of prime minister H. H. Asquith since the 1880s. But his career trajectory had differed from those Liberals who switched to Labour during and immediately after the Great War. It may have been a matter of generation. Haldane was born in 1856, the three principal Liberal converts – Buxton, Trevelyan, and Wedgwood – were born respectively in 1869, 1870, and 1872. Nor was he a conventional toff. He came from a conservative, prosperous Scottish background, both landed and professional, did not attend a major English public school, and had a reputation as a philosopher and lawyer. He was a most energetic public servant with a wide range of interests. An elderly bachelor in 1924, he had been dumped in his thirties by a girl, Valerie Munro-Ferguson, whose memory he cherished for the rest of his life. She was less charitable, and lampooned him in novels before she died, still quite young.[22]

Richard Burdon Haldane was brought up in Edinburgh and Perthshire, and in his teens studied in Germany where he developed a passion for German philosophy, literature, and culture. He co-translated the works of Spinoza and wrote a short study of the eighteenth-century Scottish economist Adam Smith. As a 'rising young lawyer',[23] he entered Parliament in 1885 as a Liberal MP when Ramsay MacDonald was still a teenager. He fell under the influence of another bookish Liberal, John Morley,[24] but, unlike Morley, saw himself as a Liberal imperialist, and supported the Boer War. In 1905 he was made secretary of state for war. He was a reforming minister, establishing an expeditionary force that could be rapidly mobilised to serve on the continent. He was made a Viscount in early 1911 and the following year became lord chancellor.

Haldane was a fluent German speaker. On the outbreak of the Great War, Asquith was secretary of state for war and for a few days Haldane took over those duties while Asquith concentrated on overall management of strategy, before the appointment to that post of Lord Kitchener. For the next year some of the Conservative press launched a vituperative personal campaign against Haldane, alleging that he sympathised with the German enemy, even suggesting that he had delayed the despatch of the Expeditionary Force in the first weekend of the war. When the Conservatives joined the Asquith coalition in May 1915 government, one of their conditions was that Haldane be dismissed. Their other demand was the removal of the first lord of the Admiralty, Winston Churchill, from a central role in the management of the war. It has been generally recognised that Churchill at the Admiralty and Haldane at the War Office had brought Britain's defences to a high level of preparedness. The Conservatives' demands did not endear them to Haldane.

From the 1890s Haldane had been a great campaigner for the extension of higher education with an emphasis on science and technology, a programme that he had derived from his experience of modern Germany. He was active in supporting efforts to build up universities in the provincial cities, with close links to industry. Education, he believed, should be for everybody, inclusive of not just technical and vocational subjects but also the humanities. This activism brought him in touch with Fabian socialists such as Sidney and Beatrice Webb.[25] Indeed he was one of the first to know about their engagement, before it was formally announced.[26] At the same time he worked with sympathetic Conservatives such as Arthur Balfour.

For the socialists and for Haldane, the campaign for a more widely available education system was a political issue, with the aim of improving the lot of the working classes. With Sidney Webb, Haldane was one of the founders of the Imperial College of Science and Technology in the University of London.[27] Webb was at that time chairman of the Technical Education Board of the London County Council.[28]

During and immediately after the Great War, Haldane's enthusiasm for public education brought him into contact with a younger generation of socialists, such as R. H. Tawney, G. D. H. Cole, Harold Laski, and Barbara Wootton, all four of whom had a profound influence on Labour Party thinking before the Second World War. Haldane's political ideas, like his philosophical ideas, had been influenced by his time in Germany. He accepted the idea of state regulation for the public good.[29] He felt detached from the older political parties, who were disdainful of political ideas and showed very little interest in public education. By the early 1920s neither wing of the Liberal Party was concerned with education, and Haldane was led to a natural sympathy with the Labour Party. By 1922 he was speaking at Labour meetings, and openly supported some Labour policies, such as the nationalisation of the coal industry.

He had known Ramsay MacDonald since the 1906 Parliament. The Kaiser Wilhelm visited England in 1907. Haldane hosted a luncheon party for him at his grand house in Queen Anne's Gate, described by the Kaiser as a 'doll's house'. The Kaiser wanted to meet people he did not normally meet, and one of the guests was Ramsay MacDonald.[30]

In December 1923, after the results of the general election indicated the probability of a Labour government, MacDonald stopped off at Haldane's home in Perthshire to discuss Cabinet appointments. There were few possible candidates for the post of Labour lord chancellor. Labour had few friends in the legal profession, and Haldane was a reassuring figure when MacDonald gave him the post.

Haldane had a high regard for MacDonald as prime minister. He 'managed his Cabinet very well,' Haldane wrote in his memoirs. MacDonald 'always read his papers and knew the points. He had a quick but not a profound mind.'[31] His respect extended to the Old Labour members of the Cabinet, who 'worked hard and came prepared. Nor were they lengthy in speech ... They made their points briefly and forcibly, trained to do so by Trade Union discipline.'[32] He persuaded MacDonald that Cabinet ministers refer to each other not by the office they held but by their surnames.[33]

Haldane had a curiosity about people and was always a genial host. He had a dry sense of humour. On one occasion, Winston Churchill, who was fond of him, prodded Haldane's portly corporation.[34]

'What is in there, Haldane?' Churchill asked.

'If it is a boy, I shall call him John. If it is a girl, I shall call her Mary. But if it is only wind, I shall call it Winston.'[35]

He had known everyone of significance in the previous forty years, and, as his fellow lawyer and lord chancellor Lord Birkenhead put it, could be 'occasionally somewhat reminiscent'.[36] Was this a polite way of suggesting that he could at times be a garrulous and monumental bore? Snowden thought he was 'a man of extraordinary capacity, one of the most powerful intellects I have ever known.'[37] He enjoyed entertaining people and was, in Beatrice Webb's words, 'a Herculean eater'.[38] He was also a heavy smoker and took little exercise, becoming prematurely stout and pasty.[39] His appearance, it has been said, would have reminded one of a prize fighter but for a certain gentleness. The Conservative politician Leo Amery recoded that his appearance and manner had something of an old-fashioned family butler.[40]

Haldane's ability to get on with people and his wish to be in the know made him suspect to the more tribal Labour politician. He maintained good personal relations with leading Conservatives such as Baldwin and Lord Birkenhead. The only person who was unable to get on with him was the saintly Lord Parmoor. In return, Haldane treated Parmoor with 'a kindly contempt'.[41]

Lord Parmoor

Lord Parmoor, like Viscount Chelmsford, had a past in the Conservative Party.

Born in 1852, Charles Alfred Cripps was the son of a leading QC and ecclesiastical lawyer. He was educated at Winchester and New College, Oxford. At Winchester he showed his force of personality when the headmaster doubted his word. Cripps objected and demanded an apology. With support from his father, he obtained it.[42] At Oxford he played football for the university team.[43] He went into the legal profession and, when appointed, was the youngest Queen's Counsel in the land.[44] He was three weeks younger than H. H. Asquith, who took silk at the same time. Another contemporary was a young Scottish Liberal, Richard Burdon Haldane.

Charles Cripps became Unionist (Conservative) MP for Stroud from 1895 to 1900, for Stretford, Lancashire, from 1901 to 1906, and for South Buckinghamshire from 1910. He was a free trader and said he stood for 'the union and co-operation of all classes, for the union of the Empire and Kingdom, and let them all be Patriots and Imperialists.'[45] A High Anglican, he was active in the politics of Church of England reform and was the first chairman of the church's House of Laity.

Prime Minister Asquith appointed him a member of the Judicial Committee of the Privy Council. He was elevated to the peerage in 1914, taking his title, Parmoor, from his Buckinghamshire estate. Not a very promising background for a future Labour minister.

Before the Great War he seemed to enjoy his success without much thought for the rest of the world. 'He delights in the freedom of the successful man', his sister-in-law tartly observed, 'to spend all he chooses on his own and his children's pleasures.'[46]

But there were hints of divergence from his privileged High Church Tory position at the heart of the Establishment, hints that accumulated during the Great War. He had a conscience and was 'wholly opposed to the declaration of war'.[47] He thought there was an 'essential inconsistency between Christian ethics and a policy based on war and force.'[48] He also felt strongly about the importance of universal free education, and reacted against Conservative values that were 'afraid of a new policy founded not on the profit of capitalism, but to encourage a general improvement of all classes in the country'. He opposed compulsory conscription and campaigned for civil rights.[49] The horrors of the war turned him into 'something like an international socialist', observed Beatrice Webb.[50] He took part in international Christian efforts to work for peace, aiming to build up a 'universal Christian conscience'.[51] He was an advocate of a League of Nations that should emphasise 'the substitution of justice for force' but also 'the restoration of science to its higher purpose of improving our control over the forces of Nature, in support of a more highly moralised civilisation'.[52] (The reference to science is interesting, for his son, Stafford, before he became a lawyer, studied chemistry at University College London – unusual for someone of his class.) After the Great War Parmoor was active in famine relief in Europe, and he campaigned for disarmament and the rights of refugees.

His views were shifting towards those of the Labour Party, but it took time before he got to know members of the party. In 1922 he took the chair at an International Peace Congress at Central Hall Westminster. One of the speakers was J. R. Clynes.[53] He had occasionally met Ramsay MacDonald before 1924 and had 'admired him as a parliamentarian, and as a leader of the Labour Party in the House of Commons'.[54]

His first wife and the mother of his five children, Theresa, was the sister of Beatrice Webb. Even when there had been political differences, he and the Webbs always got on well. Beatrice Webb thought he was cerebral, but he 'is not a leader of men', she wrote in her diary. 'His opinions do not represent the *desires* of the masses; they are the result of an attempt to deduce laws of government from certain first principles of morality.'[55] Theresa died in 1893, and he married again in 1919 to Marian, twenty-six years his junior, the daughter of a Quaker Liberal MP. She was very active in a wide range of philanthropic activity.

It was on Christmas Day 1923 that Parmoor received a letter from Ramsay MacDonald inviting him to join his government. He agreed on the condition that the government carry out 'their declared international policy of peace, arbitration and disarmament'.[56]

He was appointed lord president of the council in January 1924. In this capacity, he was ready to get his hands dirty with socialist-inspired legislation and introduced in the Lords the Minimum Wage for Agricultural Labour Bill.[57] He was a House of Lords spokesman; he and Haldane worked together, despite temperamental differences, to ensure the smooth running of government business in the House of Lords.

MacDonald also gave him responsibility for League of Nations affairs. He was allocated an office in the Foreign Office for himself and his private secretary, Philip Noel Baker. But he was not made to feel at home. 'The welcome was not cordial. I soon found that I was regarded as a cuckoo in the nest, or as a strange animal who had found his way within a sacred enclosure.'[58] However, he worked well with the prime minister, who was doubling as foreign secretary. Parmoor thought him 'dignified and impressive. He is, perhaps, somewhat in love with himself, and too much inclined towards self-pity.'[59] But together they worked on the draft of the Geneva Protocol, which could have been one of the successes of the 1924 government.

Among his sisters-in-law he was nicknamed Chin-Chin. He was, in the words of Beatrice Webb, 'a short man with broad shoulders, clear-cut features and imposing chin.'[60]

At seventy-two he was the oldest man in the Cabinet.

Lord Thomson

Christopher Birdwood Thomson, known to his friends as CB and to his family as Kit, was born in Nasik in the region of Bombay/Mumbai in India in 1875. He came from a military family. His father was a major-general who had twelve children with two successive wives. When the family moved to England, near Cheltenham, he delegated to his second wife the responsibilities of childcare and retired himself to Italy.[61] Thomson was educated at Cheltenham College and joined the Royal Engineers, receiving training at Woolwich and Chatham. At the latter he became instructor in fortifications. He saw service in South Africa, and afterwards was at the War Office, London.

He was fluent in French and loved the language. This equipped him for a diplomatic career, and he served as military attaché at the Serbian capital of Belgrade during the Balkan Wars of 1912 and 1913. On one occasion he was following the Serbian army to Salonika (now Thessaloniki in Greece), accompanied by the Italian military attaché, when a visitor called. A business card was presented. The Italian attaché became apoplectic. There were two kinds of people he could not stand: journalists and socialists. The visitor was the editor of an Italian socialist newspaper. Thomson took the card, which read 'BENITO MUSSOLINI, Editor-in-Chief, *Avanti*'. The two men met and got on well.[62]

When the Great War broke out, Thomson was appointed the official interpreter between Sir John French and Marshall Joffre, respectively the British and French military commanders. His interest and expertise in Balkan politics, however, made him, in terms of Great War strategy, an 'easterner', one believing that the Central Powers – Germany and Austria–Hungary – were vulnerable from the east, along the river Danube. This was part of the thinking behind the Dardanelles campaign, which had the objective of knocking the Ottoman Empire out of the war, wooing Romania and Bulgaria, initially neutral, and securing them on the side of the Allies. Thomson was sent to the Romanian capital, Bucharest, in early 1915 to achieve that support. He succeeded only too well. For as he got to know Romania, he realised that the country was too weak to be a military asset. Against his better judgement, he signed the country up as a belligerent. Romania faced invasion from the Central Powers, and Thomson had the task of arranging the destruction of Romanian oil wells to prevent them from falling into the German hands.

Thomson arrived in Bucharest only a few months after the attempted assassination there of his future 1924 colleague Noel Buxton. He was entranced by Romania, travelling around Bucharest and the Danube valley. After the war he wrote an affectionate account of his experiences in *Old Europe's Suicide.* In Bucharest he met Princess Marthe Bibesco, who became an intimate friend for the rest of his life. She was the daughter of a Romanian minister of foreign affairs who had been the Romanian envoy in Paris. As a girl, Marthe was brought up to be fluent in French and soaked in French culture. While still in her teens she was married to a Romanian aristocrat, Prince George Bibesco, who was more interested in fast cars and fast women than in her. But she also played the field and had very close friends, among whom was Thomson. It was believed that they were lovers.[63] They certainly corresponded for the next fifteen years and, after his death, she wrote a memoir of him.

Thanks to Prince George, Marthe had her own stately home in northern Bucharest, where Thomson was a frequent guest.

In the latter years of the war he joined General Sir Edmund Allenby in Palestine. His battalion took Jericho from the Ottomans, and he participated in the siege of Jerusalem in the autumn of 1917. He ended the war with the rank of brigadier-general and a Distinguished Service Order (DSO) medal.

After the war Thomson was part of a military delegation at the Versailles peace talks, but – as at Bucharest – he found himself at odds with British policy. He thought the terms of the peace imposed on Germany sowed the seeds of a future war.

After Versailles, Thomson left the army and decided to go into politics. Perhaps persuaded by their stand against Versailles, he joined the Labour Party and the Fabian Society.

In 1921 he was given another international mission. The Red Cross asked him to travel to Eastern Europe and to report on the refugee situation. This took him back to Belgrade, to Constantinople/Istanbul, and to Moscow where he had a meeting with the Bolshevik leader, Lenin, at his country house outside the new capital of Moscow. His impression of Lenin was that of a bloated man, overworked and unwell, and 'henpecked' by his wife, his sister, and his niece.[64] Few in Britain in the early 1920s could claim to have met both Mussolini and Lenin.

Initially he had no close friends in the Labour Party and knew none of the leaders. But he worked his passage in the movement, fighting in a by-election at Bristol and in the 1923 general election at St Albans, although he failed to get elected in both constituencies.

He then met Ramsay MacDonald, and the two men hit it off immediately. MacDonald had a good knowledge of European politics, but Thomson's expertise and experience supplemented that. Thomson was a tyro in Labour politics and posed no threat to MacDonald. He was an affable man, joining the ranks of MacDonald's new middle-class friends, and a versatile conversationalist who antagonised no one; he 'interested and amused us all'.[65] Yet, in spite of his friendship with MacDonald, he could, according to Beatrice Webb, often seem to run him down.[66]

Thomson was a guest of MacDonald at his Lossiemouth retreat in the weeks before the formation of the 1924 government. MacDonald invited him to be secretary of state for air, with a peerage. At forty-nine, Thomson was the youngest of the men of 1924.

MacDonald was, at this stage, unwilling to create hereditary peers, and as Thomson was a bachelor, a peerage would die with him. He thought carefully about the title to take, especially the territorial association. He wanted a link to the development of the aircraft industry, toying with the idea of being Lord Thomson of Croydon or Lord Thomson of Hendon, before settling on the euphonious Lord Thomson of Cardington. This was the Bedfordshire airfield where airships were researched and manufactured. It was from here six years later that Thomson, as air minister in MacDonald's second government, set off on the Airship R101. It flew over northern France and caught alight, crashing near Beauvais and killing most on board. There was an irony in the fact that the airship was on its way to India, land of Thomson's birth.

On becoming a minister, Thomson requested William Leach to be appointed as his under-secretary – he would be his spokesman in the House of Commons. Thomson wanted a businessman to assist him in negotiating commercial contracts.[67] Leach was a pacifist in the Great War, a fact that raised some eyebrows: how could a pacifist represent the Royal Air Force? This did not worry Thomson; his experiences had not encouraged him to think that war was an effective solution to international disputes.

Leach was a prominent ILP figure in Bradford, providing a balance to the more politically detached general. He was a prosperous West Riding clothing manufacturer who had once given a job to Fred Jowett. With his wife, Martha, Leach had entertained at his hospitable mansion many leading Labour figures such as MacDonald and Snowden. He had management skills, having been chairman of Bradford City Council. Short in stature, he had a 'bald egg-shaped head, sharply cocked eyebrows, and a deceiving look of innocent inquiry'.[68] As well as being opposed to the war, he espoused what were then progressive and alternative causes such as anti-vivisection and anti-vaccination, which was then a radical cause (there was a suspicion of the motives of middle-class doctors wanting to vaccinate the working class). But he was a resourceful campaigner, having the idea of acquiring cinemas on Sundays for political meetings.

Charles Trevelyan

The Trevelyans, Beatrice Webb unkindly remarked, were 'one of the oldest English families, distinguished for their lack of distinction and for their luck in marrying heiresses'.[69] The first of her assessments was not true, at least not from the mid-nineteenth century. Charles Trevelyan's grandfather, also Charles, was one of the creators of the modern civil service; this Charles married a sister of the historian Thomas Babington Macaulay. His son, our Charles's father, Sir George Otto Trevelyan, 2nd Baronet, was a statesman scholar, the biographer of Macaulay, and a historian of the American Revolution. He served in the Cabinets of Gladstone and Rosebery, wobbled over Gladstone's first Home Rule Bill for Ireland in 1886, and was briefly a Liberal Unionist. Charles's brother, George Macaulay Trevelyan, was the outstanding Liberal historian of his generation. As for the successful marriages, these led the Trevelyans to move from their original home of Cornwall to Wallington, a large estate in Northumberland.

Charles Trevelyan, the heir to the baronetcy, was born in 1870 and was educated, like Noel Buxton (and Stanley Baldwin), at Harrow and Trinity College, Cambridge. He stood as Liberal candidate in Lambeth in the general election of 1895, but he was more successful at a by-election in the Elland constituency of Yorkshire in 1899. He held this seat until 1918. In Parliament he identified with the radical wing of the Liberal Party, supporting a graduated income tax and a tax on land values. He attended meetings of the Fabian Society, and was inspired – like contemporary socialists – by the writings of John Ruskin. He was a member of a gathering of London-based radicals called the Rainbow Circle. Ramsay MacDonald was also a member of this discussion group.

Trevelyan was interested in educational reform and served – with Sidney Webb and the future Lord Chelmsford – on the London Schools Board, to which he was co-opted. During the 1890s he was close to the Webbs and indeed accompanied them on their world tour in 1898. Beatrice Webb found him good-looking, with a happy temperament, amiable and easy going, perhaps too much so, for 'he only needs real capacity for work and a dash of talent to make him a considerable politician.'[70] He was also, in spite of his presumed wealth, very slow to put his hand in his pocket to pay for incidental expenses.[71] In his defence, it must be remembered that he was totally dependent on his father for funds.

When the Liberals came to power in 1905, Trevelyan was not offered a place in the government. He was also overlooked when H. H. Asquith replaced Campbell-Bannerman as prime minister in April 1908. This lack of preferment provoked Trevelyan's father, Sir George, to write angrily to Asquith:

> Since our party came in, full recognition has been given to past services of those who, in the old days, served the country and the cause, by the employment of their sons and relatives who were worthy of a chance in the career of administration. Now that several young men have been placed in office, while my son is left out, I must protest, once for all, that I feel the exception made in our case very deeply.[72]

The protest appears to have had an impact, for, later in the year, Trevelyan was appointed under-secretary at the Board of Education where he worked hard to extend non-denominational religious education.

He opposed Britain's entry into the Great War and resigned from the government in August 1914. He felt bitter against the foreign secretary, Sir Edward Grey (whose social base was also in the north-east of England), for concealing agreements with France that committed the country to war.

He became associated with those Liberal and Labour MPs who had opposed the war. His brother, the historian, disagreed. Charles was a founder member of the pacifist National Peace Council, and worked with Ramsay MacDonald, Norman Angell, E. D. Morel, and Bertrand Russell in the Union for Democratic Control. When the Russian Tsarist regime was overthrown in March 1917, Trevelyan rejoiced. He had long campaigned against the oppressions of the old regime. Any alternative was bound to be an improvement.

In the general election of 1918 he defended his parliamentary seat at Elland. Although he had in fact joined the Independent Labour Party the previous month, he stood as an Independent. To add to the confusion, there was also an official Labour candidate. Like so many of those who had opposed the war, he lost his seat.

Three years later, in 1921, he published *From Liberalism to Labour*, which chronicled his switch in allegiance. It is an angry book. The outbreak of war in 1914 had shown up the moral and political bankruptcy of the old order of the ruling classes in Europe. Trevelyan believed that liberalism had not only been drawn into an alliance with 'Reaction', but had pursued illiberal policies. As he wrote in his book:

> [By] the end of the war Liberalism as a political force had ceased to exist ... By the Defence of the Realm Act, passed in the panic atmosphere of the first few days of the war, all safeguards for the citizen against arbitrary imprisonment by the Executive disappeared. Freedom of the Press and freedom of speech became solely a question of Government toleration. Opinions obnoxious to the Government were visited with fine and imprisonment. Criticism of the refusal to negotiate became criminal for people

> in humble station. To speak against conscription became a more dangerous offence than showing lights on the coast.[73]

The Irish Home Rule had been suspended to appease Conservatives 'whose patriotism could not have tolerated Home Rule even to secure a united Empire'.[74] And illiberalism triumphed not only at home.

> Britain becomes the central champion of the fight against all new Socialist Republics. Ireland is crushed under a military rule more scientific, and at least as ruthless as that of Austria in Italy. Savage laws are sanctioned to repress reformers in India. At home the army is prepared as the instrument of capitalism to crush strikes. The British Government takes up the discarded practices of the Tsar's tyranny, and spies and *agents provocateurs* are organised by the Government to combat political and industrial agitation.[75]

The Labour Party, he thought, was the hope of the future. He makes several observations about the exceptional nature of Labour and Socialist politics. The traditional parties relied on leaders to initiate policy. In the Labour movement policy comes from below. It was unions that organised the resistance to military action against the sending of soldiers to crush the Russian Revolution. Indeed, 1917 saw two beacons of hope for the future – the repudiation of the corrupt and brutal old regime in Russia and the proclamation of a new order of international politics from President Woodrow Wilson. The Treaty of Versailles betrayed the latter.

Trevelyan's main concerns were foreign affairs, and he noted that most of the debates at the Labour Party Conference at Scarborough in 1920 were on foreign affairs. But he was also wholly in sympathy with Labour's domestic policies. In his book he called for the nationalisation of railways, mines, and land. He even supported the capital levy, a tax on wealth to offset the national debt and to pay for the war debt. There should also, he believed, be free access to all secondary education and universities.

After his defeat in 1918, Trevelyan was selected as a candidate for a Newcastle-upon-Tyne constituency, which he easily won at the 1922 general election. The constituency was socially mixed; he was known locally, in the Geordie dialect, as 'Wor Charlie'.[76] He spoke on education during that Parliament and, when the Labour government was formed, Ramsay MacDonald appointed him appropriately as president of the Board of Education.

He was not so bookish a man as his brother George. He was more at home on the family estate at Wallington, which he was to inherit. He was a good shot, and scandalised Northumbrian neighbours by going out shooting on warm days, stripped to the waist. He told another convert from Liberal to Labour, H. B. Lees-Smith, that he 'played politics rather like a rough game of football, a lot of heavy charging and hearty tackling but not much finesse'.[77]

He was married to Molly, a half-sister of the Middle East explorer and archaeologist Gertrude Bell. Their father was Sir Hugh Bell, who had done well financially out of the nineteenth-century development of Middlesbrough. Beatrice Webb gave Molly Trevelyan advice on domestic management. However, Molly's entertainment was more generous than that of her mentor.

At Labour Party meetings, Trevelyan would identify and sit with left-wingers and address Labour colleagues as 'comrade'. With his fine intelligence, good looks, and impeccable manners there was something not quite convincing about this patrician socialist.

As president of the Board of Education, he had progressive ideas about education and was keen to push through radical measures, such as reducing class size, raising the school leaving age and cancelling the ban on nursery schools managed by local authorities. He was able to restore state scholarships for poorer students to go to university and increase the number of free places at fee-paying secondary schools. Local education authorities were empowered to raise the school leaving age to fifteen. Not many authorities implemented this measure. Trevelyan wanted to remove the restriction on pupils paying for school meals and school medical services. He had the sympathy of the chancellor of the exchequer, Philip Snowden, normally reluctant to loosen the national purse strings. Had the 1924 Labour government lasted longer, Trevelyan might have ranked with Wheatley as one of the successful reformers of that government. But his reforms were killed off by Liberal votes.

Josiah Wedgwood

Josiah Wedgwood was not an easy colleague. He had strong views about many things and was never afraid to express them. He was an individualist and not a team player. But he stands out among the men of 1924 as one whose reputation did not depend on political position, for he was a free spirit. Even party membership fitted awkwardly.

Josiah Clement Wedgwood was the only man of 1924 who was divorced. He was also – even more than Fred Jowett or John Wheatley – associated with one place. Although he died in London, he is buried within a mile or so of his birthplace at the family home in Barlaston, north Staffordshire.

He came from the distinguished family of potters, a great, great grandson of the founder of the firm Josiah Wedgwood & Sons. The Wedgwoods were related to the intellectual aristocracy of the nineteenth and twentieth centuries, a cousinhood that embraced Darwins, Huxleys, Keyneses, and Ralph Vaughan Williams. Before 1906 they had not been prominent in national political life.

Wedgwood was born in 1872 and educated at Clifton College, Bristol, where one of the teachers was the brother of H. H. Asquith. Before he became an MP at the age of thirty-three, he had already had three careers, as naval engineer, soldier, and colonial administrator. He did not go to university but trained as a naval architect and practised that craft at Armstrong's Elswick Shipbuilding Yard on Tyneside.

There was a family tradition of independence and free thinking, both in religion and politics. While in Newcastle-upon-Tyne he claimed he became a socialist, influenced by the American socialist utopian novel *Looking Backward* by Edward Bellamy, and also by his friendship with a trade unionist, John Clare, a fitter. Clare took him to the annual meeting of the Trades Union Congress in Newcastle-upon-Tyne in 1891, where he met such figures as John Burns. While in the north-east he was also in touch with contacts of his mother, a Rendel. They included the local Liberal aristocracy: Greys, Peases, Runcimans, and Trevelyans.[78] After this apprenticeship he went on to the Royal Naval College in Greenwich, where he fell in love with and married the daughter of a distinguished judge. He and his wife, based in London, used to go together to meetings of the Fabian Society.

When the South African War broke out in 1899, Wedgwood volunteered for military service and became the captain of a battery, although he did not see much actual fighting. Nonetheless he was attracted to the country and after the war offered his services to the high commissioner, Lord Milner, for administrative work in the country. He was given a post as resident magistrate in Transvaal, newly conquered and taken over by the British. He took his family there and had two very satisfying years. He had autonomy, he liked the defeated Boers and they seemed to like him. After a spell of home leave, he and his wife were returning to post when she suddenly decided that she was not going back to South Africa. They stopped at Grand Canary. Josiah Wedgwood decided, on this occasion, that his marriage was more important than his career and submitted his resignation with immediate effect, and they went back to Britain.

He decided then on a political career. He defied the leading members of the family who were then Conservative by standing as a Liberal for Newcastle-under-Lyme, the ancient independent borough, adjacent to and to the west of the Six Towns of the Potteries. He was supported by his younger brother, Ralph, who introduced him to Charles Trevelyan, Radical Liberal MP, and to the writings of Henry George.

Wedgwood's politics were vague, but one constant was the gospel of taxing land values, outlined by the American Henry George in his work *Progress and Poverty*. Wedgwood was bowled over by his reading of the work. 'From those magnificent periods, unsurpassed in the whole of British literature,' he wrote thirty-five years later, 'I acquired the gift of tongues. Ever since 1905 I have known "that there was a man from God, and his name was Henry George." I had no need thenceforth for any other faith.'[79] George's doctrine had some influence on other early British socialists, but none embraced his teachings with the enduring enthusiasm of Wedgwood.

Apart from land taxation, Wedgwood's politics were an eclectic and even inconsistent mix. He supported the railwaymen's strike in 1911 and the miners in 1913 in their major strike. He opposed Lloyd George's National Insurance Act, believing it an undue interference by the state. He disagreed with the 'collectivist' trend of Radical Liberal and contemporary socialist ideas.

Wedgwood defeated the sitting Conservative candidate in the general election of January 1906. He and his brother Ralph celebrated by draping the statue of the eighteenth-century Josiah outside the railway station in Stoke on Trent with the Liberal colours. They were removed the next morning by order of his uncle, the head of the family. Josiah Wedgwood was to hold the seat for the next nine general elections.

Later in 1906 he was made parliamentary private secretary to Walter Runciman, a junior minister in the new Liberal government. Even such a lowly government position required the holder to be loyal to the government. This was too much for Wedgwood, and he did not hold that minor position long.

He was, however, an active backbencher, seen as being on the left of the Liberal Party. He built up cordial relations with the Labour MPs, including James Keir Hardie, who told him, 'You are the only Member of this House who calls me James.'[80] He became a friend of

Philip Snowden and declared in his memoirs that he was 'in love' with Snowden's wife, Ethel.[81] He was also close to George Lansbury. Curiously for a man who not only supported the Boer War and went on to have a good record as a soldier in the Great War, he got on best with the pacifists. Wedgwood defied easy categorisation.

Wedgwood took an informed interest in foreign and colonial affairs and became a convert to the cause of Indian independence. It may be that this led to territorial jealousy on the part of Ramsay MacDonald, who prided himself on being Labour's India expert. The two men never saw eye to eye.

When he entered Parliament Wedgwood sported a distinctive drooping moustache that was virtually a male physical badge of imperialism. It came off permanently during the Great War. He also had a characteristic way of walking, as his niece wrote, 'between a swagger and a slouch, with long, loping strides'.[82] It was as if he was walking across the South African veldt.

Other MPs had reason to be wary of his unpredictability. At the end of the war, he responded to a slur from a Conservative MP, Ronald McNeill, in a manner that was more appropriate to the eighteenth century – by challenging him to a duel. The challenge was not accepted, perhaps to Wedgwood's relief, although his niece believed he was 'disappointed that he never had the chance of carrying out this interesting historic rite'.[83]

His inherited radicalism gave him a dislike for Toryism, but he made some friendships with individual Conservatives. 'If a man *must* be a Tory, at least let him be a gentleman.'[84] He was always a friend of Winston Churchill, who invited him to join the Other Club, the gathering of Churchill's male friends, mostly MPs of all parties and interesting non-politicians. They met once a fortnight at the Savoy Hotel during the parliamentary session. Here Wedgwood relaxed his normal teetotalism.[85]

Soon after the outbreak of war he was in Belgium, and then went to Gallipoli. He was a keen supporter of this doomed campaign and was brought home injured. When he recovered he was sent to

South Africa, with the idea of joining General Smuts's campaign against Germany in East Africa. But he was too late. In 1917 he travelled to the United States to add pressure on their government to join the war. After the failure of the Mesopotamia campaign, he was appointed a member of the Commission of Enquiry into that disaster. Finally he was sent on another international mission, to assess the strength of the Bolshevik Revolution in Central Asia. For this he had to travel across America and the Pacific Ocean to Tokyo and then by train to Vladivostok. He came to the conclusion that the post-war campaign in support of the White Russians against the Bolsheviks was bound to fail.

Wedgwood ended the war with a Distinguished Service Order (DSO) award and the rank of colonel. He had a good war. At the same time, paradoxically but typically, he was active in championing the rights of conscientious objectors.

On the whole, duelling aside, he was very comfortable with the twentieth century, which had, in his view, provided three great boons – the bicycle, the scout movement, and the cinema.[86]

In the general election of 1918, the 'coupon' election, he received endorsement from Lloyd George, and stood as an 'Independent Radical'.[87] He was returned unopposed. In this election he went to Blackburn to speak on behalf of the pacifist Philip Snowden. In April the following year he threw over the Liberal Party and joined the Independent Labour Party. The 1918 Parliament was, he wrote later, 'the wickedest I have known. Some called them the hard-faced men, I should have said empty-headed.'[88]

He got to know his new colleagues and wrote regularly for the ILP journal, *Forward*. One of his daughters was married to the son of the first secretary of the Fabian Society. Another daughter had married a Hungarian, and the Labour Party took advantage of this connection by sending him to Hungary to investigate atrocities committed after the fall of the Communist Béla Kun government; a future Cabinet colleague, Fred Jowett, was also a member of this mission.

Wedgwood was so combative against the post-war Lloyd George

coalition government that he was elected to the vice-chairmanship of the Parliamentary Labour Party, beating J. H. Thomas.[89] The 1918 general election had seen the defeat of several experienced Labour spokesmen, but Wedgwood was able to talk with authority on many subjects. In one parliamentary session he asked 402 questions.[90] He was the party spokesman on India, Russia, the Middle East, and the army – few could match the range of his expertise.[91] As well as going on about the land tax, he also supported the left-wing proposal of a capital levy.[92] Although this was in the Labour Party programme, the pledge was disliked by Ramsay MacDonald and never implemented. In the 1922 and 1923 general elections he stood under his new party ticket. There was no danger to his holding the seat. Being a Wedgwood was more important than a party label.

When MacDonald selected the men for his government, Wedgwood – never consulted – was offered the junior post of financial secretary to the War Office. Wedgwood refused, saying that as vice-chairman he could not take a post below Cabinet rank. He was eventually offered and accepted the sinecure of chancellor of the Duchy of Lancaster. The most important duty of this chancellor was the appointment of justices of the peace in Lancashire. It is usually given to people who might be given time-limited particular jobs. But Wedgwood was underemployed. His Cabinet colleague, Sidney Webb, observed that he was 'sullen and discontented'.[93] He could have served with distinction at the India Office, the War Office, or even the Foreign Office. Wedgwood distrusted MacDonald, who disapproved of his impulsiveness.[94]

In his Cabinet post, his main task was to be chief civil commissioner, charged with contingency planning in the event of civil or industrial unrest – a task that was neither rewarding nor appreciated.[95]

Outspoken and an awkward colleague, his interests were wide. He did not have to worry about his political base. He lacked finesse and the habit of compromise. In the general election immediately before the first Labour government he had spoken on behalf of

Hugh Dalton, who was taken aback by the way Wedgwood told his audience, using the short a's of the Staffordshire dialect, that 'Hugh Dalton and I both belong to the master class.'[96] He was seen as a man of principle with intensive enthusiasms, from Zionism to family history (especially of the Wedgwoods) and the history of Parliament. Others may have seen him as a hectoring bore.

9

In Office but not in Power

Two good books have been published about the 1924 Labour government. The first was *The First Labour Government 1924* by a (then) young American academic, Richard W. Lyman, published in 1957. The second was *Britain's First Labour Government* by two authoritative British Labour historians, John Shepherd and Keith Laybourn, published in 2006. Both studies tell the story of the nine months of the Labour government by following themes – unemployment, the economy, foreign affairs, and so on. In many ways this works well, as the reader is able to assess the performance of the government on each theme as a whole. However, reading these books can give a sense of coherence to the happenings of those months that is arguably deceptive.

In this final chapter, I have chosen a different approach. In general, I have dealt with those months in chronological order. Sometimes the government had to deal with several issues in the same week. Events are untidy things, but my objective in this approach is to give an impression of what it may have been like at the time, as events took place.

January

Ramsay MacDonald moved into Number 10, and the rest of the Cabinet and ministers moved to their government offices. After the rhetoric of the campaign and the exultation of forming a *Labour* government, hard reality set in. A government has no control over its in-tray. The lawmakers had to uphold the law, however sympathetic they may be to the law-breakers. And events kept happening within the country or in the empire for which the government now had responsibility, and which could not be ignored or wished away. There was no prescribed socialist response to an unexpected situation. This was bound to be an anticlimax for party zealots, whose expectations had been high, and a measure of disillusion soon appeared.

'What do we want?'

'The New Jerusalem.'

'When do we want it?'

'Now.'

In the first place, there is a continuity in the processes of governance, symbolised by the permanent civil service. They have been trained to carry out the wishes of the government, any government, to present options and advice on achieving the government's objectives. In 1924 a civil servant with twenty years' experience would have served Conservative, Liberal, and coalition governments.

For some in the Labour Party, this was to condemn them. But the ethos of the civil service was, in general, to cooperate and to implement, and not to thwart the policies of the new government.

A new government inherits commitments from its predecessor. There was a regular national budgetary cycle. The annual budget was introduced in April, but each government department had been in the process of its preparation over the previous six months. That process can only be modified, not ditched. It takes eighteen months for a government to have a significant impact with a budget. Any new legislation had to be drawn up in the light of existing provisions.

Overseas the restraints were greater. Colonial policy could not suddenly be reversed. There were numerous issues where little or no thought had been given by Labour thinkers, beyond a distaste for empire. J. H. Thomas became secretary of state for the colonies and reassured apprehensive staff in the Colonial Office, announcing, 'I'm here to see that there is no mucking about with the British Empire.'[1] This did not go down well with the anti-imperialists. Apart from being against it, there was no plausible policy for getting rid of it. Over the course of the year, some Labour backbenchers were conscious that Labour thinking was woefully deficient in this area. Leslie Haden-Guest, who had served in the Great War as a doctor, set up a Labour Commonwealth Group to consider the practical considerations of empire.[2] There was no rush to join up, but at least it was a start.

A similar awkwardness prevailed in the Labour Party about defence. Just as with the empire, there was no detailed policy beyond a general embarrassment. However, the lord chancellor, Lord Haldane, who had been secretary of state for war in the Campbell-Bannerman and Asquith governments, brought his experience to his additional post as chairman of the Committee of Imperial Defence.

On taking office, the government inherited an order for eight new cruisers for the Royal Navy. The first lord of the Admiralty, Lord Chelmsford, personally endorsed this and clashed with his new colleagues. A compromise was reached: five new cruisers and two new destroyers. Even so, there was no great joy on the Labour back benchers, and it fell to Charles Ammon, parliamentary secretary to the Admiralty, to defend the decision. Ammon had been a conscientious objector in the Great War and a lobbyist for the No Conscription Fellowship. He lamely explained that the work would help to reduce unemployment.

Restraints were made more acute by the fact that MacDonald had no parliamentary majority. Theoretically his government could be turned out at any time. There were constant manoeuvres, keeping his own party on board and not alienating Liberal allies too much. A core of up to a dozen Liberal MPs regularly voted against the government. MacDonald was determined not to do any deals with the Liberals. Asquith was past his best and often away from Parliament.

MacDonald did not have a high regard for him. His long-term aim was to replace Liberals rather than to be in partnership with them. Both parties were constrained by the fear of a general election, and neither could afford a third election within two years. Although MacDonald had been close to many individual Liberals before the war, he believed that Labour should take over the mantle of progressive politics, and that the British parliamentary system was basically binary. Therefore, his strategy was ultimately to destroy the Liberal Party.

Personal feelings and behaviour in the House of Commons varied. For many there was an incredulous euphoria at having a Labour government. This euphoria had to co-exist with different feelings from opposition benches. Many Conservatives' sense of entitlement had been violated. Outrage mixed with disdain, anxiety, fear, and a certain curiosity. The Conservative leader's approach seemed rather to be, 'Give 'em a chance; they'll surely screw things up in a few months, and we'll be back.'

The 1924 House of Commons was remarkable in that it was the only one in the twentieth century to have, as MPs, three former prime ministers – Asquith, Lloyd George, and Baldwin, who, between them, had fifteen years at Number 10. This may well have been daunting for the serving tenant. The situation of three former prime ministers in the House was not to be repeated until October 2022.

The government faced an unsympathetic national press. This was nothing new. But the pro-Labour press was not always supportive. The *Daily Herald*, under the control of George Lansbury, continually sniped. Lansbury had no affection for MacDonald, who had offered him a ministry outside the Cabinet. Lansbury declined, on the grounds that this offer was not equivalent to his status in the party. The ILP paper, the *New Leader*, had regular critical articles written by H. N. Brailsford and Fenner Brockway.

Where the Labour government could make its mark was in symbolic acts. MacDonald immediately recognised the Soviet Union.

This act of diplomacy went ahead in spite of previous arguments he had made for the democratic control of international affairs, which was the main thrust behind his co-founding of the Union of Democratic Control. MacDonald, acting as both prime minister and foreign secretary, did this without consulting or getting the approval from Parliament, or even the Cabinet. But it did secure approval from a large part of his parliamentary and party base. The permanent under-secretary at the Foreign Office, Sir Eyre Crowe, resisted, but eventually had to give way. A Labour MP, Sir James O'Grady, lobbied for the honour of being the first ambassador to Russia.[3] Instead, he had to be satisfied with the post of governor of Tasmania.

Bonar Law's government the previous year had erected a barrier separating Downing Street from Whitehall. It was targeted against possible demonstrations of unemployed people marching up to Number 10. This was removed.

A distinctive rhetoric emerged against, for example, profiteers. Although Snowden kept a tight control on public expenditure, there was an increase in spending on ongoing public works, such as the building of trunk roads and drainage.

Early in his occupancy of 10 Downing Street, the prime minister had a visit from a nanny working in Sussex. It was Bella, the younger sister of his mother. Amid the cares of office, it was a reminder of the simpler world of his childhood. She was so proud of him, 'Eh,' she said. 'Never did we think this was to come.'[4]

The new government inherited a number of labour disputes that highlighted one of the faultlines in the Labour Party, and especially in a Labour government. A momentum of trade union activity did not converge with the political calendar. It presented many Labour MPs with a conflict of loyalty: to their trade union representing the working class, or to the Labour government.

On the day the government was formed, the engine drivers,

members of the Amalgamated Society of Locomotive Engineers and Firemen (ASLEF), were on strike. There was a fear that the strike would spread to other unions. The new colonial secretary, J. H. Thomas, who was general secretary of the National Union of Railwaymen (NUR), appealed to his colleagues and after intensive negotiations between the unions and the Trades Union Congress – one session lasting seventeen hours – a compromise was reached and the strike was called off.

After the rail dispute was settled, there was a stoppage in the docks. Josiah Wedgwood, chancellor of the Duchy of Lancaster, was also chief civil commissioner, a post created by the previous (Conservative) government to ensure the flow of essential supplies at times of labour unrest. It was a post that, understandably, no trade unionist was eager to take on. Wedgwood had to threaten the use of troops to unload the ships. A court of enquiry was able to mediate and, under pressure from the government, the dockers' demands were met and the strike ended. The Labour government was able to use persuasion and appeals to loyalty to resolve labour disputes, but inside the velvet glove was the iron fist that it was prepared to use. Wedgwood had to work within the framework of the Emergency Powers Act, a piece of legislation that had been enacted by Lloyd George's coalition government in 1920 to bitter opposition from the Labour Party. Wedgwood's (Conservative) predecessor, J. C. C. Davidson, when handing over to Wedgwood, urged him not to change the rules.

After the Great War, Labour was very critical of the Versailles Treaty, and of punitive reparations, that is, 'making Germany pay for the war'. Such a policy was sowing the seeds of future conflict. Many in the Labour Party with foreign affairs expertise, such as E. D. Morel, were similarly critical of France, who, with Belgium, occupied the Ruhr from early 1923 in order to pressurise Germany to pay what they saw as a shortfall in the reparation payments. France was led then by the right-wing prime minister Jules Henri Poincaré, mocked as 'the Napoleon of the Ruhr'.[5] MacDonald may well have sympathised with these party sentiments, but he was keen to build up good relations with France. The League of Nations was central to his diplomacy, and MacDonald, as foreign secretary, played up his strengths of personality, charm, and curiosity by building up friendly relations with his European partners. Four days after taking office, he wrote a personal letter to Poincaré, expressing his hope that any differences between the two countries might be amicably resolved. Poincaré responded in the same spirit of goodwill.

The system of reparations payments was not working. The reparations had initially been costed in German gold marks. The early 1920s saw hyperinflation and Germany was unable to pay up. The Reparations Commission set up a committee under an American banker, Charles Dawes. The committee reported shortly before Labour took office. It proposed a rescheduling of Germany's payments and arranged for an American loan.

MacDonald welcomed the Dawes Plan, as it was known, as a basis for negotiation.

The established diplomats and officials of the Foreign Office were initially anxious about having Ramsay MacDonald as their secretary of state. Insofar as there was a 'Foreign Office policy' before MacDonald came to power, it was pro-French, anti-Russian, and was committed to upholding the Versailles agreement – even though the senior civil servant there, Sir Eyre Crowe, was himself half-German. He had first come to Britain when he was eighteen and, when angry, used to speak with a German accent. Supremely self-confident, he thought he knew more about foreign affairs than his political masters, which may well have been true. MacDonald exercised his tact and quiet determination. Over the month in office, MacDonald won Crowe's sympathy. His policies differed from some of those in his party who were much more openly critical of France and wanted a revision of the Versailles Treaty.

February

Politics resumed with the recall of Parliament after a short recess on 12 February. Ramsay MacDonald was cheered as he made his way through the gates of the Palace of Westminster to the House of Commons. Indeed, a Labour government excited a lot of public interest, and there was often a crowd of sightseers watching MPs come and go outside the Houses of Parliament.

MacDonald gave a two-hour speech, setting the tone of the government. He was resisting calls from his left-wing to introduce 'socialist' legislation that would be rejected, leading to a further general election. The issues facing the government were the national debt, reviving trade, and dealing with unemployment in a humane way. His emphasis on 'security and confidence, based on goodwill' and being 'just and worthy of respect' were not designed to stir the masses.[6]

Unemployment had been the main issue for Labour in the general election campaign. It had been the issue that had triggered the election, and Labour supporters had high hopes of a solution.

After a brief boom following the cessation of hostilities in 1918, unemployment had risen irresistibly. The causes for this arose from the Great War. Britain's global command of trade was challenged and partly replaced by the United States and Japan.

Labour had no coherent response or policy, and was only able to offer palliatives, such as a reduction in the waiting time when national insurance payments could be made. Many on the left of the party were impatient and thought that unemployment was an inseparable feature of capitalism. Once capitalism was overthrown and socialism installed, there would be no unemployment.

The government continued to sustain the previous government's programme of public works funded by the state. MacDonald argued that, together with the relief of unemployment, it was important to restore foreign trade. In his view, foreign and domestic policy were intimately linked. An export credit scheme was introduced in February, but there was no obvious impact on the figures of the unemployed.

Ramsay MacDonald had visited Egypt and was seen as sympathetic to Egyptian nationalism. There were high hopes after the nationalist Wafd Party comprehensively won elections in February under the leadership of Saad Zaghloul. He and MacDonald exchanged cordial messages. Zaghloul had not long ago been released from being detained by the British for four years after fierce anti-British riots.

During the year, British and Egyptian officials negotiated about a fresh relationship between the two countries. One sticking point was the status of the Sudan, which had been an Anglo-Egyptian condominium since 1899. Egyptian nationalists argued that Sudan should be an exclusive possession of Egypt.

The end of February provided an opportunity to test public opinion with a by-election at Burnley. (There had been two by-elections earlier, but both had been in safe Conservative seats without Labour contesting either.) The Labour candidate in Burnley was the new Home Secretary, Arthur Henderson, who had been defeated in Newcastle-upon-Tyne at the 1923 general election. Although it is desirable for Ministers to be answerable in the House of Commons or Lords, membership of Parliament is not actually a legal requirement. At the Burnley general election, Labour had won in a narrowly fought three-cornered contest. The death of the Labour MP Dan Irving had caused the by-election. The Liberal candidate was keen to fight again but was dissuaded from doing so by the party headquarters. The Liberal Party had only recently endorsed Labour in power. Henderson played up his nonconformist credentials – he was a Methodist lay preacher – in a strongly nonconformist constituency. The Conservative candidate warned of the Red Peril and received a message of support from Winston Churchill, who, less than three months earlier, had contested Leicester as a Liberal.

Arthur Henderson at one meeting caused diplomatic embarrassment by saying that a revision of the Versailles agreement was 'very much overdue'.[7] This did not improve his relationship with MacDonald, who at the time was trying to assuage France's anxiety about their own security. Nevertheless, Henderson won comfortably, with a 5 per cent swing in his favour. Analysts concluded that Labour took the required votes from the Liberals, and confirmed a trend that Labour was replacing the Liberals.

March

In March there was a strike on London transport. This was awkward because the minister of transport, Harry Gosling, not in the Cabinet, was president of the Transport and General Workers' Union. The general secretary of the union was the young and truculent Ernest Bevin. He negotiated with the prime minister, but not before the implementation of the Emergency Powers Act was averted.

The minister of labour, Tom Shaw, was under attack from left-wing backbenchers, as well as the opposition. In March he confessed, rather pathetically, 'Does anybody think that we can produce schemes like rabbits out of a hat?'[8] Ministers wrung their hands and found excuses for the lack of action. The Conservatives, to express their censure of the government, proposed that Shaw's salary be reduced.

A Cabinet committee was set up, to be chaired by the chancellor of the exchequer, Philip Snowden, to explore the subject. Unemployment was geographically patchy. It was high in shipbuilding and textile manufacturing districts, which were crucial to exports. Over the next few months Snowden's reluctance to loosen the purse strings to deal with the issue seemed to shift but any potential proposals had to be shelved with the end of the government.

In the middle of the month a by-election took place in the Abbey

Division of Westminster. Although the constituency contained some of the richest properties in the country, there were pockets of working-class areas – Vauxhall Bridge Road, Soho, and Covent Garden. Even so, at the general election of 1923, Labour did not put forward a candidate and the Conservative was returned unopposed. This time the by-election attracted enormous attention, for Winston Churchill, in his shuffle from the Liberal to the Conservative Party, declared his intention to stand as an Independent. This prompted the Labour Party to stand, putting forward Fenner Brockway, a young ILP journalist who had suffered imprisonment for opposition to the Great War and was now a stern critic of Ramsay MacDonald. He had few expectations of success, but he felt he ought 'to take up Mr Churchill's challenge to Socialism'.[9]

Churchill was also challenging the Conservative Party machine, although he gained the support of some Conservative MPs (and some Liberal MPs too) as well as the Conservative supporting the newspaper barons Beaverbrook and Rothermere. He also received the endorsement of the former Conservative prime minister, Arthur (now Lord) Balfour. It was a colourful election. Fenner Brockway canvassed the staff of the royal family in search of socialists, and Churchill was hit by a turnip in Covent Garden. Chorus girls came to address envelopes and delivered election addresses.

The result was close. At first it seemed that Churchill had won. Then the result was officially announced. Only forty-three votes separated the official Conservative, Otho Nicholson (who won), and Churchill. Brockway came a good third. Churchill was despondent at the result and confided in Brockway: 'You know, Brockway, you and I have no chance. We represent ideas – Nicholson represents the machine.'[10]

Despite the high profile of this by-election, the turnout was, at 60.2 per cent, the lowest of all the 1924 by-elections.

The Labour government had a bit of a crisis about the naval base in Singapore. A proposal to develop the base was debated.

MacDonald, who was against the development, had to face strong, wearying opposition from the first sea lord, Admiral Lord Beatty. There was, Beatty argued, a threat to our empire in the East, and to nearly £1 billion worth of trade. Fortunately for the government, the lord chancellor, Lord Haldane, with his watching brief on defence matters, backed MacDonald, who also had the more reluctant backing of the first lord of the Admiralty, Lord Chelmsford. The issue was first discussed in March but not resolved until July, when MacDonald got his way. This pleased the more pacifist wing of the party. Some Conservative MPs were vocal in impotent opposition.

In the same month some ILP MPs voted against the defence estimates: the government won, thanks to Liberal support. The ILP paper, *Forward*, referred sarcastically to 'Comrade Chelmsford'.[11]

A rebellion broke out in Bengal in March and was put down just as a previous administration would have done.

April

Philip Snowden was very lucky with his budget. To some extent his options were limited. Estimates for each government department had been submitted three months before the Labour government took office.

Snowden was the most tight-fisted chancellor of the twentieth century. He was also the most popular chancellor with the senior officials of the Treasury, who welcomed his tight fists. Snowden made no apologies for this approach. Indeed, he explained to the House of Commons his role as he saw it:

> It is no part of my job as chancellor of the exchequer to put before the House of Commons proposals for the expenditure of public money. The function of the chancellor of the exchequer,

> as I understand it, is to resist all demands for expenditure made by his colleagues and, when he can no longer resist, to limit the concession to the barest point of acceptance.[12]

His task was to balance the books and reduce the national debt, followed by a policy, if possible, of reducing indirect taxation. There was no idea of deficit management, seeing borrowing as national investment.

No taxes were raised, either of income tax or supertax. On coming into office Snowden was anticipating a budget surplus of £2 million. In fact, it was £48 million: this was from reduced expenditure and increased revenue. Some of the latter came from purchase tax on motorcars, of which there was a steady increase during the early 1920s. Extra incomings from duties on fuel and whisky were explained by the severity of the previous winter.[13] There were other lucky benefits from external circumstances. The army as a career was understandably not popular in the immediate post-war years, and few people were joining up. As a result, the army was 55,000 below strength, and so the War Office budget was underspent. The surplus gave Snowden leverage to reduce duties on tea, sugar, cocoa, coffee, and dried fruit – but not on alcoholic drinks. 'These proposals are the greatest steps ever made', he said in his budget speech, 'towards the realisation of the cherished Radical ideal of a free breakfast table.'[14] This was greeted with cheers.

Snowden, who had been a junior official in the Customs and Excise Department forty years earlier, was unquestionably Labour's expert on finance. He dominated discussions and debates with his expertise. He did not question what was seen as a Gladstonian reluctance to consider publicly funded projects as an investment. Unlike other members of the Cabinet, he had studied the subject and was respected for it. In the 1950s the last surviving man of 1924 recalled that he was 'the outstanding member of the movement'.[15]

Snowden did agree to award some money for education. The president of the Board of Education, Charles Trevelyan, was passionate about extending secondary education to working-class children. In 1924 public sector provision for elementary education for poor children extended to the age of fourteen, then the school leaving age. After that they were at work or in apprenticeships. Bright kids may be able to get scholarships to grammar schools but would usually still have to pay fees. Trevelyan had big plans for secondary education for all, but the government fell before he could implement any of his ideas, which would be realised over the next twenty or thirty years.

Snowden's budget received wide praise. The breakfasts of the poor were going to be cheaper, and the better off breathed a sigh of relief that the budget was not 'confiscatory'. The idea of a capital levy, a tax on wealth, which had been a popular policy with Labour supporters during the general election, seemed to have been quietly dropped. If the weasels had taken over Toad Hall, they were at least not nicking the silverware.

MacDonald invited the Egyptian nationalist leader, Saad Zaghloul Pasha, to come to London during the summer. The visit was delayed because of more unrest in Egypt involving the death of a British soldier.

As a leader, MacDonald, although efficient as a chairman of the Cabinet or of Cabinet committees, was awkward in personal relations with his colleagues. Although the deputy prime minister, J. R. Clynes, lived at 11 Downing Street, the two men rarely met to talk things over. MacDonald was aloof and unapproachable, and often autocratic. MacDonald had an inkling of this problem, recording in his diary on 28 April that he had a major problem in the 'co-ordinating & guidance work of the Premiership'.[16] Consequently he started to have weekly lunches with Clynes, Henderson, Snowden, Thomas, and Webb. They discussed the arrangements for the following week, and as a result there was a greater coherence in the management of government business.

Although the Labour government recognised the Soviet Union soon after it took office, serious negotiations to resolve differences started in April. MacDonald took the chair at the initial meeting with the Soviet mission, but afterwards delegated the running of it all to the parliamentary under-secretary, Arthur Ponsonby. As an Old Etonian and a former page to Queen Victoria, it would be hard for him to be portrayed as a Bolshevik sympathiser. The two main issues were settling debts to British companies that had had their Russian interests nationalised and negotiating a commercial treaty, opening up British exports to a potentially vast market that had been blocked by the Great War and the Russian Revolution. The Russians also asked for a loan. Talks continued through the summer.

On St George's Day, 23 April, King George V opened Wembley Empire Stadium. It had been built at great speed for the British Empire Exhibition, opened at the same time. Three days later the stadium hosted the Football Association Cup Final. Newcastle United beat Aston Villa 2–0. That would have bought a smile to the face of Arthur Henderson, who, over forty years earlier, had been a member of a football club that had, with others, been amalgamated to establish Newcastle United.

May

South Africa provided the cricket team to tour England in 1924. At the first test match, opening at Edgbaston on 3 May, the visiting team was bowled out for thirty on the first day in under thirteen overs.

On 9 May the minister of health, John Wheatley, received a delegation to discuss the provision of birth control advice in ministry clinics. The leading light of the delegation was Dora Russell, wife of Bertrand, a feminist, an educational reformer, and a vigorous campaigner for birth control and abortion law reform. She was accompanied in the delegation by two MPs and sympathisers such as H. G. Wells.

Birth control was a new controversial issue in post-war Britain. Progressive opinion in favour of birth control was dominated by middle-class women, such as Dora Russell. This led to some suspicion in Labour circles. People thought they should have more money rather than fewer children.[17] Some advocates of birth control were also allied to the eugenics movement, which argued for selective breeding, and for limiting the number of working-class children.

The delegation was not optimistic. John Wheatley was known for his commitment to Catholic teaching, which prohibited birth control. The delegation pointed out that it was four times more dangerous to bear a child as to work in a coal mine. Wheatley rejected the request that doctors at welfare centres should be allowed to give birth-control advice to mothers who wanted it. He argued that state or rate-funded institutions were not permitted to act on such a matter without statutory authorisation. Members of the delegation were not surprised, and the campaign was switched to lobbying MPs.

There were setbacks for campaigners on equal rights for women. Women were beginning to enter the Civil Service as clerks and secretaries. A number had been dismissed after the war to make room for returning servicemen. Women's groups failed to reverse this decision. Other issues to the benefit of women were ignored or overtaken by events, issues that had been taken up by women's organisations allied to the Labour Party. During the Great War wives of servicemen were paid allowances that were paid directly to them, and not channelled through 'the head of the family', who may have been in a trench in northern France. This was the genesis of family allowances, but the scheme was discontinued after the war and not taken up by the Labour government. The campaign for widows' pensions was similarly overlooked by the 1924 government, although it was implemented by the chancellor of the exchequer, Winston Churchill, in the next (Conservative) administration.

In other respects, attempts were made to promote 'women's issues' by the Labour government. The general election manifesto had committed the party to 'equal political and legal rights' for women.[18] An attempt was made, promoted by William Adamson, to revise the 1918 Representation of the People Act to allow women to vote on the same terms as men – that is, from the age of twenty-one. The Bill was drafted but the fall of the government prevented it becoming law. Under an Act of 1919 women were able to be justices of the peace. Few had been appointed. The chancellor of the Duchy of Lancaster, Josiah Wedgwood, one of whose few specific duties was the appointment of magistrates in Lancashire, appointed women often against local wishes.

In 1919 there had been a police strike, and many trade-union police activists had been dismissed. People in the Labour Party had campaigned for their reinstatement, but the new Labour government refused.

On 22 May a by-election was held at the West Toxteth division of Liverpool. The city had not returned any Labour MP. The majority Protestant working-class vote felt threatened by Irish Catholic immigrants undercutting their wages, and an efficient Conservative Party machine mobilised this discontent. The local Orange Order of Northern Irish Protestant Unionists came out strongly for the Conservative candidate. Labour successfully wooed the Liberal vote – there was no Liberal candidate – and a swing of 4.6 per cent won the seat for Labour, a boost for Labour morale.

The following day a by-election was held at Kelvingrove, Glasgow. This was a Conservative held seat, although their majority had been narrow in the 1923 general election. The Labour candidate was a declared communist and his agent was J. R. Campbell, acting editor of a Communist paper, *Workers' Weekly*. Labour headquarters was concerned. It did not withdraw their official endorsement, but no assistance was forthcoming. The Conservatives played on the Red Threat and won the seat with a 5.8 per cent swing. The name J. R. Campbell became better known later in the summer.

June

At the beginning of the month E. M. Forster's novel *A Passage to India* was published. A sign of changing cultural times, it presented Indians as central characters. The book may be seen as a contrast to the imperial bombast of the Empire Exhibition that was still running at Wembley.

In June Tom Shaw declared that unemployment had dropped by 240,000 since Labour had taken office, but it was pointed out that this was because of a regular rise in employment during the summer months, and that the drop in unemployment had been 280,000 the previous year.

In early June a by-election was held at Oxford, following the unseating of the Liberal MP for malpractices in the 1923 general election. The Liberals were strong in Oxford, in control of the City Council. Labour decided to contest the constituency for the first time. As a result they took votes from the Liberals, allowing the Conservative candidate to gain the seat. This did not promote Liberal–Labour cooperation.

In France the right-wing Poincaré was overturned in national elections to be replaced by the Radical former mayor of Lyons, Édouard Herriot. He accepted MacDonald's invitation to Chequers that had been intended for his predecessor.

At the end of June MacDonald had another tussle with the military, when a proposal for the Channel Tunnel became an issue, raised by an all-party parliamentary committee. The prime minister was in favour and wanted to make it a non-party issue. Opposition came from the armed forces, who thought that a tunnel would make Britain a continental power requiring a large army, and that there would have to be a concentration of forces near the entry of the tunnel.

MacDonald convened a committee, inviting all the former prime ministers – all but Rosebery took part – and service chiefs. All were opposed, and MacDonald had no alternative but to defer to their collective opinion.

July

Negotiations had proceeded during the summer leading to a revision of reparations in accordance with recommendations made by the Dawes Committee. Any concession was seen by French nationalists as bad for their country. The Chamber of Deputies was in uproar, and Herriot appealed for moral support from MacDonald. The latter dashed over to Paris on 8 July. MacDonald was able to offer some verbal guarantees for France's security but avoided any stronger commitment – that was what he had objected to in the policies of Sir Edward Grey before 1914. What Britain wanted, MacDonald wrote elliptically in a minute, was 'the closest of alliances, that which is not written on paper'.

On 9 July a by-election was held at Lewes in Sussex, following the appointment of the Conservative MP as governor of Western Australia. No Liberal had contested the seat since 1910. In 1918, 1922, and 1923 there had been a straight fight between Conservatives and Labour. Labour had edged up its share of the vote to 40 per cent in the last election. But a Liberal entered the contest, and the Conservative romped home.

At this point in the government's life, things looked good. Ministers had become used to their official cars and privileges, and a satisfactory working relationship with the civil service. There had been no government disasters, no scandals, and no resignations. The country seemed to accept the normality of a Labour government. But from the end of July the situation changed. The men of 1924 were inexperienced in dealing with crises, and responses were fumbled.

The government was able to claim, and did, that it had reduced international tension and the threat of war, and that it was laying the foundations of a new international order that would lead to both security and disarmament.[19] At home they were able to point out that 'the burden on the housewife and wage-earner' had lessened and constructive plans were under way to deal with housing and unemployment.

The party was confident and there were suggestions of a quick general election. But the sense of confident optimism did not last through the summer.

In the queen's Birthday Honours list Alexander Grant was awarded a baronetcy, a hereditary knighthood. Grant was the managing director of McVitie and Price, the makers of biscuits. It emerged in the press that Grant was, like MacDonald, a native of Morayshire. Grant's father and MacDonald's uncle had worked together on the Highland Railway.[20] The press reported that Grant had presented MacDonald with a Daimler car as well as a large number of shares in the company; he was to use the income from the dividends to maintain the car.

A small battalion of the British army was still in Germany. The secretary of state for war, Stephen 'Wee Stee' Walsh, made a visit of inspection in July. The commanding officer asked Walsh if he would like to ride a horse to make the inspection. Walsh declined. The only animal he had ridden had been a pit-pony in his days as a miner working underground, and the animal had thrown the diminutive Walsh off.[21]

British forces were also active in Iraq, where many Iraqis were unwilling to accept the League of Nations mandate awarded to Britain. British and Indian troops had been there since the Great War. It had been an expensive operation, but the use of the Royal Air Force to strafe rebel villages cut costs enormously. The war-time pacifist William Leach, representing the Air Ministry in the House of Commons, was put in the hapless role of defending these actions. The rebels, he pointed out, were blocking progress under the new monarchy. Ground action with armoured cars had meant a loss of British lives. The tribes and villagers were given notice of impending air action.

At the end of the month the question of a loan to Russia came before the Cabinet. The Russians had argued that the compensation due to bondholders depended on securing a loan. The commercial loan was guaranteed by the Cabinet, despite strong opposition from Philip Snowden.

The government's calm and confidence in the early summer started to be ruffled. What could have been a minor episode became one that engulfed the government and was a factor in its collapse.

The Red Bogey – a suspicion that Labour was identical to Bolshevism – was a theme of the mostly right-wing national press. They expressed a suspicion at MacDonald's recognition of the Soviet Union, and that the trade negotiations were linked to sympathies with Communism. At the time the Labour leadership in general, and MacDonald in particular, were hostile to the small and fairly insignificant Communist Party of Great Britain. The Communist Party had a periodical, the *Workers' Weekly*; and its acting editor was J. R. Campbell, who had been the Labour agent at the Glasgow Kelvingrove by-election in May. On 25 July, the *Workers' Weekly* published an article calling on the police and troops not to allow themselves to be called on to fire on strikers. Four days after the publication a Conservative MP raised the matter in the House of Commons. A few days later the attorney general, Sir Patrick Hastings, instructed the director of public prosecutions to charge Campbell with offences under the Incitement to Mutiny Act of 1797. This led to angry protests by some Labour backbenchers in the House of Commons. The Cabinet then discussed the matter, and it was decided that no prosecution with political implications should happen without Cabinet approval. It was also decided to abandon the prosecution. Campbell was only the *acting* editor. It turned out that he had had a good war, was on a disability pension – he had lost all his toes in action – and had been awarded the Military Medal. It was all great publicity for *Workers' Weekly*, who produced a banner headline, 'Working Class Agitation Forces Government Surrender'.[22] If the case had gone ahead, the paper would have called on the prime minister himself to be a witness. Ten years earlier, MacDonald had defended Tom Mann, later a founding member of the Communist Party, on a similar charge.

The withdrawal of the prosecution suggested dithering on the government's part. Conservative MPs and press suggested that Communist pressure was behind it all. The issue would dog the government for the rest of its life.

At the end of the month a by-election was held at the Holland-with-Boston constituency in Lincolnshire, following the death of the Labour MP W. S. Royce, who had been a prominent local Conservative before the war. He had switched parties and taken the seat for Labour from the Liberals in the 1923 general election in a straight fight. In this by-election the Liberals entered the fray. There were only 800 votes between the victorious Conservative and the Labour candidate (Hugh Dalton), but the Liberals polled over 7,500 votes, coming third. It was the only Labour defeat in a by-election in 1924.

August

The issue of the Russian loan dragged on. Over the night of 3–4 August, a nineteen-hour session between the two sides argued over the precise wording of the loan agreement. Eventually two loosely worded drafts were agreed, the first a general commercial treaty and the second providing a framework for further negotiations on compensation.

Although Labour MPs were in general supportive, it was strongly attacked by Lloyd George

The indirect administration of India became a great responsibility. The Indian nationalist Mahatma Gandhi had been imprisoned four years earlier for 'sedition'. He was released on grounds of ill health. This was a crumb of comfort to Indian nationalists who had been disappointed by a tough letter sent by MacDonald, saying that he would not be intimidated by 'threats of force or policies designed to bring the Government to a standstill'.[23] It was a letter that could have been written by any Conservative minister and was particularly disappointing as MacDonald had visited India and was seen to be sympathetic to the nationalists.

On 7 August the Housing Act, regarded as Labour's major achievement, received the royal assent.

Although there had been state intervention in housing since the 1870s, the involvement became much more pressing after the Great War. It was realised that the health of the nation depended on salubrious housing.

The Housing Act was Wheatley's brainchild. Although the idea had not featured in the general election campaign, it had grown over the previous ten years as a result of Wheatley's experiences in Glasgow. The city had witnessed rent strikes, and Wheatley realised that the only answer to provide security of tenure was public control of housing.

Lloyd George had called for 'Homes fit for Heroes' after the Great War. Slums had to be cleared away and new houses built. Christopher Addison, minister of health in Lloyd George's coalition government, and Neville Chamberlain, minister of health in the subsequent Conservative governments, both tackled the issue with Housing Acts. The Addison Housing Act granted government subsidies for local authorities to build houses for the working-class to rent; this was in operation for two years but ended in 1921 with cutbacks in government expenditure, which had spiralled because of inflation in the costs of house building. Chamberlain's Housing Act of 1923 provided subsidies of £6 per house to local government authorities and private builders over a period of twenty years. (It cost £500 to build a house.) It was intended that houses built were for sale. This meant it was providing homes for middle-class people who could afford to buy them.

John Wheatley had been active in issues of municipal housing enterprises in Glasgow and criticised the Chamberlain proposals from the opposition benches in 1923. He argued that the provision of working-class housing for rent should 'in the future be a public enterprise'.[24]

A fortnight after his appointment as minister of health, Wheatley convened a committee consisting of both sides of the building industry. They were to report on the present position with regard to labour and materials. The committee reported in early April and Wheatley, together with his parliamentary secretary Arthur Greenwood, then brought in representatives of local government authorities.

In June legislation was introduced. In order to offset the fluctuations of trade costs, Wheatley wanted his scheme to be a long-term project. And so, there was to be an annual subsidy over thirty years of £9 a house – more for rural areas – for the construction of houses with prescribed specifications. Conscious of his own upbringing, the houses had to have space and indoor toilets. The rents were to be controlled by the local government authority, and the houses were not to be for sale. The ratio of financial support from the Treasury and from the local government authorities was two to one.

Three features characterised the Housing Act. First, unlike the previous acts, it was designed to produce housing for rent and not for purchase. By locking local authorities into the scheme it gave the project durability. Second, it involved the private and public sectors, the building trades and local as well as national government. And third, it was an example of planning that went beyond one financial year. It lasted, albeit in limited form, until 1932. The legislation was formally opposed by the Conservatives, but it was difficult for them, as Wheatley's Bill was an extension of previous legislation. Indeed, in speaking on the Bill, Wheatley said it was a capitalist and not a socialist measure.[25] The spokesman for the Opposition was Lord Eustace Percy, not one of their leading stars. On the final reading of the Bill only 128 Conservatives voted against it. Neville Chamberlain offered criticism only on details.

The impact of the Act took time to mature. But three years after 1924 nearly a quarter of a million houses were built under Wheatley's scheme, compared with 86,000 in 1923/24.[26] But it laid the foundation for the construction of the housing estates between the wars, and in spite of modifications by later governments, stood as the outstanding achievement of the 1924 Labour government. One lasting legacy of the Act was that it established a consensus among all parties that the public sector had a responsibility for the provision of housing. This consensus lasted until the 1970s.

On 14 August the government contested its last by-election at Carmarthen. It was, and remained, a secure Liberal seat, with little variation in the poll since the general election of 1923.

September

On 11 September the *Daily Mail* published details of MacDonald's financial support from Alexander Grant and his baronetcy. Lloyd George had been embroiled in a scandal of selling honours for cash. Labour had condemned this, but the Grant affair looked as if the prime minister was guilty of the same offence. When MacDonald addressed political meetings after this exposure, he was greeted with cries of 'Biscuits' by hostile elements. MacDonald may have been gullible and naive, but it looked bad for him.

In the middle of the month the postponed visit of Zaghloul Pasha finally took place. Talks did not lead anywhere, and the hopes of the Egyptian nationalists for a fresh approach from MacDonald were dashed. No further progress in Anglo-Egyptian relations was possible in the government's remaining six weeks.

One of the recommendations of the Union for Democratic Control (UDC) had been that international disputes should be settled by arbitration. As foreign secretary, MacDonald promoted this concept at the League of Nations in Geneva. His deputy, the parliamentary under-secretary Arthur Ponsonby, was busy dealing with the Russian negotiations, and for League of Nations work MacDonald relied on the septuagenarian lord president of the council, Lord Parmoor.

During his talks with the French prime minister, MacDonald agreed that they should work together on security and disarmament, all the time taking into consideration France's apprehensions about Germany.

In September MacDonald travelled to Geneva and addressed the Fifth Assembly of the League of Nations in a speech outlining his ideas. The speech was greeted with loud applause. Germany should be admitted to the league. He emphasised the idea of collective security and proposed a disarmament conference. An international agreement on disarmament was another UDC policy. By the end of the month officials worked out an agreement that became known as the Geneva Protocol.

Then the problems started. On MacDonald's return to London, the Cabinet discussed the proposals. Haldane and Chelmsford, the first lord of the Admiralty, were opposed. The defence service departments were fearful of commitments that might involve British armed forces. The strong backing of Arthur Henderson and Lord Parmoor was not enough. The status of the Protocol was unclear. Was it mandatory or just a recommendation? In the end it went nowhere, but even the discussion was an advance on pre-1914 international relations.

Yorkshire won the county cricket championship for its third successive year.

October and the End

Many Scottish Labour MPs, not excluding the secretary of state for Scotland, William Adamson, were sympathetic to the idea of some form of Scottish devolution. A commission was set up to investigate the issue. The government fell before it reported.

In early October a vote of censure was brought against the government about the withdrawal of the prosecution of J. R. Campbell of the *Workers' Weekly*. Had MacDonald misled Parliament by saying that he did not know about the dropping of charges? His answer was evasive and not very convincing. The secretary of the Cabinet, Sir Maurice Hankey, described it as a 'bloody lie'.[27] All party leaders contributed to the debate, and in the final vote Liberals combined with Conservatives to defeat the government. Although it was not constitutionally obligatory, MacDonald saw it as a vote of no confidence.

The morning after the vote, 9 October, MacDonald went to Buckingham Palace and asked King George V for a dissolution of Parliament. The king wanted to announce that he did this with reluctance, but MacDonald advised him that that would seem too political. 'Then,' MacDonald wrote in his diary, 'we talked about a variety of things from the Red Flag, the Marseillaise and other revolutionary songs, the 1886 Trafalgar square riots, Cunningham Graham [*sic*], Ireland, Grey's remarks about an Irish Republic. He remarked, "you have found me an ordinary man, haven't you?"'[28]

In the general election campaign, held in the weeks up to polling day, Wednesday, 29 October 1924, MacDonald threw himself into intense activity. He made two long tours of the country speaking to large crowds. It was the first general election when leaders made speeches over the new wireless medium. MacDonald's speech at a Glasgow rally was broadcast live. This was not effective. By contrast the Conservative leader, Stanley Baldwin, gave some thought to the technique of broadcasting from a studio. He spoke in quiet, confidential, intimate tones as if he were in the listener's own home. It was far more effective.

The Conservatives conflated the Anglo-Soviet negotiations with the Campbell case, arguing that the Labour Party and the Labour government were prisoners of the Communists. Their candidate in the Abbey Division of Westminster told his prospective constituents that a 'vote for the Socialists is a vote for the Communists. They pretend to be separate, but at every crisis we find them together.'[29] Even the former Conservative foreign secretary, Lord Curzon, could say on the eve of poll, 'Anyone who voted Labour tomorrow was voting for handing this country over to the Communists and to Moscow.'[30] *The Times* thought that Labour's proposal to set up a national electricity grid would have been 'dear to Lenin'.[31]

On the Saturday, four days before polling day, the *Daily Mail* published what purported to be a letter from Grigory Zinoviev, the president of the Communist International, to a British Communist Party official, calling on the Communist Party to stir up revolution. The *Daily Mail* published it with the headline, 'Civil War Plot by Socialists' Masters: Moscow Orders to Our Reds: Great Plot

Disclosed'.[32] The letter had been intercepted by the Foreign Office. MacDonald had seen it and asked the Foreign Office to check its authenticity. When it was published in the *Daily Mail*, MacDonald was electioneering in Manchester. The Foreign Office had sent a letter of protest to the Russian government, a protest that had been approved by MacDonald, who at the time regarded the matter as an irritant but otherwise routine. MacDonald was ready for the Zinoviev letter to be published,[33] but obviously not in the sensational manner of the *Daily Mail*. On receiving the press coverage, he felt as if he had been 'sewn in a sack and thrown into the sea'.[34]

J. H. Thomas was also in Manchester and realised the potential damage of the story. 'We're sunk,' he said when he saw MacDonald.[35]

The *Daily Mail* was a strong supporter of the Conservatives in the election campaign. The Conservatives found a theme on which to construct a narrative. The swift recognition of the Soviet Union and the eagerness for a loan to and a treaty with Russia showed that the government was either complicit with the Bolsheviks, or were their dupes – useful idiots. The Campbell case and the Zinoviev letter only confirmed this narrative.

The full details of the origins of the Zinoviev letter have never been established. No original of the letter has been seen, and such a letter seems improbable. Zinoviev denied that he wrote it. At any rate, the Communist Party of Great Britain was a revolutionary party. It did not need a letter from Moscow to incite them to insurrection. Inside the Labour Party, the belief was that there had been collaboration between public servants who could not accept the legitimacy of a Labour government, and the *Daily Mail*. As late as 1999, at the prompting of the Labour foreign secretary, Robin Cook, the Foreign and Commonwealth Office issued an exhaustive report that was unable to establish responsibility. It was suggested that there was collusion between White Russian exiles and some British intelligence operatives.

But what impact did it have on the outcome of the general election? Labour lost over forty seats, but held their ground in the

Midlands, Yorkshire, and Scotland. One Cabinet minister, F. W. Jowett, lost his seat in Bradford, and Labour lost seats in Greater London. But the greater loss was suffered by the Liberal Party. This continued the trend that had been revealed at by-elections. Their leader, H. H. Asquith, was defeated at Paisley, and Liberals lost over a hundred other seats. Labour put up more candidates and there was great enthusiasm among Labour supporters. The total Labour vote in fact increased by over a million, but the Conservative vote increased by double that. The Liberals were the greatest victims. They lost 118 seats and almost one-third of the 4.3 million votes they had secured less than a year earlier. If the publication of the Zinoviev letter had any effect, it seemed to have pushed former Liberal voters into the arms of the Conservatives.

Labour found other crumbs of comfort. MacDonald's strategy of Labour replacing the Liberals as the progressive party had succeeded. The two realistic alternatives were now Labour and Conservative. The raw experience of nine months in office had made Labour supporters confident that their time would come again.

Results of the general election became public on Thursday and Friday, 30 and 31 October. It was soon clear that the Conservatives, with a gain of 155 seats, had scored their biggest triumph for over a generation.

Labour was disappointed but not downhearted. 'We still remained on the threshold of power,' wrote the party's secretary, Arthur Henderson.

> Labour in office but not in power was an interesting, useful, and instructive experiment. It gave added prestige to Labour as well as training and experience in administration to a good proportion of the personnel of the Parliamentary Party. From a House of Commons standpoint Labour has nothing to fear at the prospect of finding itself responsible, at no distant date, for the conduct of national affairs as a free and independent agent.[36]

MacDonald travelled from Aberavon, his South Wales constituency, to London, on Thursday, 30 October. He called on Sir Eyre Crowe, permanent under-secretary at the Foreign Office, who was ill in bed. Relations had warmed between them over the year and Crowe was, according to MacDonald's diary, 'heartbroken'.[37]

Relations between MacDonald and Snowden, never cordial, became embittered after the fall of the government. Snowden told Fred Jowett, who, in spite of political differences, was always a friend and confidant, that they 'had wantonly and recklessly thrown away ... [the greatest opportunity] by the most incompetent leadership which ever brought a Government to ruin'.[38] The following month his bitterness went further:

> You know that I have never trusted JRM, but he has added to the attributes I knew, during the last nine months, an incapacity I never thought of. He has thrown away the greatest opportunity which ever came to a party and he has landed us with five years of a Tory Government. And his colossal conceit prevents him being in the remotest measure conscious of what he has done.

Josiah Wedgwood – Colonel Wedgwood as he was then known – handed the office back to Davidson, newly reappointed chancellor of the Duchy of Lancaster and chief civil commissioner. He was able to reassure him: 'I haven't destroyed any of your plans. I haven't done a bloody thing about them.'[39]

The Cabinet met on Saturday morning, and an acrimonious discussion was held about the election. It met again for the last time on Tuesday, 4 November. It was agreed that MacDonald should submit their resignation to the king – not that any alternative course was possible. Haldane proposed a motion expressing appreciation of the 'invariable kindness and courtesy' the prime minister had shown.[40]

At 5:30 p.m. MacDonald saw King George V and submitted the

resignation of himself and his government. Stanley Baldwin was invited to form his second government.

As soon as he could, the ex-prime minister set off on a walking tour in the West Country. 'If friends fail,' he wrote in an article in *Forward* the following month, 'the hill road never does.'[41]

Notes

Introduction

1 Quoted in A. J. P. Taylor, *The Origins of the Second World War* (Hamish Hamilton: London, 1961), 231.

1. Tuesday, 22 January 1924

1 Quoted in Richard W. Lyman, *The First Labour Government 1924* (Chapman and Hall: London, 1957), 98–9.
2 Roy Hattersley, *David Lloyd George* (Abacus: London, 2012), 275.
3 Hugh Dalton, *Call Back Yesterday* (Frederick Muller: London, 1953), 146.
4 John Bew, *Citizen Clem* (Riverrun: London, 2017), 10.
5 Stephen Roskill, *Hankey, Man of Secrets* (Collins: London, 1972), II, 353.
6 J. H. Thomas, *My Story* (Hutchinson: London, 1937), 75.
7 Harold Nicolson, *King George the Fifth* (Constable: London, 1952), 388.
8 MacDonald's diary, quoted in David Marquand, *Ramsay MacDonald* (Jonathan Cape: London, 1977), 304.
9 Quoted in Nicolson, 384.
10 Kenneth Rose, *King George V* (Phoenix: London, 2000), 330.
11 Quoted in Nicolson, 389.
12 Philip Viscount Snowden, *An Autobiography* (Ivor Nicholson and Watson: London, 1934), II, 608.
13 J. R. Clynes, *Memoirs* (Hutchinson: London, 1937), 341.
14 Dalton, 145.

15 Henry 'Chips' Channon, *The Diaries*, ed. Simon Heffer (Hutchinson: London, 2021–2), I, 255.
16 Marquand, 313.
17 Snowden, 606.
18 Roger Moore, *The Emergence of the Labour Party, 1880–1924* (Hodder and Stoughton: London, 1978), 192.
19 Moore, 192.
20 Beatrice Webb, *The Diary of Beatrice Webb*, Norman and Jeanne MacKenzie (eds) (Virago: London, 1982–5), IV, 10.
21 Dalton, 146.
22 Webb, IV, 14. There seems to have been no discussion of the allocation of jobs.
23 Roy Jenkins, *The Chancellors* (Macmillan: London, 1998), 275.
24 Webb, III, 436.
25 Thomas, 75. I think Thomas exaggerates his rôle in the appointments. He was a great raconteur, unwilling to let veracity get in the way of a good story.
26 Webb, III, 436.
27 Quoted in David Howell, 'William Adamson' in *Oxford Dictionary of National Biography*, accessed online 5 January 2021.
28 Snowden, II, 761.
29 Webb, III, 347.
30 Clynes, II, 21.
31 Webb, IV, 28.
32 Snowden, II, 604.
33 Patrick Hastings, *The Autobiography* (William Heinemann: London, 1948), 229.

2. The Arrival of Labour

1 H. G. Wells, *The New Machiavelli* (Penguin Books: London, 2005), 225.
2 Thomas Johnston, *Memories* (Collins: London, 1952), 245.

3 J. R. Clynes, *Memoirs* (Hutchinson: London, 1937), I, 120.
4 Gerald Kaufman, 'John Hodge' in Alan Haworth and Dianne Hayter (eds), *Men Who Made Labour* (Routledge: London and New York, 2006), 93.
5 G. H. Roberts, 'Philip Snowden' in Haworth and Hayter (eds), 129.
6 Wells, 250.
7 Philip Viscount Snowden, *An Autobiography* (Ivor Nicholson and Watson: London, 1934), I, 124.
8 Fenner Brockway, *Inside the Left* (George Allen & Unwin: London, 1942), 222.
9 Peter Clark, *Churchill's Britain* (Haus Publishing: London, 2020), 215.
10 Emanuel Shinwell, *The Labour Story* (Macdonald: London, 1963), 62.
11 Lord George Hamilton, *Parliamentary Reminiscences and Reflections, 1868 to 1885* (John Murray: London, 1917), 323.
12 Roger Moore, *The Emergence of the Labour Party, 1880–1924* (Hodder and Stoughton: London, 1978), 7.
13 Herbert Tracey, *The Book of the Labour Party* (Caxton Publishing: London, 1925), 68.
14 Moore, 74.
15 Moore, 41.
16 Moore, 54.
17 Johnston, 32.
18 Moore, 6.
19 Snowden, I, 73.
20 David Clark, *Voices From Labour's Past* (Lensden Publishing: Kendal, 2015), 83.
21 Quoted in David Clark, 84.
22 Snowden, II, 542–4.
23 Quoted in Keith Laybourn, *The Labour Party 1881–1951* (Alan Sutton: Gloucester, 1988), 31.
24 Quoted in *Men Who Made Labour*, 15.

25 David Clark, 83.
26 G. T. Garratt, *The Mugwumps and the Labour Party* (Hogarth Press: London, 1932), 13, 88.
27 Frank Hodges, *My Adventures as a Labour Leader* (George Newnes: London, 1925), 24.
28 Garratt, 104.
29 David Clark, 37.
30 E. J. Hobsbawm, *Labouring Men* (Weidenfeld and Nicolson: London, 1965), 247.
31 Hobsbawm, 250, 257.
32 W. Stephen Sanders, 'Rt Hon Lord Olivier. BA, LLD, KCMG, CB' in Herbert Tracey, *The Book of the Labour Party* (Caxton Publishing: London, 1925), III, 232.
33 Quoted in Tracey, I, 95.
34 Peter Clark, 234.
35 Moore, 99.
36 Moore, 100–1.
37 Webb, III, 196.
38 Webb, III, 19.
39 Webb, III, 79.
40 Haworth and Hayter, 6.
41 Webb, III, 196.
42 Moore, 117.
43 Moore, 109.
44 Lord Shepherd, 'Labour's early Days' in Haworth and Hayter (eds), 249.

3. From Pressure Group to Government in Waiting

1 Mary Agnes Hamilton, *Remembering My Good Friends* (Jonathan Cape: London, 1944), 63.
2 Quoted in Robert E. Dowse, *Left in the Centre: The Independent Labour Party, 1893–1940* (Longmans: London, 1966), 96.

3 Hugh Dalton, *Call Back Yesterday* (Frederick Muller: London, 1953), 160.
4 Catherine Ann Cline, *Recruits to Labour* (Syracuse University Press: New York, 1963), 9.
5 Hamilton, 104.
6 Cline, 69.
7 Bertrand Russell, *Justice in Wartime* (National Labour Press: Manchester and London, 1915), 82.
8 Russell, 32.
9 G. Lowes Dickinson, *The European Anarchy* (George Allen & Unwin: London, 1914), 144.
10 Dickinson, 78.
11 Russell, 29.
12 Hamilton, 74.
13 Hamilton, 75.
14 A. J. P. Taylor, *The Trouble Makers* (Hamish Hamilton: London, 1957), 135.
15 Taylor, 134.
16 Taylor, 143.
17 Fenner Brockway, *Inside the Left* (George Allen & Unwin: London, 1942), 66.
18 David Kirkwood, *My Life of Revolt* (George G. Harrap: London, 1935), 168.
19 David Clark, *Voices from Labour's Past* (Lensden Publishing: Kendal, 2015), 87.
20 Quoted in Clark, 119.
21 Hamilton, 79.
22 D. H. Lawrence, *Lady Chatterley's Lover* (Penguin Books: Harmondsworth, 1960), 251.
23 Giles Radice and Lisanne Radice, *Will Thorne, Constructive Militant: A Study in New Unionism and New Politics* (George Allen & Unwin: London, 1974), 72.
24 C. E. Bechhofer Roberts ('Ephesian'), *Philip Snowden* (Cassell: London, 1929), 176.

25 Alan Haworth, 'David Shackleton' in Alan Haworth and Dianne Hayter (eds), *Men who Made Labour* (Routledge: London and New York, 2006), 206, 177.
26 Quoted in Roy Hattersley, *David Lloyd George* (Abacus: London, 2012), 483.
27 Ken Coates (ed.), *British Labour and the Russian Revolution* (The Bertrand Russell Peace Foundation: Nottingham, 1975), 24.
28 Coates, 29.
29 William Gallacher, *Revolt on the Clyde* (Lawrence and Wishart: London, 1948), 52–3.
30 Emanuel Shinwell, *The Labour Story* (Macdonald: London, 1963), 92.
31 Roberts, 185–6.
32 Harry Pollitt, *Serving My Time* (Lawrence and Wishart: London, 1940), 132, 136.
33 Quoted in Richard W. Lyman, *The First Labour Government 1924* (Chapman and Hall: London, 1957), 184.
34 Philip Viscount Snowden, *An Autobiography* (Ivor Nicholson and Watson: London, 1934), I, 500.
35 Roger Moore, *The Emergence of the Labour Party, 1880–1924* (Hodder and Stoughton: London, 1978), 131.

4. Steps to Downing Street

1 A. J. P. Taylor, *English History, 1914–1945* (Oxford University Press: Oxford, 1965), 126.
2 Taylor, 127.
3 Emanuel Shinwell, *The Labour Story* (Macdonald: London, 1963), 99.
4 John Shepherd and Keith Laybourn, *Britain's First Labour Government* (Palgrave Macmillan: Basingstoke, 2006), 25.
5 Taylor, 12.
6 Shepherd and Laybourn, 8.

7 Quoted in Roger Moore, *The Emergence of the Labour Party, 1880–1924* (Hodder and Stoughton: London, 1978), 179.
8 Quoted in Moore, 189.
9 Arthur Henderson, 'Labour as it is To-day' in Herbert Tracey (ed.), *The Book of the Labour Party* (Caxton Publishing: London, 1925), I, 32.
10 The Labour Party, *Report of the 23rd Annual Conference*, 101.
11 Philip Viscount Snowden, *An Autobiography* (Ivor Nicholson and Watson: London, 1934), II, 574.
12 Andrew Thorpe, *A History of the British Labour Party* (Palgrave Macmillan: Basingstoke, 2008), 59.
13 L. MacNeill Weir, *The Tragedy of Ramsay MacDonald* (Secker & Warburg: London, 1938), 108.
14 Weir, 109.
15 David Kirkwood, *My Life of Revolt* (George G. Harrap: London, 1935), 201.
16 Thomas Johnston, *Memories* (Collins: London, 1952), 47.
17 Johnston, 226.
18 Oswald Mosley, *My Life* (Nelson: London, 1970), 409.
19 The Labour Party, 113.
20 Johnston, 230.
21 Henderson, 21.
22 The Labour Party, 45.
23 The Labour Party, 45.
24 Shepherd and Laybourn, 26.
25 Peter Clark, *Churchill's Britain* (Haus Publishing: London, 2020), 20.
26 Shepherd and Laybourn, 15.
27 The Labour Party, 2.
28 L. S. Amery, *My Political Life* (Hutchinson: London, 1953–5), II, 280.
29 Emanuel Shinwell, *The Labour Story* (Macdonald: London, 1963), 106.

30 Hugh Dalton, *Call Back Yesterday* (Frederick Muller: London, 1953), 140.
31 Shepherd and Laybourn, 28.
32 Shepherd and Laybourn, 30.
33 Quoted in Shepherd and Laybourn, 31.
34 The Earl of Oxford and Asquith, *Memories and Reflections* (Cassell: London, 1928), II, 208–9.
35 Roy Jenkins, *Asquith* (Collins: London, 1964), 500.
36 Roy Jenkins, *The Chancellors* (Macmillan: London, 1998), 275.
37 J. C. C. Davidson, *Memoirs of a Conservative*, Robert Rhodes James (ed.) (Weidenfeld and Nicolson: London, 1969), 191.
38 Quoted in Shepherd and Laybourn, 56.

5. The Leader

1 C. R. Attlee, *As It Happened* (Odhams Press: London, 1953), 90.
2 L. MacNeill Weir, *The Tragedy of Ramsay MacDonald* (Secker & Warburg: London, 1938), 18.
3 Thomas Johnston, *Memories* (Collins: London, 1952), 216.
4 Lord Elton, *The Life of James Ramsay MacDonald (1866–1919)* (Collins: London, 1939), 31.
5 Hugh Dalton, *Call Back Yesterday* (Frederick Muller: London, 1953), 187.
6 Beatrice Webb, *The Diary of Beatrice Webb*, Norman and Jeanne MacKenzie (eds) (Virago: London, 1982–4), III, 427.
7 Dalton, 187.
8 David Marquand, *Ramsay MacDonald* (Jonathan Cape: London, 1977), 5.
9 Weir, 16.
10 Elton, 35.
11 Elton, 36.
12 Elton, 27.

13 Quoted in Marthe Bibesco, *Lord Thomson of Cardington* (Jonathan Cape: London, 1932), 216.
14 Dalton, 238.
15 Elton, 240.
16 Elton, 224.
17 Elton, 225.
18 Elton, 44.
19 Elton, 53.
20 Elton, 62.
21 Marquand, 22.
22 Elton, 65.
23 Elton, 70.
24 Marquand, 42.
25 Marquand, 26.
26 Elton, 75.
27 Quoted in Roger Moore, *The Emergence of the Labour Party, 1880–1924* (Hodder and Stoughton: London, 1978), 117.
28 Marquand, 131.
29 J. Ramsay MacDonald, *Margaret Ethel MacDonald* (Hodder and Stoughton: London, 1912), 136.
30 MacDonald, *Margaret Ethel MacDonald*, 116.
31 Marquand, 72.
32 MacDonald, *Margaret Ethel MacDonald*, 234.
33 Elton, 126.
34 Elton, 196.
35 Elton, 200.
36 Elton, 190.
37 Elton, 234.
38 Elton, 248.
39 Elton, 263.
40 Raymond A. Jones, *Arthur Ponsonby: The Politics of Life* (Christopher Helm: London, 1989), 97.
41 Elton, 298.

42 Mary Agnes Hamilton, *Remembering My Good Friends* (Jonathan Cape: London, 1944), 136.
43 Elton, 318–19.
44 David Kirkwood, *My Life of Revolt* (George G. Harrap: London, 1935), 164.
45 Kirkwood, 87.
46 Kirkwood, 164–5.
47 Elton, 337.
48 Elton, 355.
49 Marquand, 275.
50 Kirkwood, 197.
51 John Bew, *Citizen Clem* (Riverrun: London, 2017), 125.
52 MacDonald, *Margaret Ethel MacDonald*, 20.
53 Philip Viscount Snowden, *An Autobiography* (Ivor Nicholson and Watson: London, 1934), I, 93.
54 Fenner Brockway, *Inside the Left* (George Allen & Unwin: London, 1942), 35.
55 Brockway, 65.
56 Arnold Bennett, *Journals*, Norman Flower (ed.) (Cassell: London, 1933), III, 46.
57 Johnston, 217.
58 Webb, III, 39.
59 Brockway, 151.
60 Brockway, 152.
61 Roy Hattersley, *David Lloyd George* (Abacus: London, 2012), 585.
62 Webb, IV, 181.
63 Oswald Mosley, *My Life* (Nelson: London, 1970), 214.
64 Dalton, 289.
65 Richard Burdon Haldane, *An Autobiography* (Hodder and Stoughton: London, 1929), 331.
66 Quoted in Dalton, 144.
67 Haldane, 327.
68 Haldane, 328.

69 Haldane, 333.
70 Elton, 159, 170.
71 Lord Snell, *Men, Movements and Myself* (J. M. Dent: London, 1935), 252.
72 Elton, 223.
73 Webb, IV, 92.
74 J. H. Thomas, *My Story* (Hutchinson: London, 1937), 249.
75 Webb, IV, 35.
76 Kevin Morgan, *Ramsay MacDonald* (Haus Publishing: London, 2016), 106.
77 Hamilton, 127.
78 J. Ramsay MacDonald, *The Socialist Movement* (Williams and Norgate: London, 1911), 27.
79 Elton, 137.
80 Elton, 140.
81 MacDonald, *The Socialist Movement*, 89.
82 MacDonald, *The Socialist Movement*, 90.
83 MacDonald, *The Socialist Movement*, 116.
84 Catherine Ann Cline, *Recruits to Labour* (Syracuse University Press: New York, 1963), 33.
85 Quoted in Elton, 180.
86 Mosley, 241.
87 Quoted in David Clark, *Voices from Labour's Past* (Lensden Publishing: Kendal, 2015), 160.
88 Marchioness of Londonderry, *Retrospect* (Frederick Muller: London, 1938), 224.
89 Morgan, 105.
90 Londonderry, 227.
91 Garratt, *The Mugwumps*, 94, 104.
92 Dalton, 179.
93 Dalton, 226.
94 Dalton, 176.
95 Dalton, 179.

96 Martin Gilbert, *Winston S. Churchill: Prophet of Doom, 1922–1939* (Minerva: London, 1990), 197.
97 MacDonald, *The Socialist Movement*, 112.
98 MacDonald, *The Socialist Movement*, 154.
99 MacDonald, *The Socialist Movement*, 235.
100 Egon Wertheimer (trans.), *Portrait of the Labour Party* (G. P. Putnam: London, 1929), 174.
101 J. Ramsay MacDonald, *Parliament and Revolution* (National Labour Press: London, 1919), 97.
102 MacDonald, *Parliament and Revolution*, 102–3.
103 Hamilton, 110.
104 Morgan, 100.
105 Hamilton, 110.
106 Morgan, 101.
107 H. W. Nevinson, quoted in Morgan, 101.
108 Elton, 225.
109 Quoted in Cline, 78.
110 Jones, 141.
111 Kenneth Rose, *King George V* (Phoenix: London, 2000), 329.
112 Quoted in Marquand, 306.
113 Marquand, 307.

6. The Big Four

1 Tony Judge, *J. R. Clynes: A Political Life* (Alpha House Books: London, 2015), 13.
2 Judge, 16–17.
3 Judge, 19.
4 J. R. Clynes, *Memoirs* (Hutchinson: London, 1937), I, 31–2.
5 Clynes, I, 45.
6 Judge, 26.
7 Judge, 31.
8 Egon Wertheimer (trans.), *Portrait of the Labour Party* (G. P. Putnam: London, 1929), 183.
9 Giles Radice and Lisanne Radice, *Will Thorne, Constructive*

Militant: A Study in New Unionism and New Politics (George Allen & Unwin: London, 1974), 45.

10 Clynes, I, 65.
11 Judge, 45.
12 Judge, 207.
13 Tony Lloyd, 'J. R. Clynes' in Alan Haworth and Dianne Hayter (eds), *Men Who Made Labour* (Routledge: London and New York, 2006), 41.
14 Judge, 66.
15 Judge, 69.
16 Judge, 80.
17 Judge, 84.
18 Judge, 90.
19 Judge, 96.
20 Clynes, I, 204.
21 Clynes, I, 264.
22 Clynes, I, 294.
23 Clynes, I, 301.
24 Judge, 106.
25 Judge, 106.
26 Judge, 136.
27 Judge, 113.
28 Philip Viscount Snowden, *An Autobiography* (Ivor Nicholson and Watson: London, 1934), II, 531–2.
29 Judge, 121–2.
30 Judge, 126.
31 Roger Moore, *The Emergence of the Labour Party, 1880–1924* (Hodder and Stoughton: London, 1978), 187.
32 Hugh Dalton, *Call Back Yesterday* (Frederick Muller: London, 1953), 190–1.
33 David Kirkwood, *My Life of Revolt* (George G. Harrap: London, 1935), 197.
34 Beatrice Webb, *The Diary of Beatrice Webb*, Norman and Jeanne MacKenzie (eds) (Virago: London, 1982–4), III, 408.

35 Kirkwood, 198.
36 Dalton, 193.
37 Webb, IV, 18.
38 Judge, 144.
39 Judge, 146; J. R. Clynes, *Memoirs* (Hutchinson: London, 1937), II, 23.
40 Clynes, II, 27.
41 Webb, III, 385.
42 Richard S. Grayson, 'Arthur Henderson' in Greg Rosen, *Dictionary of Labour Biography* (Politicos: London, 2001), 276.
43 Alan Haworth and Dianne Hayter (eds), *Men Who Made Labour* (Routledge: London and New York, 2006), 14.
44 Derek Foster, 'Arthur Henderson' in Haworth and Hayter (eds), 84.
45 Chris Wrigley, *Arthur Henderson* (University of Wales Press: Cardiff, 1990), 42.
46 Wrigley, 11.
47 Wrigley, 17.
48 Wrigley, 19.
49 John Saville, 'Arthur Henderson' in Joyce M. Bellamy and John Saville (eds), *Dictionary of Labour Biography* (August M. Kelley: New Jersey, 1972), I, 161.
50 Wrigley, 21.
51 Wrigley, 52–3.
52 Philip Viscount Snowden, *An Autobiography* (Ivor Nicholson and Watson: London, 1934), I, 125.
53 Wrigley, 60.
54 Wrigley, 64.
55 Mary Agnes Hamilton, *Arthur Henderson* (William Heinemann: London, 1938), 224.
56 Dalton, 172, 190, 193–4.
57 Wrigley, 74.
58 Wrigley, 71.

59 Wrigley, 81.
60 Wrigley, 93–4.
61 Wrigley, 98.
62 Wrigley, 102.
63 Wrigley, 114.
64 Dalton, 189.
65 Saville, 162.
66 Hamilton, 234.
67 Webb, III, 347.
68 Wrigley, 140.
69 Dalton, 42–3.
70 Wrigley, 155.
71 Webb, III, 352, 432.
72 Dalton, 126.
73 Dalton, 190.
74 Lord Elton, *Among Others* (Hutchinson: London, 1938), 220.
75 Webb, IV, 254.
76 Webb, IV, 359.
77 Frank Hodges, *My Adventures as a Labour Leader* (George Newnes: London, 1925), 25.
78 J. H. Thomas, *My Story* (Hutchinson: London, 1937), 265.
79 Mary Agnes Hamilton, *Remembering My Good Friends* (Jonathan Cape: London, 1944), 110–11.
80 Snowden, I, 13.
81 C. E. Bechhofer Roberts, *Philip Snowden* (Cassell: London, 1929), 86.
82 Quoted in Dalton, 189.
83 Thomas Johnston, *Memories* (Collins: London, 1952), 229.
84 Roy Jenkins, *The Chancellors* (Macmillan: London, 1998), 260.
85 Colin Cross, *Philip Snowden* (Barrie and Jenkins: London, 1966), 62.
86 Quoted in David Clark, *Voices from Labour's Past* (Lensden Publishing: Kendal, 2015), 185.

87 Webb, IV, 145.
88 Webb, IV, 254.
89 Earl Lloyd George, *Lloyd George* (Frederick Muller: London, 1960), 231–4.
90 Hamilton, 114.
91 Webb, IV, 11.
92 Webb, IV, 46.
93 L. MacNeill Weir, *The Tragedy of Ramsay MacDonald* (Secker & Warburg: London, 1938), 446.
94 Jack Straw, 'Philip Snowden' in Haworth and Hayter (eds), 184.
95 Weir, 370.
96 Snowden, II, 657.
97 Webb, IV, 184.
98 Thomas, 248.
99 Philip Whitehead, 'J. H. Thomas' in Rosen, 576.
100 Gregory Blaxland, *J. H. Thomas* (Frederick Muller: London, 1964), 17.
101 Earl of Birkenhead, *Contemporary Personalities* (Cassell: London, 1924), 6.
102 Henry 'Chips' Channon, *The Diaries*, Simon Heffer (ed.) (Hutchinson: London, 2021–2), 251.
103 Thomas, 20–1.
104 Blaxland, 51.
105 Blaxland, 61.
106 Blaxland, 84.
107 Dalton, 193.
108 Quoted in Blaxland, 290.
109 Blaxland, 152.
110 Blaxland, 113.
111 Blaxland, 142.
112 Channon, I, 108.
113 Thomas, 234.
114 Thomas, 15.

115 Thomas, 32.
116 Thomas, 247.
117 Thomas, 205.
118 A. G. Gardiner, *Certain People of Importance* (Jonathan Cape: London, 1926), 255.
119 Thomas, 69.
120 Thomas, 70.
121 Dalton, 192.
122 Thomas, 262.
123 Thomas, 30.
124 Blaxland, 211.
125 Dalton, 102.
126 Snowden, II, 739.
127 Blaxland, 211.
128 Edward Marsh, *A Number of People: A Book of Reminisces* (Heinemann: London, 1939), 402.
129 Raymond A. Jones, *Arthur Ponsonby* (Christopher Helm: London, 1987), 230.
130 Blaxland, 213.
131 Webb, IV, 369.
132 Dalton, 147.

7. Old Labour

1 David Howell, 'William Adamson' in *Oxford Dictionary of National Biography*, accessed online 5 January 2021.
2 Howell.
3 Beatrice Webb, *The Diary of Beatrice Webb*, Norman and Jeanne MacKenzie (eds) (Virago: London, 1982–4), III, 329.
4 Quoted in A. J. A. Morris, *C. P. Trevelyan* (Blackstuff Press: Belfast, 1977), 147.
5 Webb, III, 330–1.
6 William Gallacher, *Revolt on the Clyde* (Lawrence and Wishart: London, 1949), 266.
7 Quoted in Howell.

8 Greg Rosen, 'William Adamson' in Greg Rosen (ed.), *Dictionary of Labour Biography* (Politico's: London, 2001), 6.
9 Thomas Johnston, *Memories* (Collins: London, 1952), 101.
10 Johnston, 103.
11 Philip Viscount Snowden, *An Autobiography* (Ivor Nicholson and Watson: London, 1934), II, 736.
12 Kenneth O. Morgan, *Labour People* (Oxford University Press: Oxford, 1987), 69.
13 Greg Rosen, 'Vernon Hartshorn' in Rosen (ed.), 266.
14 Peter Stead, 'Vernon Hartshorn: Miners' Agent and Cabinet Minister', *Glamorgan Historian* (2006), VI, 90; Duncan Tanner et al., *The Labour Party in Wales 1900–2000* (University of Wales Press: Cardiff, 2000), 95.
15 Roger Moore, *The Emergence of the Labour Party, 1880–1924* (Hodder and Stoughton: London, 1978), 131–2.
16 Quoted in Stead, 86.
17 James Griffiths, *Pages from Memory* (J. M. Dent: London, 1969), 18; Joyce Bellamy and John Saville, 'Vernon Hartshorn' in Joyce Bellamy and John Saville (eds), *Dictionary of Labour Biography* (August M. Kelley: New Jersey), I, 151.
18 Stead, 90.
19 Stead, 91.
20 Hywel Francis and David Smith, *The Fed: A History of the South Wales Miners in the Twentieth Century* (Lawrence and Wishart: London, 1981), 141.
21 Herbert Tracey, *The Book of the Labour Party* (Caxton Publishing: London, 1925), III, 226.
22 Morgan, 76.
23 Fenner Brockway, *Socialism Over Sixty Years* (George Allen & Unwin: London, 1946), 111.
24 Marsha Singh, 'Fred Jowett' in Alan Haworth and Dianne Hayter (eds), *Men Who Made Labour* (Routledge: London and New York, 2006), 114.

25 John H. Grigg, 'Fred Jowett 1864–1944', in *Labour Heritage* (Spring 2018), 7.
26 Matthew Seward, 'Frederick Jowett' in Rosen (ed.), 330.
27 Singh, 115.
28 Brockway, *Socialism*, 62.
29 Brockway, *Socialism*, 322–4.
30 Philip Viscount Snowden, *An Autobiography* (Ivor Nicholson and Watson: London, 1934), I, 303.
31 Singh, 117.
32 Brockway, *Socialism*, 187.
33 Quoted in Brockway, *Socialism*, 323.
34 Grigg, 11.
35 Brockway, *Socialism*, 210.
36 Margaret Olivier, *Sydney Olivier* (George Allen & Unwin: London, 1948), 31.
37 Greg Rosen, 'Sydney Haldane Olivier (Lord Olivier)' in Rosen (ed.), 451.
38 Webb, I, 316.
39 Webb, II, 166.
40 Olivier, 134.
41 Olivier, 93.
42 Snowden, II, 611.
43 Maurice Cowling, *The Impact of Labour* (Cambridge University Press: Cambridge, 1971), 379.
44 Olivier, 18.
45 Snowden, II, 610.
46 J. S. Middleton, revised by Marc Brodie, 'Thomas Shaw' in *Oxford Dictionary of National Biography*, accessed online 7 January 2021.
47 Spartacus Educational, 'Tom Shaw', accessed online 3 April 2022.
48 Tracey, III, 188.
49 Middleton.

50 Greg Rosen, 'Rt Hon Tom Shaw MP CBE' in Rosen (ed.), 551.
51 Webb, III, 294.
52 Middleton.
53 J. H. Thomas, *My Story* (Hutchinson: London, 1937), 282.
54 Snowden, I, 130–1; John Bew, *Citizen Clem* (Riverrun: London, 2017), 132.
55 Ian McCartney, 'Stephen Walsh' in Haworth and Hayter (eds), 201.
56 A. E. Watkin, revised by Marc Brodie, 'Stephen Walsh' in *Oxford Dictionary of National Biography*, accessed online 8 January 2021.
57 John Saville, 'Stephen Walsh' in Joyce Bellamy and John Saville, 'Vernon Hartshorn' in Joyce Bellamy and John Saville (eds), *Dictionary of Labour Biography* (August M. Kelley: New Jersey), IV, 87.
58 Snowden, I, 303.
59 J. R. Clynes, *Memoirs*, I (Hutchinson: London, 1937), 127.
60 Keith Feiling, *The Life of Neville Chamberlain* (Macmillan: London, 1946), 68.
61 Watkin.
62 Watkin.
63 Randolph S. Churchill, *Lord Derby, King of Lancashire* (Heinemann: London, 1959), 507.
64 Churchill, 567–8.
65 W. Golant, 'C. R. Attlee in the First and Second Labour Governments', *Parliamentary Affairs*, XXVI (1973).
66 Bew, 134.
67 Tracey, III, 220.
68 Golant, 318–19.
69 C. R. Attlee, *As It Happened* (Odhams Press: London, 1953), 75.
70 Bew, 132.

71 Quoted in Oswald Mosley, *My Life* (Nelson: London, 1970), 216.
72 Webb, I, 317.
73 Snowden, II, 794.
74 Webb, I, 317.
75 Quoted in Webb, I, 318.
76 Margaret Cole, *Makers of the Labour Movement* (Longman Green: London, 1948), 231.
77 Cole, 233.
78 Quoted in Cole, 227.
79 Webb, II, 204.
80 Mary Stocks, *Commonplace Book* (Peter Davies: London, 1970), 57.
81 Mary Agnes Hamilton, *Remembering My Good Friends* (Jonathan Cape: London, 1944), 260.
82 Brockway, *Inside the Left*, 123.
83 Arnold Bennett, *The Journals*, III, Norman Flower (ed.) (Cassell: London, 1933), 29.
84 Webb, II, 23.
85 Cole, 238.
86 Webb, II, 159.
87 Webb, III, 205.
88 Webb, III, 417.
89 John Brown, 'Sidney and Beatrice Webb (1st Baron and Lady Passfield)' in Rosen (ed.), 598.
90 Webb, IV, 38.
91 Webb, I, 417.
92 Norman and Jeanne Mackenzie, 'Introduction to Part V' in Webb, I, 317.
93 Webb, I, 357.
94 Webb, I, 224.
95 Mosley, 174.
96 Quoted in John Hannan, *The Life of John Wheatley* (Spokesman: Nottingham, 1988), 123.

97 Brockway, *Inside the Left* (Allen & Unwin: London, 1942), 194.
98 Charles Masterman, quoted in Ian S. Wood, *John Wheatley* (Manchester University Press: Manchester, 1990), 139.
99 Emanuel Shinwell, *The Labour Story* (Macdonald: London, 1963), 110.
100 Wood, 7.
101 Hannan, 1.
102 John McGovern, *Neither Fear Nor Favour* (Blandford Press: London, 1960), 65.
103 Wood, 10.
104 McGovern, 65.
105 Wood, 127.
106 Hannan, 31.
107 Quoted in Wood, 29.
108 Quoted in Chris Bryant, 'John Wheatley' in Rosen (ed.), 604.
109 Robert Blake, *The Unknown Prime Minister* (Eyre and Spottiswood: London, 1955), 394.
110 Wood, 113–14.
111 John T. Scanlon, 'Rt Hon John Wheatley, MP' in Tracey, III, 211–12.
112 Wood, 119.
113 Roy Jenkins, *Gallery of Twentieth Century Portraits* (David and Charles: Newton Abbot and London, 1988), 73.
114 Scanlon, 216.
115 Dalton, 147.
116 Wood, 120.
117 L. MacNeill Weir, *The Tragedy of Ramsay MacDonald* (Secker & Warburg: London, 1938), 139.
118 Wood, 120.

8. New Labour

1 Mosa Anderson, *Noel Buxton* (George Allen & Unwin: London, 1952), 30

2 Anderson, 31.

3 Victoria de Bunsen, *Charles Roden Buxton* (George Allen & Unwin: London, 1948), 63.

4 Anderson, 67.

5 Anderson, 103.

6 Anderson, 105.

7 Anderson, 111.

8 George Edwards, *From Crow-Scaring to Westminster* (Larks Press: Dereham, 2008), 128.

9 Oswald Mosley, *My Life* (Nelson: London, 1970), 217.

10 Beatrice Webb, *The Diary of Beatrice Webb*, Norman and Jeanne MacKenzie (eds) (Virago: London, 1982–5), IV, 120.

11 Quoted in Robert Ingham, '1st Viscount Chelmsford (Frederic John Napier Thesiger)' in Greg Rosen (ed.), *Dictionary of Labour Biography* (Politico's: London, 2001), 115.

12 Wilfred Thesiger, *The Life of My Choice* (Collins: London, 1987), 59–60.

13 Thesiger, 77.

14 Webb, III, 348.

15 Webb, II, 320.

16 Hugh Dalton, *Call Back Yesterday* (Frederick Muller: London, 1953).

17 Quoted in Ingham, 117.

18 Philip Viscount Snowden, *An Autobiography* (Ivor Nicholson and Watson: London, 1934), II, 607.

19 Stephen Gosling and John Saville, 'Frederic John Thesiger, 3rd Baron and 1st Viscount Chelmsford' in Joyce Bellamy and John Saville (eds), *Dictionary of Labour Biography* (Macmillan: London, 1979), V, 214.

20 L. S. Amery, *The Leo Amery Diaries*, John Barnes and David Nicholson (eds) (Hutchinson: London, 1980), I, 365.
21 J. H. Thomas, *My Story* (Hutchinson: London, 1937), 65.
22 Webb, II, 113.
23 Webb, I, 338.
24 Webb, I, 345.
25 Richard Burdon Haldane, *An Autobiography* (Hodder and Stoughton: London, 1929), 114.
26 Webb, I, 360.
27 Haldane, 91–2.
28 Haldane, 125.
29 Jean Graham Hall, *Haldane, Statesman, Lawyer, Philosopher* (Barry Rose Law Publishers: Chichester, 1996), 340.
30 Haldane, 224.
31 Haldane, 333.
32 Haldane, 327.
33 Snowden, II, 705.
34 Webb, IV, 150.
35 John Campbell, *Haldane* (Christopher Hurst: London, 2022), 3.
36 Earl of Birkenhead, *Contemporary Personalities* (Cassell: London, 1924), 81.
37 Snowden, II, 704.
38 Webb, II, 236.
39 Webb, III, 145.
40 Hall and Martin, 1–2.
41 Webb, IV, 50.
42 Webb, I, 60.
43 Lord Parmoor, *A Retrospect* (William Heinemann: London, 1936), 28.
44 Webb, I, 322.
45 Quoted in Greg Rosen, 'Baron Parmoor of Frith (Charles Alfred Cripps)' in Rosen (ed.), 459.
46 Webb, II, 348.

47 Parmoor, 64.
48 Parmoor, 101.
49 Snowden, II, 609.
50 Webb, III, 346.
51 Parmoor, 131.
52 Parmoor, 138.
53 Parmoor, 173.
54 Parmoor, 186.
55 Webb, I, 123.
56 Parmoor, 188.
57 Parmoor, 16.
58 Parmoor, 197.
59 Parmoor, 208.
60 Webb, I, 59.
61 Marthe Bibesco, *Lord Thomson of Cardington* (Jonathan Cape: London, 1932), 23.
62 Bibesco, 57.
63 Henry 'Chips' Channon, *The Diaries*, Simon Heffer (ed.) (Hutchinson: London, 2021–2), II, 82.
64 Bibesco, 142.
65 Lord Elton, *Among Others* (Hutchinson: London, 1934), 149.
66 Webb, IV, 229.
67 Maurice Cowling, *The Impact of Labour* (Cambridge University Press: Cambridge, 1971), 371.
68 Mary Agnes Hamilton, *Remembering My Good Friends* (Jonathan Cape: London, 1944), 164.
69 Webb, I, 194–5.
70 Webb, II, 286.
71 Webb, II, 182.
72 A. J. A. Morris, *C. P. Trevelyan* (Blackstaff Press: Belfast, 1977), 74.
73 Charles Trevelyan, *From Liberalism to Labour* (George Allen & Unwin: London, 1921), 45, 48–9.
74 Trevelyan, 53.

75 Trevelyan, 10.
76 Morris, 152.
77 Dalton, 196.
78 Richard Gorton, 'Josiah Wedgwood MP', *Labour Heritage* (Autumn 2020), 1.
79 Josiah C. Wedgwood, *Memoirs of a Fighting Life* (Hutchinson: London, 1940), 60.
80 Wedgwood, 78
81 Wedgwood, 78.
82 C. V. Wedgwood, *The Last of the Radicals* (Jonathan Cape: London, 1951), 79.
83 C. V. Wedgwood, 119.
84 Dalton, 197.
85 C. V. Wedgwood, 96.
86 C. V. Wedgwood, 221.
87 C. V. Wedgwood, 126.
88 Josiah C. Wedgwood, 146.
89 Gorton, 3.
90 Gorton, 3.
91 Josiah C. Wedgwood, 183.
92 C. V. Wedgwood, 149.
93 Gorton, 3.
94 Gorton, 4.
95 C. V. Wedgwood, 153.
96 Dalton, 197.

9. In Office but not in Power

1 Quoted in Richard W. Lyman, *The First Labour Government 1924* (Chapman and Hall: London, 1957), 106.
2 Lyman, 216.
3 L. MacNeill Weir, *The Tragedy of Ramsay MacDonald* (Secker & Warburg: London, 1938), 173.
4 David Marquand, *Ramsay MacDonald* (Jonathan Cape: London, 1977), 306.

5 Quoted in Lyman, 158.
6 Quoted in Marquand, 312.
7 Quoted in Marquand, 334.
8 Quoted in Lyman, 137.
9 Quoted in Chris Cook, 'By-elections of the first Labour Government' in Chris Cook and John Ramsden (eds), *By-elections in British Politics* (UCL Press: London, 1997), 45.
10 Quoted in Peter Clark, *Churchill's Britain* (Haus Publishing: London, 2020), 9.
11 Marquand, 320.
12 Quoted in Roy Jenkins, *The Chancellors* (Macmillan: London, 1998), 278.
13 Jenkins, 279.
14 Quoted in Bernard Mallet and W. Oswald George, *British Budgets 1921–22 to 1931–32* (Macmillan: London, 1932), 108.
15 Charles Trevelyan, quoted in Lyman, 144n.
16 Quoted in Marquand, 325.
17 Dora Russell, *The Tamarisk Tree* (Elek/Pemberton: London, 1975), 170.
18 John Shepherd and Keith Laybourn, *Britain's First Labour Government* (Palgrave Macmillan: Basingstoke, 2006), 76.
19 *Six Months of Labour Government* (Independent Labour Party Information Committee: London, 1924), 23.
20 Marquand, 357.
21 W. Golant, 'C. R. Attlee in the First and Second Labour Governments', *Parliamentary Affairs* (1973), XXVI, 320.
22 Shepherd and Laybourn, 167.
23 Quoted in Lyman, 214.
24 Quoted in Shepherd and Laybourn, 97.
25 I am grateful to Professor Steve Schifferes for this point.
26 Lyman, 121.
27 Quoted in Marquand, 371.
28 Quoted in Marquand, 378.
29 Quoted in Lyman, 258.

30 Quoted in Lyman, 259.
31 Quoted in Marquand, 378.
32 Quoted in Shepherd and Laybourn, 181.
33 Marquand, 384.
34 MacDonald's diary, quoted in Marquand, 387.
35 Shepherd and Laybourn, 182. David Marquand gives a variation of this story, according to which Thomas was staying with Philip Snowden. He saw the papcr first, hammered on Snowden's door. 'Get up, you lazy devil,' he shouted. 'We're bunkered.' (Marquand, 381.)
36 Arthur Henderson, 'Introductory: Labour as it is To-day' in Herbert Tracey (ed.), *The Book of the Labour Party* (Caxton: London, 1925), 33.
37 Marquand, 387.
38 Quoted in Fenner Brockway, *Socialism Over Sixty Years* (George Allen & Unwin: London, 1946), 222.
39 Quoted in Shepherd and Laybourn, 70.
40 Marquand, 388.
41 Quoted in Marquand, 388.

Acknowledgements

I cannot remember a time when I was not interested in the subject of this book. My paternal grandparents, Lilian and William Clark, were Labour Party activists in the unpromising constituency of Southend-on-Sea in the 1920s. William Clark was born in Banff and brought up in Elgin, where we had a family holiday when I was seven years old. We went several times to Lossiemouth. 'Ramsay MacDonald, Labour's first prime minister, came from here,' I was told when we visited.

Since my teens I have been an avid reader of books on the political history of Britain in the nineteenth and twentieth centuries. At Keele University I did the special subject of Labour History with Frank Bealey. One of my closest friends was a grandson of one of the men of 1924, and through him I met several close relatives of Josiah Wedgwood. But in the next few decades other interests and careers took over. Writing this has been like sorting out in my mind a familiar story.

I have been grateful to many friends and relatives. Dave Cope of the Kendal bookshop Left on the Shelf has provided me with some essential books. The London Library has carried out an excellent service, sending books through the post to Somerset during the COVID-19 lockdown. Several friends have made helpful comments on various chapters, to whom I give my thanks – Thomas Clark, Simon Gamble, Edmund Marsden, John Payne, Colin Thomas, Ruth Windle, and Professor Steve Schifferes of City University. Feedback from a talk I gave to the Frome Society for Local Study has also been useful.

I am indebted to Gabriel Clark and Nathaniel Clark for technical advice and guidance relating to the word processor; and to Colin Thomas and Jane and Jonathan Rendel for the loan of books.

Above all, I thank Theresa Clark, who has provided unfailing love, support, encouragement, and punctilious comments on every sentence of the text. I am so lucky to be married to her.

Finally, I wish to thank the team at Haus: Barbara Schwepcke, Harry Hall, Ella Carr, Daisy Wilkins, Edoardo Braschi, and Luz Aguilera. It has been a pleasure to work with them.

Bibliography

Adonis, Andrew, *Ernest Bevin, Labour's Churchill* (Biteback: London, 2021).

Amery, Leo, *The Leo Amery Diaries*, John Barnes and David Nicholson (eds) (Hutchinson: London, 1980).

Amery, Leo, *My Political Life*, 3 vols (Hutchinson: London, 1953–5).

Anderson, Mosa, *Noel Buxton: A Life* (George Allen & Unwin: London, 1952).

Attlee, C. R., *As It Happened* (Odhams Press: London, 1953).

Bennett, Arnold, *The Journals of Arnold Bennett, Volume 3: 1921–1928*, Norman Flower (ed.) (Cassell: London, 1933).

Bew, John, *Citizen Clem* (Riverrun: London, 2017).

Bibesco, Marthe, *Lord Thomson of Cardington: A Memoir and Some Letters* (Jonathan Cape: London, 1932).

Birkenhead, Earl of, *Contemporary Personalities* (Cassell: London, 1924).

Blake, Robert, *The Unknown Prime Minister: The Life and Times of Andrew Bonar Law 1858–1923* (Eyre & Spottiswoode: London, 1955).

Blaxland, Gregory, *J. H. Thomas: A Life for Unity* (Frederick Muller: London, 1964).

Brockway, Fenner, *Inside the Left* (George Allen & Unwin: London, 1942).

Brockway, Fenner, *Socialism Over Sixty Years: The Life of Jowett of Bradford (1864–1944)* (George Allen & Unwin: London, 1946).

Channon, Henry 'Chips' in *The Diaries*, 3 vols, Simon Heffer (ed.) (Hutchinson: London, 2022).

Churchill, Randolph S., *Lord Derby 'King of Lancashire': The Official Life of Edward, Seventeenth Earl of Derby 1865–1948* (Heinemann: London, 1959).

Clark, David, *Voices from Labour's Past: Ordinary People, Extraordinary Lives* (Lensden Publishing: Kendal, 2015).

Clark, Peter, *Churchill's Britain: From the Antrim Coast to the Isle of Wight* (Haus Publishing: London, 2020).

Cline, Catherine Ann, *Recruits to Labour: The British Labour Party 1914–1931* (Syracuse University Press: New York, 1963).

Clynes, J. R., *Memoirs*, 2 vols (Hutchinson: London, 1937).

Coates, Ken (ed.), *British Labour and the Russian Revolution* (The Bertrand Russell Peace Foundation: Nottingham, 1975).

Cole, G. D. H., *Socialism in Evolution* (Penguin Books: Harmondsworth, 1938).

Cole, Margaret, *Makers of the Labour Movement* (Longman, Green: London, 1948).

Cowling, Maurice, *The Impact of Labour: The Beginning of Modern British Politics* (Cambridge University Press: Cambridge, 1971).

Cross, Cross, *Philip Snowden* (Barrie and Jenkins: London, 1966).

Dalton, Hugh, *Call Back Yesterday: Memoirs 1887–1931* (Frederick Muller: London, 1953).

Davidson, J. C. C., *Memoirs of a Conservative*, Robert Rhodes James (ed.) (Weidenfeld and Nicolson: London, 1969).

de Bunsen, Victoria, *Charles Roden Buxton: A Memoir* (George Allen & Unwin: London, 1948).

Dickinson, G. Lowes, *The European Anarchy* (George Allen & Unwin: London, 1916).

Dilks, David, *Neville Chamberlain*, 2 vols (Cambridge University Press: Cambridge, 1984).

Dowse, Robert E., *Left in the Centre: The Independent Labour Party 1893–1940* (Longmans: London, 1966).

Edwards, George, *From Crow-Scaring to Westminster: An Autobiography* (Larks Press: Dereham, 2008).

Elton, Lord, *Among Others* (Hutchinson: London, 1938).

Elton, Lord, *The Life of James Ramsay MacDonald (1866–1919)* (Collins: London, 1939).

Feiling, Keith, *The Life of Neville Chamberlain* (Macmillan: London, 1946).

Francis, Hywel, and Smith, David, *The Fed: A History of the South Wales Miners in the Twentieth Century* (Lawrence and Wishart: London, 1981).

Gallacher, William, *Revolt on the Clyde* (Lawrence and Wishart: London, 1948).

Gardiner, A. G., *Certain People of Importance* (Jonathan Cape: London, 1926).

Garratt, G. T., *The Mugwumps and the Labour Party* (Hogarth Press: London, 1932).

Gilbert, Martin, *Winston S. Churchill: The Prophet of Doom, 1922–1939* (Minerva: London, 1990).

Glasgow, George, *MacDonald as Diplomatist: The Foreign Policy of the First Labour Government in Great Britain* (Jonathan Cape: London, 1925).

Graham, Thomas N., *Willie Graham* (Hutchinson: London, 1948).

Griffiths, James, *Pages from Memory* (J. M. Dent: London, 1969).

Haldane, Richard Burdon, *An Autobiography* (Hodder and Stoughton: London, 1929).

Hall, Jean Graham, Martin, Douglas, *Haldane: Statesman, Lawyer, Philosopher* (Barry Rose Law Publishers: Chichester, 1991).

Hamilton, Lord George, *Parliamentary Reminiscences and Reflections 1868– 1885* (John Murray: London, 1917).

Hamilton, Mary Agnes, *Arthur Henderson: A Biography* (Heinemann: London, 1938).

Hamilton, Mary Agnes, *Mary Macarthur: A Biographical Sketch* (Leonard Parsons: London, 1926).

Hamilton, Mary Agnes, *Remembering My Good Friends* (Jonathan Cape: London, 1944).

Hannan, John, *The Life of John Wheatley* (Spokesman: Nottingham, 1988).

Hastings, Patrick, *Autobiography* (Heinemann: London, 1950).

Hattersley, Roy, *David Lloyd George: The Great Outside* (Abacus: London, 2012).

Haworth, Alan, and Hayter, Dianne (eds), *The Men Who Made Labour: The PLP of 1906 – The Personalities and the Politics* (Routledge: London and New York, 2006).

Hobsbawm, R. J., *Labouring Men: Studies in the History of Labour* (Weidenfeld & Nicolson: London, 1965).

Hodges, Frank, *My Adventures as a Labour Leader* (George Newnes: London, 1925).

Jenkins, Roy, *Asquith* (Collins: London, 1964).

Jenkins, Roy, *The Chancellors* (Macmillan: London, 1998).

Jenkins, Roy, *Gallery of Twentieth Century Portraits* (David and Charles: Newton Abbot and London, 1988).

Johnston, Thomas, *Memories* (Collins: London, 1952).

Jones, Raymond A., *Arthur Ponsonby: The Politics of Life* (Christopher Helm: London, 1987).

Judge, Tony, *J. R. Clynes: A Political Life* (Alpha House Books: London, 2015).

Kirkwood, David, *My Life of Revolt* (George G. Harrap: London, 1935).

Lawrence, D. H., *Lady Chatterley's Lover* (Penguin Books: Harmondsworth, 1960).

Laybourn, Keith, *The Labour Party 1881–1951: A Reader in History* (Alan Sutton: Gloucester, 1988).

Lee, Francis, *Fabianism and Colonialism: The Life and Political Thought of Lord Sydney* (Defiant Books: London, 1988).

Lloyd, Lord, *Egypt Since Cromer*, 2 vols (Macmillan: London, 1933–4).
Lloyd George, Earl, *Lloyd George* (Frederick Muller: London, 1960).
Londonderry, Marchioness of, *Retrospect* (Frederick Muller: London, 1938).
Lyman, Richard W., *The First Labour Government 1924* (Chapman and Hall: London, 1957).
McCallum, R. B., *Asquith* (Duckworth: London, 1935).
MacDonald, J. Ramsay, *Margaret Ethel MacDonald* (Hodder and Stoughton: London, 1913).
MacDonald, J. Ramsay, *Parliament and Revolution* (The National Labour Press: London, 1919).
MacDonald, J. Ramsay, *The Socialist Movement* (Williams and Norgate: London, 1911).
MacDonald, J. Ramsay, *Wanderings and Excursions* (Jonathan Cape: London, 1932).
McGovern, John, *Neither Fear nor Favour* (Blandford Press: London, 1960).
Macleod, Iain, *Neville Chamberlain* (Frederick Muller: London, 1961).
Mallett, Bernard, and George, C. Oswald, *British Budgets 1921–22 to 1932–33* (Macmillan: London, 1933).
Marquand, David, *Ramsay MacDonald* (Jonathan Cape: London, 1977).
Marsh, Edward, *A Number of People: A Book of Reminiscences* (Heinemann: London, 1939).
Moore, Roger, *The Emergence of the Labour Party, 1880–1924* (Hodder and Stoughton: London, 1978).
Morgan, Kenneth O., *Labour People, Leaders and Lieutenants, Hardie to Kinnock* (Oxford University Press: Oxford, 1987).
Morgan, Kevin, *Ramsay MacDonald* (Haus Publishing: London, 2006).

Morris, A. J. A., *C. P. Trevelyan, Portrait of a Radical* (Blackstaff Press: Belfast, 1977).

Mosley, Oswald, *My Life* (Nelson: London, 1970).

Pollitt, Harry, *Serving My Time: An Apprenticeship in Politics* (Lawrence and Wishart: London, 1940).

Olivier, Lord, *White Capital and Coloured Labour* (Hogarth Press: London, 1929).

Olivier, Margaret, *Sydney Olivier* (Allen and Unwin: London, 1948).

Oxford, Earl of, and Asquith, K. G., *Memories and Reflections 1857–1927*, 2 vols (Cassell: London, 1928).

Parmoor, Lord, *A Retrospect* (Heinemann: London, 1936).

Radice, Giles, and Radice, Lisanne, *Will Thorne, Constructive Militant: A Study in New Unionism and New Politics* (George Allen & Unwin: London, 1974).

Roberts, C. E. Bechhofer ('Ephesian'), *Philip Snowden: An Impartial Portrait* (Cassell: London, 1929).

Rose, Kenneth, *King George V* (Phoenix: London, 2000).

Rosen, Greg (ed.), *Dictionary of Labour Biography* (Politico's: London, 2001).

Russell, A. K., *Liberal Landslide: The General Election of 1906* (David and Charles: Newton Abbot, 1973).

Russell, Bertrand, *Justice in Wartime* (National Labour Press: Manchester and London, 1915).

Russell, Dora, *The Tamarisk Tree: My Quest for Liberty and Love* (Elek/Pemberton: London, 1975).

Shepherd, John, *George Lansbury: At the Heart of Old Labour* (Oxford University Press: Oxford, 2002).

Shepherd, John, and Laybourn, Keith, *Britain's First Labour Government* (Palgrave Macmillan: Basingstoke, 2006).

Shinwell, Emanuel, *Conflict Without Malice* (Odhams Press: London, 1955).

Shinwell, Emanuel, *The Labour Story* (Macdonald: London, 1963).

Sloane, Nan, *The Women in the Room: Labour's Forgotten History* (I. B. Tauris: London and New York, 2018).
Snell, Lord, *Me, Movements and Myself* (E. J. Dent: London, 1936).
Snowden, Philip Viscount, *An Autobiography*, 2 vols (Ivor Nicholson and Watson: London, 1934).
Stocks, Mary, *My Commonplace Book* (Peter Davies: London, 1970).
Tanner, Duncan, et al., *The Labour Party in Wales 1900–2000* (University of Wales Press: Cardiff, 2000).
Tawney, R. H., *The Radical Tradition: Twelve Essays on Politics, Education and Literature* (Penguin Books: Harmondsworth, 1966).
Taylor, A. J. P., *English History, 1914–1945* (Oxford University Press: Oxford, 1965).
Taylor, A. J. P., *The Origins of the Second World War* (Hamish Hamilton: London, 1961).
Taylor, A. J. P., *Politicians, Socialism and Historians* (Hamish Hamilton: London, 1980).
Taylor, A. J. P., *The Trouble Makers: Dissent in Foreign Policy, 1792–1939* (Hamish Hamilton: London, 1957).
Thesiger, Wilfred, *The Life of My Choice* (Collins: London, 1987).
Thomas, J. H., *My Story* (Hutchinson: London, 1937).
Thomas, J. H., *When Labour Rules* (W. Collins: London, 1920).
Thorpe, Andrew, *A History of the British Labour Party* (Palgrave Macmillan: Basingstoke, 2008).
Thurtle, Ernest, *Time's Winged Chariot* (Chaterson: London, 1945).
Trevelyan, Charles, *From Liberalism to Labour* (George Allen & Unwin: London, 1921).
Webb, Beatrice, *The Diary of Beatrice Webb, Volume 1, 1873–1892: Glitter Around and Darkness Within*, Norman and Jeanne MacKenzie (eds) (Virago: London, 1982).
Webb, Beatrice, *The Diary of Beatrice Webb, Volume 2, 1892–1905:*

All the Good Things of Life, Norman and Jeanne MacKenzie (eds) (Virago: London, 1983).
Webb, Beatrice, *The Diary of Beatrice Webb, Volume 3, 1905–1924: The Power to Alter Things*, Norman and Jeanne MacKenzie (eds) (Virago: London, 1984).
Webb, Beatrice, *The Diary of Beatrice Webb, Volume 4, 1924–1943: The Wheel of Life*, Norman and Jeanne MacKenzie (eds) (Virago: London, 1985).
Wedgwood, C. V., *The Last of the Radicals: Josiah Clement Wedgwood, MP* (Jonathan Cape: London, 1950).
Wedgwood, Josiah Clement, *Memoirs of a Fighting Life* (Hutchinson: London, 1940).
Weir, L. MacNeill, *The Tragedy of Ramsay MacDonald* (Secker & Warburg: London, 1938).
Wells, H. G., *The New Machiavelli* (Penguin Books: London, 2005
Wertheimer, Egon (trans.), *Portrait of the Labour Party* (G. P. Putnam's Sons: London, 1929).
Williams, Francis, *A Prime Minister Remembers* (Heinemann: London, 1961).
Wood, Ian S., *John Wheatley* (Manchester University Press: Manchester, 1990).
Wrigley, Chris, *Arthur Henderson* (University of Wales Press: Cardiff, 1990).
Yeowell, Nathan (ed.), *Rethinking Labour's Past* (I. B. Tauris: London and New York, 2022).

Chapters and Articles

Bellamy, Joyce, and Saville, John, 'Vernon Hartshorn' in Joyce M. Bellamy and John Saville (eds), *Dictionary of Labour Biography* (August M. Kelley: New Jersey, 1972), I, 150–2.
Black, Duncan, 'C. P. Trevelyan' in Greg Rosen (ed.), *Dictionary of Labour Biography* (Politico's: London, 2001), 587–90.

Brown, John, 'Sidney and Beatrice Webb (1st Baron and Lady Passfield)' in Greg Rosen (ed.), *Dictionary of Labour Biography* (Politico's: London, 2001), 596–9.

Bryant, Chris, 'John Wheatley' in Greg Rosen (ed.), *Dictionary of Labour Biography* (Politico's: London, 2001), 604–5.

Carter, Matt, 'Richard Burdon Haldane (1st Viscount Haldane of Cloan)' in Greg Rosen (ed.), *Dictionary of Labour Biography* (Politico's: London, 2001) 247–50.

Clark, Peter, 'J. R. Clynes: Number Two in Labour's First Government', *Labour Heritage* (Summer, 2022), 12–15.

Cook, Chris, 'By-elections of the First Labour Government' in Chris Cook and John Ramsden (eds), *By-elections in British Politics* (UCL Press: London, 1997), 37–58.

Fisher, Trevor, 'Labour's 1918 Transformation', *Labour Heritage* (Winter 2021), 11–13.

Foster, Derek, 'Arthur Henderson' in Alan Hawarth and Dianne Hayter (eds), *Men Who Made Labour: The PLP of 1906 – The Personalities and Politics* (Routledge: London and New York, 2006), 83–9.

Golant, W., 'C. R. Attlee in the First and Second Labour Governments', *Parliamentary Affairs*, XXVI (1973), 318–35.

Gorton, Richard, 'Josiah Wedgwood MP', *Labour Heritage* (Autumn 2016, 1–6).

Gosling, Stephen, and Saville, John, 'Frederic John Thesiger, 3rd Baron and 1st Viscount Chelmsford' in Joyce M. Bellamy and John Saville (eds), *Dictionary of Labour Biography* (Macmillan: London, 1979), V, 213–15.

Grayson, Richard S., 'Arthur Henderson' in Greg Rosen (ed.), *Dictionary of Labour Biography* (Politico's: London, 2001), 276–8.

Griffiths, Clive, 'Noel Buxton (Lord Noel-Buxton of Aylesham)' in Greg Rosen (ed.), *Dictionary of Labour Biography* (Politico's: London, 2001), 94–6.

Grigg, John H., 'Fred Jowett, 1864–1944', *Labour Heritage* (Spring 2018), 7–13.

Howarth, Alan, 'David Shackleton' in Alan Hawarth and Dianne Hayter (eds), *Men Who Made Labour: The PLP of 1906 – The Personalities and Politics* (Routledge: London and New York, 2006), 171–8.

Howell, David, 'William Adamson' in *Oxford Dictionary of National Biography*, accessed online 6 January 2021.

Ingham, Robert, '1st Viscount Chelmsford (Frederic John Napier Thesiger)' in Greg Rosen (ed.), *Dictionary of Labour Biography* (Politico's: London, 2001), 115–17.

Kaufman, Gerald, 'John Hodge' in Alan Hawarth and Dianne Hayter (eds), *Men Who Made Labour: The PLP of 1906 – The Personalities and Politics* (Routledge: London and New York, 2006), 171–8, 91–6.

Knox, William, and Saville, John, 'William Adamson' in Joyce Bellamy and John Saville, *Dictionary of Labour Biography* (Macmillan: London, 1984), VII, 4–8.

Laybourn, Keith, 'Philip Snowden (1st Viscount Snowden)' in Greg Rosen (ed.), *Dictionary of Labour History* (Politico's: London, 2001), 536–8.

Lloyd, C. M., 'The Poor Law' in Herbert Tracey (ed.), *The Book of the Labour Party* (Caxton Publishing: London, 1925), 3–18.

Lloyd, Tony, 'J. R. Clynes' in Alan Haworth and Dianne Hayter (eds), *Men Who Made Labour: The PLP of 1906 – The Personalities and Politics* (Routledge: London and New York, 2006), 39–45.

McCartney, Ian, 'Stephen Walsh' in Alan Haworth and Dianne Hayter, eds, *Men Who Made Labour: The PLP of 1906 – The Personalities and Politics* (Routledge: London and New York, 2006), 201–4.

Middleton, J. S., revised by Marc Brodie, 'Thomas Shaw' in *Oxford Dictionary of National Biography*, accessed online 7 January 2021.

Rosen, Greg, 'C. B. Thomson (Lord Thomson of Cardington)' in Greg Rosen (ed.), *Dictionary of Labour Biography* (Politico's: London, 2001), 573–4.

Rosen, Greg, 'Baron Parmoor of Frith (Charles Alfred Cripps)' in Greg Rosen (ed.), *Dictionary of Labour Biography* (Politico's: London, 2001), 459–60.

Rosen, Greg, 'Stephen Walsh' in Greg Rosen (ed.), *Dictionary of Labour Biography* (Politco's: London, 2001), 594–5.

Rosen, Greg, 'Sydney Haldane Olivier (Lord Olivier)' in Greg Rosen (ed.), *Dictionary of Labour Biography* (Politico's: London, 2001), 451–2.

Rosen, Greg, 'Rt Hon Tom Shaw MP CBE' in Greg Rosen (ed.), *Dictionary of Labour History* (Politico's, London, 2001), 510–11.

Rosen, Greg, 'Vernon Hartshorn' in Greg Rosen (ed.), *Dictionary of Labour Biography* (Politico's: London, 2001), 265–6.

Rosen, Greg, 'Willie Adamson' in Greg Rosen (ed.), *Dictionary of Labour Biography* (Politico's: London, 2001), 6–7.

Saville, John, 'Arthur Henderson' in Joyce M. Bellamy and John Saville (eds), *Dictionary of Labour Biography* (Augustus M. Kelley: New Jersey, 1972), I, 161–5.

Saville, John, 'Stephen Walsh' in Joyce M. Bellamy and John Saville (ed.), *Dictionary of Labour Biography* (Macmillan: London, 1977), IV, 87–90.

Seward, Matthew, 'Frederick Jowett' in Greg Rosen (ed.), *Dictionary of National Biography* (Politico's: London, 2001), 330.

Shepherd, Lord, 'Labour's Early Days' in Alan Haworth and Dianne Hayter, eds, *Men Who Made Labour: The PLP of 1906 – The Personalities and Politics* (Routledge: London and New York, 2006), 241–62.

Singh, Marsha, 'Fred Jowett' in Alan Haworth and Dianne Hayter (eds), *Men Who Made Labour: The PLP of 1906 – The Personalities and Politics* (Routledge: London and New York, 2006, 113–18.

Stead, Peter, 'Vernon Hartshorn: Miners' Agent and Cabinet Minister', *Glamorgan Historian*, VI (1969), 83–94.

Straw, Jack, 'Philip Snowden' in Alan Haworth and Dianne Hayter (eds), *Men Who Made Labour: The PLP of 1906 – The Personalities and Politics* (Routledge: London and New York, 2006), 181–6.

Thorpe, Andrew, 'Josiah Wedgwood (the 1st Baron Wedgwood of Barlaston)' in Greg Rosen (ed.), *Dictionary of Labour Biography* (Politico's: London, 2001), 599–600.

Watkin, A. E., revised by Marc Brodie, 'Stephen Walsh' in *Oxford Dictionary of National Biography*, accessed online 8 January 2021.

Whitehead, Philip, 'J. H. Thomas' in Greg Rosen (ed.), *Dictionary of Labour Biography* (Politico's: London, 2001), 569–73.

Wrigley, Chris, 'John Robert Clynes' in Greg Rosen, ed., *Dictionary of Labour Biography* (Politico's: London, 2001), 124–5.

Index

B

N

O

P

R

S

Z